Leading Ladies

Leading Ladies

Sharing Our Stories of Inspiration and Faith

Treva Gordon
Foreword Written by
Tennessee State Senator Thelma Harper

Copyright © 2013 by Treva Gordon.

Library of Congress Control Number:		2013906821
ISBN:	Hardcover	978-1-4836-2638-3
	Softcover	978-1-4836-2637-6
	Ebook	978-1-4836-2639-0

All rights reserved. No part of this book may be reproduced or transmitted in any form or by any means, electronic or mechanical, including photocopying, recording, or by any information storage and retrieval system, without permission in writing from the copyright owner.

This book was printed in the United States of America.

Rev. date: 05/16/2013

To order additional copies of this book, contact:
Xlibris Corporation
1-888-795-4274
www.Xlibris.com
Orders@Xlibris.com
125728

Contents

Foreword—Tennessee State Senator Thelma Harper 9
Letter of Introduction—Dr. Dorinda Clark-Cole 11
Letter of Introduction—Katherine Purnell 13
Introduction Letter from the founder—Treva R. Gordon 15

1—Evangelist Almeta Scott 17
2—Andrea Perkins 24
3—Angella Banks 30
4—Audra Buchanan 37
5—Honorable Beth Harwell 43
6—Betty Burchett 49
7—Elder Beverly A. Kirby 56
8—Buena Montgomery 63
9—C. Lynne Tate-Shakeenab 71
10—Christine Jolie Littleton 78
11—Connie F. Booker 85
12—Cynthia Pitts 91
13—Dara Smith 99
14—Darlene James-Runnels 105
15—DaShaunda L. Turner 112
16—Demeshia 119
17—Dionne Jermeia 126
18—Evangelist Eva Bronaugh Barnes 133
19—Evangelist Regina Relliford Spivey 140
20—Gloria Leavell 149
21—Jacqueline L. Knight 157
22—Jamie Figueroa 164
23—Janine Folks Edwards 171
24—Jennifer Kay Miller 179
25—Jennifer Rawls 184
26—Kelly Gore 191
27—LaTrina Renee' Alfred 198
28—LaTosha Roberson 205

29—Laura E. Payne	211
30—LaVon Bracey	218
31—Lisa Lewis-Balboa	224
32—Mayor Carolyn P. Bowers	231
33—Mayor Kim McMillan	239
34—Minister Suzanna Reese-Wilson	246
35—Monica Dunnagan	252
36—Nicole R. Scott	259
37—Omni Mandela Camilla Walker	270
38—Pastor Diana S. Washington	277
39—Pastor Dr. Jane W. Garland	284
40—Pastor Judy D. Quarles	291
41—Pastor Yolanda Morgan	299
42—Servella Lee Terry	306
43—Sha Jackson	314
44—Tameshia Mayfield	321
45—Tamika Christian	327
46—Tangie Conecha Smith-Singleton	332
47—Tiffinea Reid-Breaux, LCSW	339
48—Treva R. Gordon	346
49—Deaconess Winsome W. Brown-Blackford	355
50—Yvonne Hill	361
Thoughts of a Leading Lady	367
Rosetta Perry	367
Cheryl "Action" Jackson	369
Janis F. Kearney	371
First Lady Mary Curlin	373
Pastor Ginger Luffman	375
Memorable Photos of Leading Ladies	377
Leading Ladies: Our First Conference	383
"I am a Leading Lady."	385

I would like to thank every woman for their written contribution and work inside *Leading Ladies: Sharing Our Stories of Inspiration and Faith*. May each woman be forever blessed and your families too. This book is dedicated to women everywhere. Special thanks to our many families and friends who bless us daily with their unending love and support. Words alone cannot express how thankful we are for your loving support. Philippians 4:13.

Foreword

Tennessee State Senator Thelma Harper

Great leaders are often born out of adverse climates and unusual circumstances. When we think of leadership, we normally think of individuals of such great status, they appear almost unattainable. However, to the contrary, we are all born with the *leadership gene*. It is solely our choice as to whether we decide to allow this trait to lie dormant or to activate it. We must make a conscious decision in our daily living to strive to lead others by our own example. Not only must we lead with great vision, integrity, and humility, but our leadership must also motivate others to strive for greatness as well.

Moreover, in a predominately male-dominated society, it is oftentimes challenging for females to have a leading voice. Many women find themselves in a constant *battle of the sexes* and become so engulfed with competition that all focus is lost. It is essential for individuals to find their own unique leading voice that stands apart from all others and simultaneously motivates their world around them to do the same.

Leading Ladies continually venture the unknown with confidence and courage. We must use every life experience, whether good or bad, as our motivation to motivate. In our weak moments, it is imperative that we draw inspiration from our fore leaders as well as those who look to us for guidance.

As mothers, daughters, sisters, and friends, we must strive to always move forward.

Senator Thelma Harper
State Senator
19th Senatorial District
State of Tennessee

LETTER OF INTRODUCTION

Dr. Dorinda Clark-Cole

Leading Ladies Event

A Leading Lady means to me a strong woman that stands out front and empowers others to follow and to have great aspirations for her future, depending solely on example and spiritual principles.

Dr. Dorinda Clark-Cole is a legendary icon in gospel music. She is known throughout the world as the Rose of Gospel, the Church Girl, and the Evangelist. But more than anything else, she is a three-time Grammy Award winner. She is a two-time Stellar Awards winner and is truly a Leading Lady.

Dr. Cole is the host of TCT Network's *Dorinda Show*. She has a clothing and jewelry line, as well as an impressive singing career. She has worked in the office of an evangelist for more than twenty years and continues to spread the Good News. She is a wife, mother, and business leader. Her mother, the late great Dr. Mattie Moss-Clark, saw the gift that was in her from a small child. She is thankful for her sisters, the legendary Clark Sisters. Together they have ministered all over the world. In 2012, Dr. Cole was the keynote speaker at the Michigan Leading Ladies Conference. She ministered hope and inspired every woman in the room. Dr. Dorinda Clark-Cole is a Leading Lady.

Contact Information
http://www.dorindaclarkcole.net
http://www.lightrecords.com
http://www.twitter.com/DORINDATHEROSE

Letter of Introduction

Katherine Purnell

As a leader in higher education, I am excited to see that women are entering and graduating from college in greater numbers. Women are also advancing to leadership positions. Today more than 18 percent of top executives are women.

I want to pay tribute to Sally Helgesen, one of the earliest advocates who told us that the way women lead is "the female advantage." Increasingly we have research from prestigious sources (MIT, Harvard Business School, Pepperdine

University) to support that women in leadership result in higher profitability and more effective problem solving and that employees respect their women leaders and like working for them.

According to a new study conducted by Caliper, a Princeton-based management consulting firm, women leaders share a strong profile; they are more assertive and persuasive, have a stronger need to get things done, and are more willing to take risks than male leaders.

My own leadership style centers around communication and positive working relationships. I encourage and emulate an upbeat and can-do attitude. This has resulted in success for me.

Women have made incredible progress over the past twenty-five years; however, we have more work to do. Our salaries are still lower than men in similar positions, and 18 percent of top executives being women is not high enough.

The strong leadership exhibited by the women featured in this Leading Ladies book is admirable. I am certain their words will encourage and inspire you. It is an honor to introduce them.

Katherine Purnell
Campus President
Daymar Institute—Clarksville
www.daymarinstitute.edu

Introduction Letter from the Founder

Treva R. Gordon

What a blessing this Leading Ladies book project has been for me. I have been inspired by the Holy Spirit to put this book together and bring together some amazing women. God spoke to me about this book, and I immediately went to work at it. Then as He began directing my path and giving me the blueprint and the number of women to be inside this book, I began seeking out women to share their stories, and yes, they did. I would like to thank my husband, Robert, and my children for always motivating me. Special thanks to my sisters and my dad for their never-ending love and support; to my pastor, my church, and everyone for their support, I appreciate you greatly. God is good. I believe every single person living today has a story to share. I am so thankful for each and every woman in this book. They inspire me daily. For in life, we have struggles, yet we are determined to *win* daily.

The stories we share together are inspirational, and I am honored to be a part of something that is so powerful, strong, and much bigger than me. I totally get it. God is good. This book will minister to the total man. There is something in this book for everyone.

As a Leading Lady myself, like many of these women you will read about in this book, I, too, faced several challenges in life, but God always made the way. Don't sit around waiting for somebody else to pave the way for you.

You've got to move yourself first. Get busy working toward your goals. Finish and stay true to the course. God bless you and keep you are my daily prayers.

Much love,

Treva R. Gordon
Leading Ladies, Inc., Founder and President
www.TrevaGordon.com

1

Evangelist Almeta Scott

He that dwelleth in the secret place of the most High shall abide under the shadow of the Almighty. I will say of the Lord, He is my refuge and my fortress: my God; in him will I trust. Surely he shall deliver thee from the snare of the fowler, and from the noisome pestilence. He shall cover thee with his feathers, and under his wings shalt thou trust: his truth shall be thy shield and buckler. Thou shalt not be afraid for the terror by night; nor for the arrow that flieth by day; Nor for the pestilence that walketh in darkness; nor for the destruction that wasteth

at noonday. A thousand shall fall at thy side, and ten thousand at thy right hand; but it shall not come nigh thee. Only with thine eyes shalt thou behold and see the reward of the wicked.

—Psalms 91:1-8, King James Version

I was born in 1933, in Dillon, South Carolina, to Rueben Jasper McKellar and Betsy McKellar. My mother was the mother of ten children. There were five boys and five girls.

Life back home, people were hungry, but we were blessed with food. I had so many wonderful memories and times growing up. My father was a farmer, and he planted collards, peas, and everything that we could eat. He also raised hogs and chickens. There was always food for us; even when food was rationed, we always had food and love. God always made a way. We would can food like apples and peaches to make jelly. Mother canned watermelon rinds. Back in those days' people saved everything they could. They rationed sugar and many other things. Back then there was a little hand machine that they would use to make sausages and sausage pudding. Often times I would go into the barn when father wasn't looking and get a piece of sausage pudding. I remember they would put the potatoes in a hill form when they collected them. The smell would be so good. Daddy would clean fish, like mullet, and put them in the smokehouse, and Mother would then cook them with grits. I would also love to make cracklin' cornbread with collards. We ate ham and many good things. We were blessed. I also learned a lot from my grandmother. She taught us about church and how to be good wives. She later took ill in life and had to be cared for.

I am most thankful that my mother was a good mother and stayed home with us. My mother knew where we were. Most parents today don't know where their children are. My mother let us know that she loved us. It is a different world today. Even as an adult, I learned so much from my mother, and it helped me to be a better mother to my very own children. I also wanted to know that my children were safe in the house before going to bed.

My father built our home with his own hands. My oldest brother Ruben was in the navy and helped him. I had some good old times at home. We would play baseball. I was blessed to hit the ball very far out in the yard running and playing. My father would teach us about the Bible. He would write many things in his Bible. My mother always stayed at home raising the children. She was a Christian woman. Our parents took us to church. If you didn't go to church, you didn't go anywhere else. Our parents were very strict. We had to be obedient. I am thankful for the good life we had as children coming up. My father was Methodist, and my mother was in Holiness. Our church was right down the street. The name of my church was New Jerusalem Holiness Church. We had many instruments in the church—the washboard, drums, piano or organ, cymbals, and more. I always enjoyed going to church.

I was married at sixteen years old to Charles Blue. Ten children were born, and one was a stillborn. It was a joy raising my children. We were married for nearly fifty years before he passed away. I remained a virtuous woman until I remarried. I later married Elijah Scott. We were married for ten years, and he passed away.

When I got saved, the Lord called me into ministry. I did not want to preach and didn't preach for years. Back in those days, it was hard for women preachers. It was not acceptable. If it hadn't been for women, the church doors would have still been closed. I organized a group of singers, and we would go around singing at different churches. There was a woman named Gladys Ray who first led us around singing. I enjoyed this time. She later moved to New Jersey, and our group continued to sing. We were called the Family Gospel Singers. This group was made up of all my children.

God called me as an evangelist in the ministry. I was a Jonah and did not want to preach, but after my sickness, I obeyed God after He healed me. I am a teacher. Most of all, I call people over the phone and read scriptures to them and have prayer. I have had a phone ministry for many years. God blessed this ministry by bringing people to the Lord. People who didn't even know God learned about Him. I taught Sunday school and Bible study throughout the years. I was always in the church doing something. I love doing for the Lord. I love the preaching and the teaching. We also had a noonday prayer in the home where we would just pray. It made us closer to the Lord. Where there is a praying Christian, you will find a strong Christian. We used to have prayer from house to house. We had prayer every day. There was always something to do for the Lord. Prayer makes you strong. Prayer changes things. When something was troubling me, I always prayed because God can solve things. Instead of worrying, try praying. As a mother, I always prayed for my children. Even in my womb, I prayed for my children. Many times I would get the neighborhood children to come and go to church with me, and they would. Every time I asked them, they would come. Just like the song says, "Bringing in the sheep." It was a blessing to see the children come to church. The children learned to come to Sunday school, and I taught them the Word of God. They were happy.

> Train up a child in the way he should go: and when he is old, he will not depart from it. (Prov. 22:6, KJV)

To this day, I remember things my mother taught me from way back then. There is nothing that God cannot do. He is almighty and powerful if you trust Him. He has been so good to me. Proverbs 31 talks about how a woman builds her house. She lives a clean and holy life. That is why she is called a virtuous woman. When her spouse dies she remains clean and holy, and you cannot find many today. What is a virtuous woman? She loves the Lord.

Who can find a virtuous woman?

> Who can find a virtuous woman? For her price is far above rubies. The heart of her husband doth safely trust in her, so that he shall have no need of spoil. She will do him good and not evil all the days of her life. She seeketh wool, and flax, and worketh willingly with her hands. She is like the merchants' ships; she bringeth her food from afar. She riseth also while it is yet night, and giveth meat to her household, and a portion to her maidens. She considereth a field, and buyeth it: with the fruit of her hands she planteth a vineyard. She girdeth her loins with strength, and strengtheneth her arms. She perceiveth that her merchandise is good: her candle goeth not out by night. She layeth her hands to the spindle, and her hands hold the distaff. She stretcheth out her hand to the poor; yea, she reacheth forth her hands to the needy. She is not afraid of the snow for her household: for all her household are clothed with scarlet. She maketh herself coverings of tapestry; her clothing is silk and purple. Her husband is known in the gates, when he sitteth among the elders of the land. She maketh fine linen, and selleth it; and delivereth girdles unto the merchant. Strength and honour are her clothing; and she shall rejoice in time to come. She openeth her mouth with wisdom; and in her tongue is the law of kindness. She looketh well to the ways of her household, and eateth not the bread of idleness. Her children arise up, and call her blessed; her husband also, and he praiseth her. Many daughters have done virtuously, but thou excellest them all. Favour is deceitful, and beauty is vain: but a woman that feareth the Lord, she shall be praised. Give her of the fruit of her hands; and let her own works praise her in the gates. (Prov. 31:10-31, KJV)

In March 2011, I suffered a severe stroke. I wasn't feeling good. I believe I was stressed. The doctor told me that the stroke I had was very serious. The Lord spared my life. The doctors said that I would never walk, talk, or live. Or if I lived, I would have Alzheimer's. Doctors saw bleeding in my brain. My daughter Pastor Diana Washington and Minister Susan Phillips also were at the hospital. I was unconscious for quite some time. They said when I awoke I was preaching. The doctors said that the bleeding wouldn't stop, and I would have to have an operation. My daughter told the doctor that the bleeding would stop and she laid her hands on me and prayed. Praise God. I am alive today because of God.

I am seventy-nine years old and alive and well. I love serving God. I love to do things in the church and teach people about the Lord. If you serve the Lord, He promises a long life if you are obedient. However, I believe that when it is your time, it is your time. I believe His Word. We don't know God's ways.

If you desire a closer walk with the Lord, if you pray, He will draw you closer. Get up in the morning to pray. It's wrong not to take out time for God. If you can give your time to other things, you can also give your time to God. The first thing I do in the morning is lift my hands and give my all to God. There is a sign on my wall that says, "Good morning God will be handling all your problems today, so you relax and have a good time." People sometimes just start out and go on in their day without thanking God or talking to Him. Always pray when you wake up in the morning. The Lord wants you to seek Him first.

> But seek ye first the kingdom of God, and his righteousness; and all these things shall be added unto you. (Matt. 6:33, KJV)

The Bible says that when we sleep, God sends His angels to watch over us while we are sleeping. There is a song that says, "The angels watching over me."

My son Michael drives trucks, and I pray for God to send an angel to keep him safe over the dangerous highways and that the angels watching over him will take care of him. I pray for people who are on the road, asking the Lord to take care of them. Fasting is good. If you want God to move on your behalf, then you should fast. I often fast as long as I can, and that is sometimes all day. Your mind has to be made up. You can't do anything on your own. If you want a blessing, then fast and pray for God to bless you.

I keep a bottle of anointing oil in my house. If I get sick, I anoint myself and pray. A lot of times, I anoint myself, and the sickness goes away. Now you must believe in prayer. Everyone does not believe in prayer. I used to see my mother many times kneel down, and I would hear her pray. I would also gather my children and pray. It made us closer. If my children were afraid, I would say to them to ask the Lord to not make them afraid. When you pray, don't doubt in your heart but believe. Believe that God will do what you are asking Him to do.

In my hometown I am a well-known evangelist. Well-known as a woman who will get a Word from God. I have traveled to many places. I have ministered in several conferences and churches. I have preached in Dillon, South Carolina, and other places too. I am known there for my evangelism. I am not afraid to stand up for the Gospel. God doesn't want no coward soldiers. Even after my stroke, I still speak what the Lord says. I have preached several times in Clarksville, Tennessee, at my daughter's church, at their women's conferences. God gave me a sermon: "wrapped up, tied up, and tangled up in Jesus" and "you got what you wanted and lost what you had." God doesn't dwell in sin. When King David took Uriah's wife, he was wrong. David stopped walking in God's way when he sinned. Stay in the will of God. Being outside the will of God, you will not be in His protection. As long as David walked in the will of God, he was blessed; but when he walked outside the will of God, he suffered in his flesh. II Samuel 12:1-13.

Each day I pray for life, health, and strength. I pray for food, and I thank Him for those who are less fortunate and those who do not have much. I pray for His special-needs children too. For many years, I would give to the mission ministries on TV to help the hungry children. I thank God for everything He has blessed me with. I thank God for keeping my children well and not sick. I ask the Lord to bless them. I have twenty-three grandchildren, fifteen great-grandchildren, and several great-great-grandchildren. They are in several states—Tennessee, New Jersey, South Carolina—and outside the U.S., in Germany.

I just love to pray. I have prayed for thousands of people over my lifetime. A praying Christian is a strong Christian. But you have to have the faith. Some people never pray. They never even thank the Lord for their blessings when they sit down to eat. My father never sat down at the supper table without blessing his food. Always thank God and pray over your food. Never eat without thanking God for your food. Let the Lord know that you are thankful for everything.

Once a tornado hit, I said, "Lord, if it be your will, turn the tornado and don't let it hit," and it went in another direction. I also prayed that it wouldn't hurt the people. I was scared, but the Lord protected us.

I believe the Lord is on His way back. With the way the world is today, I know He's coming back, and like a thief in the night. People have become so wicked. They don't believe that the Lord is coming. People say, "I heard that a long time ago." Well, no man knows the day nor the hour that He shall return. He's on His time and not ours. It won't be rain this time. It is going to be fire. I believe hell is real. It wasn't made for Christians. It was made for the devil and his angels. Hell is just as real as heaven.

If you don't know the Lord, please turn to Him and get saved while you have a chance. The Lord will save you anytime, and all you have to do is to accept Him. Romans 10:9. The Lord does not hear a sinner's prayer. I believe that if a sinner comes to God and repents, God will hear your prayer and save you.

When a person is saved, he or she will serve God. I believe Jesus is the way. I believe there is one God. You can make a god out of worshipping idols or whatever you desire to turn into your god, but that does not mean that is the real God. Leviticus says there is not another god. People have things they worship and call it god. I once knew a girl that said the sunshine was her god. I say the Son shining is God. Leviticus 19.

I want to thank you for reading my chapter. I want you to learn more about God. If you miss out on God, then you will miss out on heaven just like the man Lazurus, who was in hell and tormented. Luke 16:23. There are men and women of God on this earth to tell you about God.

> Blessed are they which do hunger and thirst after righteousness: for they shall be filled. (Matt. 5:6, KJV)

The Lord says that if you hunger and thirst after Him, you shall be filled. Be filled with the Spirit. Many people don't know the Spirit of God.

Contact Information
Evangelist Almeta Scott
Remnant of God Outreach Ministries
1208 ½ Paradise Hill Road, Clarksville, TN 37040

＃ 2

Andrea Perkins

I have so much to thank God for, all of His wonderful blessings, every opened door, and brand-new mercies along with each new day. That's why I praise Him, and for this, I give Him praise because I never would have made it without Him. I would have lost it all, but now I see how He was there for me, so I can truly say, THANK YOU, LORD, FOR ALL YOU'VE DONE FOR ME! How God made something out of nothing.

Hopefully, in my you will see my ups and downs, faults and failures, my good and bad and take action to govern yourself accordingly. I grew up in a home with two working parents, and I didn't feel as though they didn't love me, but I felt as though something was missing in my life. As a child, I was sweet. I never complained, although I got pushed around and beat up, and yet back then I still kept a smile on my face. Then one day, because I was also a big girl, a group of girls jumped on me in the park and pulled down my tube top, and the boys got a kick out of that, and that's when my life changed. That's when I became a fighter. Looking back on the issues of my life, my dearly beloved father inflicted a major pain on me by informing me that all I was going to be good for was to lie on my backside and have babies. Yes, at the time I was a hot mess because I was deceiving myself into thinking that when a male noticed me or called me in the midnight hour to come visit, that meant he loved me and cared about me. I also was foolish to believe that even though he had someone else and chose to call me, I was special. When I grew up and saw the real picture for what it truly was, I could no longer mistake longing for male attention, sex abuse, and lies for love. Believe me, it is what it is no matter how you try to dress it up. I now thank God for the pain that my father inflicted on me, but at the time, I was very devastated. I couldn't imagine in my mind why or how you could speak such words to your own child. Yet in my pain, with God's help, I took full advantage of this situation to make a liar out of my daddy; and praise God, my daddy got to see that he was wrong in his perception of me.

Now, I work at the same place he retired from, just on the other side. I was a mother's girl. My mother meant the world to me. Even after I had my children, my mother still meant a lot to me. However, although my mother was my best reason for living, my mother hurt me when she told me I could not stay at their house at the time we were facing financial crisis. I suggested that if she allowed me to move in with them, we could save some money and put it together and help each other. My mother—the Bible base, loving all, and would do anything for anybody no matter what—shocked my whole world and boldly told me I couldn't stay at her house. At the time, I couldn't understand it. Surely I misunderstood what my mother said, but no, I didn't. I was so out of it. I threatened my mother by telling her I was going to tell her pastor that she wouldn't let me stay in her house, but she wasn't even feeling what I was saying because she was standing by her decision. I felt my mother's decision was wrong, but she knew it was right, and years later, as I grew up a little more, I came to realize that what she did was not to hurt me but to make me and keep her house in order.

She knew that if my father would have done or say anything wrongful or hurtful to her, it was going to be a problem, and my mother was not going to allow her house to be out of order, even if it killed her. My father was different. I didn't understand why he treated my mother the way he did. I also didn't understand why my mother allowed him to do so, and that's another reason why I'm grateful to God today that He allowed me and my father to gain a better relationship before he passed away.

It was after my mother passed when I and my father became closer. You see, God does work in mysterious ways. Most people who know us say I look like my mother, and at times I act like her, but they haven't seen my father's mother. One of my aunties brought my father a picture of his mother, and he thought they took a picture of me that I could be her identical twin. I was afraid I was going to die when I was twenty-seven years old because I was told that was how old my grandmother was when she died. I can do bad all by myself. I don't want to be alone, but I'm not going to accept no more disrespect by being treated like a punching bag. I am a woman of God, and I refuse to be treated any other way than as such.

When you enter into a relationship, have something to offer other than your physical frame. My first marriage was referred to as a shotgun wedding, which means I got married because I was with child and didn't want to put shame on the family name. Believe me, love had nothing to do with it. I think those days are truly over, so we don't have to worry about that. I was underage, was still in school, never worked, couldn't drive, didn't know how to wash clothes or cook. I was still under Mama's care, so I was totally lost on how to be a real wife. My husband at the time took full advantage of the situation. I was beaten often when he got mad. He would take out his frustrations on me instead of the person whom he was mad at. I was under his management per se. Finally, one day I let him know I wasn't going to take it anymore, and I started standing up for myself. Ladies, love doesn't abuse or use you; please note that as a true fact. Then I got another chance at marriage with a great man. However, since I was used to the bad, I didn't know how to accept and appreciate the good. Now I've learned my lesson that when God gives you a gift, you better take extremely good care of it and treat it as a treasure because that's what it is. Don't be like me and miss it when it's gone and start thinking about the should, could, and would haves. Be proactive, not reactive; a marriage destined by God is a blessing. Don't lose your blessing fooling around with trash. Keep your family matters within your home and with God. You really never know who's out to help you destroy your home. Luther Vandross sings it best, "A house is not a home." I fully agree. You can live in the same house and be many miles apart, like the other singer sung, "Your body's here with me, but your mind is on the other side of town." Don't get caught up in the mess. You really can't judge a book by its cover.

Though my brother and my sister are older than me, I, through my ups and downs and how I dealt with them, look like I'm way older than them. I really wanted people to like me and care for me. At least that's what I thought. In school I was the child left behind until one very special, caring guidance counselor, Marie Young, had me in her office one day. She ordered me to get out of the level-three classes. I thought to myself, *Why now, why do you care after all these years?* I had been in high school longer than most people because I had all my children before I graduated. One teacher informed my dearly beloved mother that this was the year that I really improved, and they couldn't believe it. Why do people say that if they had the opportunity to change things, they wouldn't? Doesn't that defeat the purpose of making the statement? Better yet, that could just be a flat-out lie. I believe that's the real reason we can't. If we could, we truly would. I know that if I could, I wouldn't have had any children until I was more prepared on how to raise them. I wasn't the best nor the worst parent, but because I didn't know what love was myself and how to love myself, I didn't know how to love my children, and we all suffered for that. But thank God for giving me the opportunity to improve. I thought what my children wanted and needed was something that I could buy, but when I came to the realization of what they really wanted and needed, I realized it was my love, time, care, and patience, which are priceless. The damage had already been done. Money can't buy everything you need.

I have had mixed emotions about doing this chapter. There were times when I was so excited, and then there were times I thought, *Why in the world am I doing this?* Even until this present moment, January 31, 2013, I was still undecided about doing this chapter. When I first heard about it, I talked with my brother, Mr. Ronald Terry Ogburn, and he encouraged me on some subjects, and then I would get in gear and then get back out. One of my biggest issues is that I wanted to be real and open, but also keeping in mind that once you put yourself out there, you can't take it back. That's one thing that really kept me from moving forward in doing this, yet I wanted to hopefully keep someone from making the errors in life that I made, and that would make writing this worth it all. That's my real goal for doing this. I spoke with Loverne Forman this morning about my struggles in doing this, and she said something that helped me choose to go ahead and get it on the way. At this point, I've got over five pages written down. See what an encouraging word can do for you even though sometimes you have to encourage yourself?

I'm a person who really hates injustices. I feel more like Malcolm X than Martin. I get really disturbed when two people do the same thing, but one person, per se, gets away with it and the other gets the death penalty. Or when they say or do what they can and then say it has nothing to do with the color of your skin. Then they say it isn't personal. I hate it when people can do what they will and cannot and then say it's not racial. When they like you, know it's nothing but a lie. Writing this in this book does not make me a Leading Lady. People calling you a Leading Lady won't make you a Leading Lady. I want to be more than a Leading Lady; I want to be one of God's Leading Ladies, and that's something only God can predestine you to be. So please, don't get it twisted when people start giving you tittles and positions because people are so quick to change and be fake and phony, but God is unlike us. He is real, and when He does something, you can count on it.

One godly Leading Lady in my life was my mother, Annie Belle Jones Ogburn. There were many days I wanted to be like her, and many days, I was grateful that I wasn't her. She was a true instrument used by God. In the early seventies, she lost her leg due to a blood clot; and although I didn't see it, I was told that they used a saw to cut her leg off, and that just amazed me. How strong of a godly woman she was. Then she had chosen to put up with my father's abusive words and actions and still chose to keep the wedding vows she made to him and the Lord until her passing on July 15, 2004. Now I know that I'm not as strong as my mother was because I wouldn't have put up with the stuff she put up with from him or anybody else for that matter. I'm just keeping it all the way real. Although my father had his issues as we all do, I believe he really loved my mother in his own way that only God could understand. When my mother passed, my father tried to pass with her. My father loved my mother more than he or his children would ever know.

There were two things my father loved, and that was delivering the mail and drinking. When my father retired from the United States Postal Service from being a city carrier, he basically died within. He loved the Postal Service so much he really didn't want to leave, but it was in his best interest to leave. His other love that caused him and us so much pain was his love for alcohol. I can't mess with it today after seeing how it affected my family. And the only reason why my father didn't die drinking was because he was in a nursing home and couldn't get it on a regular basis and not because he didn't want it. I really miss both of my parents. My father's passing was different than my mother's. I guess it could be because he was the last parent I had left. It could be because I miss going down to the nursing home from time to time discussing the Postal Service with him and getting a kick out of letting him know that I'm still there after he made it a point to tell me I wasn't going to be good for anything but having babies. I was wrong, but I did enjoy it at times. Then he would listen to me and give me some very important insight. Some good words of wisdom were something I really didn't get from him as a child living with him. So I'm grateful of the renewed relationship with him before he passed on July 10, 2011. There are two things I do regret about my father's passing. One is I wasn't there, and two is I felt like my father just gave up on life. I'm sure he knows that we did love and care for him despite our childhood memories of him. I truly believe he died knowing that we, his children, love him, and maybe that's why he was ready to go.

I'm glad that God can and will use whomever He so chooses without them having to be 100 percent perfect and 100 percent right. That's why the song says, "He saw the best in me when everyone else would only see the worst in me. He's the only one that can and will look beyond my faults and see my needs." That's why "Amazing Grace" shall always be the song of praise, for it was grace that bought my liberty. I do not know just why He came to love me so. He looked beyond my faults and saw my needs. My goal for me is to be able to be a doer of His holy divine Word and not just a reader and listener. My back up is Philippians 4:13, "I can do all things through Christ who strengthens me." Now let the church say amen, for God has spoken. Let the church say amen. God has not promised me sunshine—that's not the way it is going to be—but a little pain mixed with God and sunshine make me appreciate the good times. Be grateful because he keeps blessing me over and over. When I woke up this morning, hallelujah, I was closed in my right mind. When I looked all around me, my family was doing fine. I'm going to thank Him because of how he kept me. I want to thank Him because he has never left me. I can tell the world that I am blessed.

Andrea Perkins

Contact Information
E-mail: ayvette35@hotmail.com

3

Angella Banks

God Will Deliver
A Promise Worth Living For

God will not fail you
God cannot fail you
If you stand on his promise
You shall receive your blessing

For unto whomsoever much is given, of him shall be much required: and to whom men have committed much, of him whey will ask the more.

—Luke 12:48, KJV

About Me

My name is Angella Banks. I am a native of Brownsville, Tennessee. I am married to my husband, supporter, and friend, Michael, and have a beautiful ten-year-old daughter, Aniya. I am the founder and president of Xcellence, Inc., a nonprofit organization that supports community leaders, churches, and small businesses. I also teach business management and marketing at the collegiate level. I am currently obtaining my doctoral degree in business administration with a marketing specialization from Capella University. I enjoy traveling, reading, outreach, teaching seminars, and spending quality time with my family and friends.

Special Dedication

I would like to dedicate this story to my mother, Mary Ann Palmer, who is and has always been the first Leading Lady in my life! I am blessed to have a natural and spiritual mother who has spent her life developing and training me to be the woman I am today, a mother, a wife, a philanthropist, a woman of Xcellence, and a *Leading Lady*!

Introduction

From the little girl to the woman I am today, I have always known I was different. How so? Different in my posture, different in my talk, different in my attitude, and different in my vision. It was not until much later in my life that I came into the knowledge that God had created me different by design. God had made me different while yet in my mother's womb. My entire life story is written from beginning to end. I've never in my life been content with being the status quo; I've always desired more for myself, my parents, my family, and my friends.

I was barely an adult when I made the first steps to move beyond my comfort zone and trust God. During this time in my life, I had tried several careers—manufacturing, part-time retail, and college—but was yet unfulfilled. Little did I know that God was working on a plan and that my life would take many turns to realize it.

At the age of twenty-two, I felt that I was ready to step out on faith and see what else was in store for my life beyond the small city limits of my hometown. My first destination was to Freeport, a small city on the northern tip of Illinois, close to Rockford. Although, it was my first move away from home, I was surrounded by family and loved ones. I was excited. I was moving for what I thought was my first managerial position. I took a relocation package as an assistant credit manager with the then national furniture-giant Heilig-Meyers.

Upon arriving at the store, they never trained me for my new role and continuously had me to work on systems that I was already previously trained on, only to find out two weeks later that they were scheming to keep me out of their front office. I will never forget that day. As I walked in to work, the manager called me into his office along with the credit manager and two younger white males and said, "We're sorry, but the position that you applied for is no longer available, and the lady that previously held that job is coming back." He proceeded to say, "We can give you a sales job on the floor, making commission only, and that is it."

What was I going to do? I was distraught as a young woman. I had moved over nine hours away from home. I had a new car and had moved into my own apartment. I declined the offer and left in tears. I no longer had a job nor any way to pay my rent and bills. It did not take me too long to understand what had happened. I had grown up in the South all my life, worked and interacted with all races, only to leave home and be discriminated against.

I never interviewed for the job face-to-face but opted for a phone interview instead. Based upon my poised tone and grammar, they assumed that I was Caucasian. Instead I was this young lady of African-American decent. As a young girl in school, I was pulled from my classes for speech therapy. I was ashamed because I did not feel that I sounded any different from the other kids. They would laugh as the therapist, Cindy Smith, would come and call my name among a few others out of class. Being embarrassed did not last long because she was funny and the sweetest. I have lived in several cities in my life, and I am complimented repeatedly on my grammar. To this day, my colleagues up North cannot believe I am from the South, and my colleagues from the South think I am originally from up North. Today, I count it all joy! I know now that even in my moments of shame, God was giving me a lifetime gift.

I pursued a legal case against the company and won a small settlement. It was not about the money; it was about the principle. You do not treat people wrong! I received a job as an underwriting assistant with MetLife through a staffing agency. I managed for a little while, but after nine short months of struggling to make ends meet, I knew that this season of my life was over. Although I walked away from the job, I would again work for the company full-time in three different states. I viewed it then as a misfortune, but the opportunity has granted me more than sixteen years of experience in the insurance and financial industry. I did not know what was next, but I knew I had to keep moving forward. I felt I was searching for something but had no clue what it was.

I returned home to Tennessee for a couple of months, and it was one of my dearest friends, Vatisha, that said, "Hey, girl, come go back with me to see if you like it!" Being young and having nothing to lose, I took her up on the offer and moved to Indianapolis, Indiana. I loved my new city. It was filled with unlimited opportunities for a young person to excel. I became a young American corporate leader and was blessed as a young woman to gain knowledge that could never be taken away. Through transitions in life and additional career opportunities, I was also blessed to live in Alpharetta, Georgia, and St. Louis, Missouri. I was able to secure leadership positions with several Fortune 500 companies. As I resided in these cities, I met key people that would continue to shape my life for years to come and still today. They became my family away from home. Looking back today at my life, even those relationships were strategically planned for His promise.

The Journey

In 2003, I received one of God's most precious gift, the gift of motherhood, a beautiful baby girl. It was at that moment that my entire life changed. I had been given the assignment to shape and mold another individual's life. A life that held my DNA. I instantly became more responsible in my actions, decisions, and my relationship with God. It was a turning point in my life. The time had come for me to impart, teach, and train my daughter (my legacy) everything that had been imparted to me. I wouldn't say that I was a bad person, but I was a lost person! Lost from His guidance, His will, and His purpose for my life. I grew up in the Church of God in Christ (COGIC) all my life, was exposed to God's Word and truth from my spiritual parents, Superintendent Stephen Biddle and Mother Ida Rule Biddle (Tennessee) and Superintendent Ezell Jackson and Mother Everlyn Jackson (Illinois), but had never fully internalized what it meant to be saved and to live my life through Him and for Him.

After nearly a decade, in 2005, I returned home to Tennessee to care for my dad, Curtis L. Palmer Sr., after hearing that his struggle with diabetes had become debilitating. I was happy to be home to care for my dad, but I was also struggling with the feelings of failure. After a seven-year-long relationship, I was a single mother; and after years of building a solid career, I was back in the place where I had started from. It was in this season of my life that I would challenge God for my return home, ask him what was next for my life and what were I to do while waiting. After months of praying for strength, guidance, and vision, my life shifted to a new dimension. I returned to college, secured a comfortable position in management at Regions Bank, and purchased my first home.

Things were good in my life, I felt restored. I was secure and felt that my life was moving in the right direction. I didn't understand until later that this is how the enemy wants us to feel. That our lives are all about having nice things and nice careers, buying nice homes, driving nice cars, going to church routinely, and helping others every now and then when we feel like it and when there's no financial challenge to do so. There's nothing wrong with having nice things as I have been abundantly blessed in my life; however, my life is not defined by what I have but by the life that I live and to whom I serve. God's vision for our lives is so much greater than materialistic things and impromptu actions. "Now unto him that is able to do exceeding abundantly above all that we ask or think, according to the power that worketh in us" (Eph. 3:20, KJV).

On August 3, 2007, I lost my dad to a massive heart attack. My short-lived gratification was once again gone. I was once again no longer fulfilled at my job, not even at the thought that I was the first college graduate from my family. That void that I had fought so hard to fill had once again resurfaced. I wanted more for my life. I had felt this way shortly after the birth of my daughter and this time after the death of my father. An overwhelming desire to live a meaningful life, give back, and live with assignment and purpose took precedence. It was time for me to build my legacy, and it began by acknowledging what God wanted for my life. It's not about me but all about Him. I recalled a simple prayer that I would always pray as a little girl: Lord use me as a vessel for the kingdom. I remember saying this even though I wasn't fully exposed to the full realm of what I was speaking. I would hear the church mothers and saints say it, so I guess it just landed in my spirit as a seed, and I began quoting it almost daily. I truly believe that the Lord heard my prayer and the sincerity of my heart and felt it was time to release his vision and purpose for my life.

The Promise

It did not take much longer after that, as I lay in bed sound asleep, that God imparted me a vision through a dream. I remember waking up and starting to write. I did not know how I was going to fulfill it, but I knew that I could trust Him. I wanted to be obedient to what He had called me to do. He had showed up in my life so many times before that I had no reason to doubt Him now. I was so excited that I could hardly wait for daylight to come. As soon as it was 5:00 a.m., my time, I phoned my best friend, Audra Buchanan, in the hope that she would answer the phone. She lived in Indianapolis, Indiana, and it was an hour ahead of my time. I began to share with her the vision; it was the birthing of my life's purpose, Xcellence Inc. An organization that would unite people, support those individuals striving to make a difference in the world, including community leaders, churches, and business owners that have made a commitment to move forward with their vision or calling. It was spoken in His Word that this would become a national organization. I was in awe and questioned, "National. Are you sure, Lord?" Again, it was confirmed. "If you trust me, my child, I'll make provision!" God had me a promise, and I had made the decision to stand, trust, and believe in His Word.

Xperiencing the Shift

If I was going to be sincere, there were changes that needed to be made. I prayed and made plans to move forward with what I had been called to do. It was a time of hardship and sacrifice, but for every storm, there is also calm thereafter. It gets real quiet and peaceful, then the sun shines, and if blessed, you may even get to see a rainbow. For every season changes four times a year, and as beautiful as they are, they all have advantages and disadvantages, but all four are designed with a specific purpose and are needed for our ecological system. If God designed it for our ecological system, then you can be assured that He did it for our human system as well. The challenges, trials, hurts, and pain we have experienced in our lives come to strengthen and redirect us to stay the course of His master plan. I resigned from Regions Bank, stepped out on faith; and here today, I am embarking on five years of living a life of purpose, giving back and helping others.

The Overflow

On September 10, 2011, I married my husband, Michael Banks. I was blessed with an opportunity to begin teaching at the collegiate level and will complete my doctoral degree spring 2015. My daughter is beautiful and amazing! She has her own personal relationship with God even at the tender age of ten. Xcellence, Inc., has touched my life and many others. We have a presence in six states with aggressive plans to have additional. On January 1, 2013, we launched national chapters, new community programs, and the Xcellence Community Magazine. Our initiatives, programs, and people are growing every day, for we realize that it is not about us but about servitude and living the life that God has envisioned for each of us and for those we serve!

Reflections

Before inception and birth, God's plan for our lives was already created. In His Word, "Being confident of this very thing, that he which hath begun a good work in you will perform it until the day of Jesus Christ" (Phil. 1:6, KJV). Regardless of where you are in life, know that it is never too late to walk in purpose and assignment. It just takes a humbling spirit to realize that there is more to life than where you are and that God has called you to be greater. Your vision is unique and comes with its own personal identification number assigned to it. No one else's number matches yours. You are important to the body of Christ and to the people in your life. Pray to God for direction, guidance, and understanding; we are not waiting on Him, but He is waiting on us! Just as He had a promise for me, He also has a promise for you. Believe in His Word, activate your faith, move forward into your calling, and lastly, stand on His promise!

Closing

I pray that you have been both inspired and empowered by my testimony. I would love the opportunity to visit with you, your organization, or your business and impart with you what God has done and is doing in my life. If you are not currently affiliated with Xcellence, Inc., and would like to start a or join us, we would love to have you. May you move forward, and Godspeed in the endeavors of your life, reaching for and restoring everything that the enemy thought he had deprived from you!

If you would like to learn more about our organization or make a donation, please visit our website: www.xcellenceinc.com.

Please feel free to contact me. Remember I am here to serve you!

Angella Banks, MBA
Founder and President
Xcellence Incorporated
E-mail: angellabanks@xcellenceinc.com
 Like us at http://www.facebook.com/xcellenceinc
 Follow us @xcellbizgrp

4

Audra Buchanan

Sunshine after the Rain

But those who trust in the Lord will find new strength. They will soar high on wings like eagles. They will run and not grow weary. They will walk and not faint.

—Isaiah 40:31, New Living Translation

When I was a young girl growing up, I would sing the song "Rain, rain, go away, come again another day." For a long time, that was the theme of my life—rainy days. Why? Because it seemed as if the torrential rains never stopped for very long. Have you ever felt as if the rain would never stop in your life? I'm here to share my story with you to let you know that even though it may be raining in your life right now, the sun will shine again.

I grew up in one of the large cities in the state of Michigan. I was basically raised by my mother, who was and still is a devout Jehovah's Witness. Life for me always seemed so complicated. In my opinion, I was never able to live life the way "normal" people lived. It was when I entered my teenage years when it started raining in my life. My parents separated due to my father's substance-abuse problems. At times I would just sit and cry and try to make sense of why things were the way they were. I would pray and ask God to make the pain go away. My family life had fallen apart, and I felt lost. My mother had now become a single parent, and with me being the oldest of three children, all the responsibilities of helping to raise my siblings fell on me.

I fell into a hole of despair. I never got the opportunity to be a teenager and experience life the way my friends did. I was a caretaker of my siblings, and because of my mother's religion, I wasn't able to do anything. I wasn't able to participate in sports or anything that required me to stay after school. I couldn't participate in any holiday activities; no parties or dances, not even my senior prom. Isolation became my best friend. No one ever really knew how much I was hurting, because I did then, what I've done all my life, and that is to smile and pretend as though all is well.

I would always secretly pray that my dad would come back and that maybe we could be a real family. He would come home for a while but would never stay for very long. I envied my girlfriends who had their mom and dad in the home. I always wanted a dad that would be there for me and protect me and teach me things. I knew my dad loved me, but his addiction trumped everything else. It's just something about the love and protection from a dad that girls need . . . I can only imagine. My mother was very strict and sometimes even a bit cold. I tried to be close to my mom, but there just seemed to be always something between us that never really allowed us to be close. Our relationship wasn't bad, but we just weren't close. She was very hard on me about everything; maybe it's because I was the oldest. I just felt like I could never do anything right. The words *I love you* were not common in my household.

For the most part, I felt as if I really didn't matter much when I was growing up. At the age of thirteen, a major storm hit my life. I was attacked and physically and sexually assaulted. My attacker beat me with a hammer and broke several bones. That day changed my life in a way that I can't describe. I couldn't understand why something like that would happen. "God, why did this happen to me?" For a long time I would struggle with myself trying to figure out what I had done wrong. When you're thirteen, all you can really think about is the embarrassment and shame of what happened. The only positive thing that came out of that horrible situation was that my dad came around more often. Oh, how I wanted him to come back home to love and protect me, but he didn't.

There was one person in my life who I knew, without a shadow of a doubt, loved me unconditionally, and that was my granny. She was the best granny in the world to me. She always made me feel special and wanted. It seemed as if she just really understood me. She always took the time to listen to me and give me good, sound advice. Granny just always knew how to make me feel that everything was going to be all right no matter how bad things appeared to be. When God called her home in 2002, it left a hole in my heart that can never be filled by anyone else. I found myself questioning God and asking Him, "Why would you take away the only person I had in my life who I felt really loved me?" As I've gotten older, I realized that it was her appointed time to leave this earth, and I just thank God for allowing me to have her for as long as I did. She was truly a phenomenal woman.

I so desperately wanted someone in my life that I could be close to and trust. When I was eighteen, my dad left Michigan and moved to California to start a new life. He didn't even tell us he was leaving town; he just disappeared. It was several years later before we heard anything from him. His addiction had landed him in prison. It would be fourteen years later before I would see my dad again. To this day I still fight against the feelings of abandonment. I would ask myself, "Why would he just go away and leave us? What did we do wrong?" For most of my life, I have always felt that I did something wrong. *Why is it so hard for someone to love me?* As I entered my twenties, I was really hoping and praying that I could start a new life; and maybe, just maybe, I could have someone in my life that would truly love me.

My son's father and I had known each other as young kids but didn't become involved with each other until after graduation from high school. On September 6, 1989, we became the proud parents of a son. I was so happy because I thought that now I was going to have the family that I had always wanted. I wanted my son to grow up with a mom and dad. Unfortunately, my happiness and joy didn't last very long. It started out as a slap across the face and with the promise that it would never ever happen again. I knew in the beginning that he was a heavy drinker, but I didn't realize that he was an alcoholic and that his father, too, was an alcoholic. All I knew was that he said he loved me and would never leave me. I spent the next ten years of my life being abused. When you are dealing with an alcoholic, you learn to walk on a tight rope because you never know what will set them off. For years, I lived in fear and hid the abuse with makeup covering the black eyes and bruises.

One evening I had put my son to bed and was up watching television. His father stopped by, and he appeared to be sober. At this point, I had found the courage to end my relationship with him, but he didn't want to accept it. He started pressuring me for sex, and when I refused, he pulled me off the couch by my hair and proceeded to beat me worse than he ever had before. Somehow he got me in a choke hold, and I could not breathe. I fought for as long as I could, but I could feel the life leaving my body, and I was getting weaker and weaker. I was praying, "Lord Jesus, please help me!" All I could think of was what was going to happen to my son when I'm gone. Then everything went black. When I came to and opened my eyes, he was standing over me with this glassy look in his eyes, as if he was frozen. He didn't move; he just stood there looking down at me, and then he turned and walked out of the room without a word. I got to my feet and went to living room, and he had opened the door and walked out and never looked back. It's as if something or someone (thank you, Jesus) had literally forced him to stop and made him leave. I was able to close and lock the door and call 911 for help. That was the last time he ever put his hands on me. I later found out that he had openly confessed to a family member that he came there that night with the intention to kill me. I will go to my grave knowing and believing that God intervened that night to save my life.

When I made the decision to leave the Jehovah's Witness organization, it completely ended my relationship with my mother and my siblings. No communication of any kind. All I had was my son, and all he had was me. A year later, I was led to the Lord and gave my life to Christ in May 1997. About a year or so later, I met someone. I really thought that maybe I could have another chance at being happy and loved by a man. He was twelve years older than me and was stable. He was saved and active in the church, and he really seemed to love my son. I so wanted him to have a father—something that I never really had. We were married in a beautiful church ceremony. Things were good for a while.

During the course of our marriage, my husband became an ordained deacon. Even though at church it seemed as if all was well, home life was another story. He was very mean and controlling, nothing like the man that had courted me. He became extremely jealous of my relationship with my son, and he isolated me from my friends and family. His temper was so bad that at times I was afraid for me and my son's safety. I knew that because I had been through so much with my son's father that I refused to continue to live in a situation like this. I went to my grandfather for financial help and started making plans to leave. I had to make plans to sneak away because I was so afraid of his temper. My son and I were able to get out and try to start a life on our own. My now ex-husband stalked and harassed me from the time I left until our divorce was final. He eventually found out where we lived, and one Sunday afternoon, after our divorce was finalized, he proceeded to my apartment, climbed up on the balcony (in his church suit), and went inside my house. He sexually assaulted me and then begged me to forgive him. I laid there on the floor thinking to myself, *I can't believe that I was married to this man. How could he do this to me? He's a deacon in the church. How can this be happening?* Eventually he was charged, convicted, and punished for his crime.

I have been abused physically, emotionally, mentally, and financially. All I ever really wanted was to be loved and protected. It seemed like the more I wanted it and looked for it, the worse things got. One day a very dear friend and I were having a conversation, and she told me that I needed to learn to love myself first. WOW! It was as if someone was speaking to me in a foreign language. Love myself first? I am being 100 percent real when I say to you that I had never in my life been told that or even shown how to do that. I always thought that if I gave enough and tried enough and endured enough, someone would love me. I had never thought about loving myself first. I always believed that I loved myself. I like to shop and buy nice things, get my hair and nails done, travel . . . You know, I do all the outward things to show that I love myself. However, the person on the inside is longing to be loved and appreciated.

Have you ever found yourself at a place in life where you know that you are not loving yourself and living the life that God intended for you to live? If you have, then believe me, I do understand. I am an ordinary woman just like you, but I serve an extraordinary God that has the power to change anything in your life—including you. The first and most important way to start loving yourself is to seek God for direction. There is an answer in His Word, the Bible, for every issue or problem that we may be faced with in life.

Most of the time, we just don't want to do the things or give up the things that we know we need to. I am forty-five years young, and I have spent the majority of my life in fear. I've made a lot of bad choices and had to suffer great consequences because I was afraid of being alone or of being abandoned by a man. God's Word reassures us: "Even if my father and mother abandon me, the Lord will hold me close" (Ps. 27:10, NLT).

My personal life experiences have taught me that the best way to conquer fear is with faith and forgiveness. It's not always easy to do, but it's necessary. I had to open up my heart and forgive my father. Seven years ago, my father was living in a homeless shelter in Atlanta. As far back as I can remember, he has struggled with drug addiction. I brought him from Atlanta to Indianapolis, into my home, to take care of him; and seven months later, he suffered a massive stroke. Had he still been living in shelters, undoubtedly he would not be here today. I continue to take care of and look after my father. My siblings have turned their backs on him, but because of my love for Christ, I must do the right thing. My dad and I have a good relationship now, and I thank God for that. I was also able to forgive my son's father and my ex-husband. They both have recently struggled with homelessness and major health issues. By forgiving them, I am able to open my heart to sincerely pray for them. Even though I don't have a relationship or any communication with my mother or siblings to this day, I continue to pray for them and their salvation.

The enemy knows our weaknesses, and he will always try to use them against us because he knows that he has no real true power over the saints of God. He tries to appear powerful by means of deception and trickery. I am a living and breathing testament that when God has a plan for your life, and He does have a plan for everyone's life, no matter what you must go through in life, you can be an overcomer. I've spent all my life looking for someone to love me, want me, appreciate me, and protect me; and all along, the Lord has been there with His arms wide open, saying, "Here I am." God loves us so much and desires to give us His very best. Be encouraged and know that if I can make it, then so can you. I am presently pursuing my bachelor of arts in business at Marian University and will graduate this year. I am the cofounder of Xcellence Incorporation. If you are in a domestic relationship or would like me to share my testimony with your group, please send an e-mail to the address below. Please visit our website at www.xcellenceinc.com.

Contact Information
AudraBuchanan@xcellenceinc.com

5

Honorable Beth Harwell

Speaker of the Tennessee House of Representatives

When people say to me, a woman's place is in the home, I say, with enthusiasm, it certainly is, but if she truly cares about her home, that caring will take her far and wide.

—Eleanor Roosevelt

My Story, Inspiration, and Those Who Helped Me along the Way

I grew up in a very small town in northern Pennsylvania, and I am the youngest of five children. I had a good, happy home life there but certainly wanted to strike out on my own. After graduating high school a year early, I began to think about colleges. I was raised Church of Christ, and it was important to me and to my parents that I attend a Church of Christ university. As it happened, David Lipscomb was the closest one. After high school I packed my bags for Nashville and never looked back. I fell in love with Nashville and with Tennessee.

I was not raised in a particularly political household, so it certainly wasn't something I thought about pursuing when I was younger. But God has His ways of presenting something to you in a unique way—and that's certainly what happened to me. At various times in my life, there were strong women who inspired me. Had it not been for a summer with my grandmother, I may never have considered a life in public service.

The summer after I finished high school, my grandmother came to live with us because she was bedridden. The nurse that cared for her would take an hour for lunch every day, and it was my responsibility to sit with her during that time and keep her company. As fate would have it, the only thing on television that summer was the Watergate hearings and the coverage of the U.S. Senate Watergate Committee. We watched it together every day.

I thought it was fascinating. I was enthralled with the characters, the system, the findings of investigation—I found the entire process to be fascinating. My grandmother decided her new hero was Senator Sam Ervin from North Carolina, who served as the chairman of the committee. My hero quickly became Senator Howard Baker, who was the ranking Republican on the committee. I told my grandmother, "I just love the way he talks!" His accent was so unique to me—growing up north of the Mason-Dixon line, I really wasn't accustomed to that gentle Southern drawl.

I remember telling my grandmother I would meet both of those men someday. She really encouraged me, fostering some of the passion that eventually led me into politics. Years later, after I had come to Nashville, I did meet them. When I was doing my graduate work at Vanderbilt University, Senator Ervin came to Nashville for a forum. I told him the story of my grandmother, and he sent her a note. Later, I met Howard Baker through local politics in Nashville, and so I was able to meet them before my grandmother passed away. I owe her a lot when it comes to my entrance into politics.

Although my interest in politics came from watching the Watergate hearings, I still did not think about running for office. At that point, I aspired to teach political science and pursued my degree in that field, but I did want to get involved in some way.

I volunteered on a local Metro Council campaign, and I was honored to do some work for an organization on Capitol Hill tracking bills—that really got me hooked. I secured an internship with the Tennessee General Assembly, really working closely with members every day. I saw legislators working together each day to address very serious issues that really had an impact on people's daily lives, and I really came to appreciate their work. After those experiences, I did go on to realize my goal of teaching political science at Belmont University for several years.

Fast forward a few years: My state representative decided to run for Congress against Bill Boner, vacating his Statehouse seat. I thought I should consider practicing what I'd been preaching, so to speak. There really is something to be said for being young, naive, and energetic. I was not aware that I wasn't *supposed* to win that House seat. I was still teaching political science at the time, and I didn't know a lot of people in Nashville. Most of the people I did know were students, and not all of them liked me! But I ventured out every day, thinking, "I can do this."

I ran a hard campaign. I got out and met a lot of great people and realized I really enjoyed getting out into my community and hearing from people directly what their issues and concerns were—that does not come across in a textbook; you can't teach that.

I learned a valuable lesson in that campaign: every vote really does count. I lost by just a few dozen votes. I didn't let it get me down; in fact, I was inspired. I tried again two years later, and that time, I won. It is really humbling to think back to when I came in; I was not only a member of the minority party but also a member of the minority party from Middle Tennessee, and there weren't many of us back then.

A lot has changed since I first came to the Tennessee General Assembly. Nashville and the surrounding areas have seen a lot of population growth;

the political landscape is, of course, vastly different; the issues facing the state have changed. One thing that remains, though—and something of which I am particularly proud—is the spirit of crossing party lines to get our work done. The Tennessee General Assembly is a place where there is true debate, give-and-take, and understanding that although we disagree on specifics, we are all working toward the same end goal. That fosters a lot of great things for Tennesseans. Since becoming Speaker, I have tried to focus on continuing that tradition.

The Capitol in Nashville is a special place, and there is a lot of history in the House chamber that is not lost on me. When I was first elected, I never really saw myself as Speaker; but in 2011, the time was right. And now, I love the job, and I am inspired every single day. I think about all the people that came before me in this position and all of the history that has happened in the House chamber, and it is very humbling.

For example, a neat fact of history is how important Tennessee was to the women's movement. By 1920, thirty-five states had ratified the Nineteenth Amendment, which was one state short of the number needed to amend the U.S. Constitution to give women the right to vote.

A special session of the Tennessee General Assembly was called to consider ratification. A pivotal vote belonged to Representative Harry Burn, who was considered undecided. On the morning of the vote, Representative Burn received a note from his mother, who asked her son to vote in favor of ratification. When the time for the vote came, the House clerk called Representative Burn's name. He did what any good son does by making his mother proud. He voted aye.

My great-aunt was in the gallery—the very one I sit in every day. Her mother, anticipating it could be a historic day, let her skip school to witness it. As I sit in the same chamber as the first female Speaker of the House, I remember those who came before us.

When I think back to those struggles of the women who came before me, it puts things in perspective. Even for my mother's generation, doing something like this, leading the House of Representatives, was really out of the realm of possibility. Women just simply did not have the opportunity to do something like this. It is so inspiring to think of how far we have come. I think even my generation can sometimes take for granted how much the women before us struggled—and it was a long struggle.

I really get inspired by the members and the legislative process. I love hearing from the members—what is important to them and their districts—it helps me to understand the different perspectives from all over the state, which is a very healthy thing for leaders at any level.

My kids and my family also inspire me. I always think of my kids while I work in Nashville, and I know they are always watching me, and that makes me aspire to do good in all that I do. I was a legislator before I was a mother, but I am a better legislator now that I am a mother. I think more deeply of what our actions today mean for future generations. I more carefully consider the impact our decisions will have on my kids.

I keep a picture of my beautiful daughter's eyes on my desk at the Capitol—it reminds me to always remember that I want to make her proud and that we must always be thoughtful that the policies we implement will have an effect on future generations. Are we making them proud? Will they inherit a better state than we did?

I always strive for balance in my life, but I am reminded that it means different things at different times. When my dad was sick, I left my family here and cancelled speaking engagements—which I really dislike doing to people who have been gracious enough to ask me to visit with them—to be by his side and care for him. During that time, my life was not in perfect balance in a traditional sense. I probably was not meeting every need of children or my professional commitments. But that was where I needed to be, and for me, that was balance.

I try to keep that in perspective and enjoy every stage of life. Sometimes we have a tendency to always assume that the next stage will be better, more fun, more fulfilling, or less chaotic, but my advice is to enjoy what is in front of you. Appreciate where you are right now.

This life truly is about service, and when you lose sight of that, you're no longer a good public servant. It is an awesome responsibility, and public service is so important. When young women tell me they are interested in the political arena, I encourage them to look to their community. If you are connected to your community as a whole, public service is a natural progression of being involved in civic organizations, your church, a local public school, or any other kind of activism.

At this point in my life, I am very happy, satisfied, and deeply honored to serve as Speaker of the House. I consider it such a great honor to walk in the footsteps of some very extraordinary Leading Ladies that came before me on other roles that led me to where I am. I cannot say enough of their service to our state and nation and of their commitment to see that women everywhere were considered equal and valued.

I have had the privilege and honor of watching extraordinary women do extraordinary things. One thing I know we're all asked is "how do you do it?" Squeezing in life's little joys: kids, pets, exercise, church, volunteer work—whatever it is that makes our lives feel whole—it can seem a monumental task. But we do it. We do it because we all want to live full lives, and because of it, we are better people and our communities are stronger, safer, and richer.

Contact Information:
Speaker Beth Harwell
Legislative Plaza, Suite 19
Nashville, Tennessee 37243
speaker.beth.harwell@capitol.tn.gov

6

Betty Burchett

As children, many of us were told a story of three young men who were thrown by their king into a fiery furnace. The trial they faced seemed hopeless. Yet we see the king saying, *"Was it not three men we cast bound into the midst of the fire? Look! I see four men loosed and walking about in the midst of the fire without harm"* (Dan. 3:24-25, New American Standard Bible). This is the story of my life. I have been thrown into many fires bound, but I thank God that I have come through them loosed and walking about without harm.

My name is Betty Burchett. I am assessor of property for Montgomery County government. I am married to my soul mate, Robert Burchett. We have two children—Robert Jr. and Bracey—as well as one precious granddaughter, Ellie.

I was born in the fifties as the middle of five children to parents who were hardworking farmers. No one was more of an introvert than I. If you have ever seen a child shy away from a teacher, then you get a picture of what I was like. Because I would cry if I was asked to speak, I constantly hid from the teacher. I struggled throughout my school years. My parents sent me to a private all-girl school from the seventh through twelfth grades. Many times I know it was only prayer that got me through to graduation.

When I attended college, my freshman year was easy. My years of high school had already exposed me to everything I was required to take during my first year of college. Then my sophomore year was a major whirlwind. Not only were the classes harder, but I also became sick and was absent from class many days. When I went home for Christmas break, my mom made an appointment with my internist. He discovered that I had a tumor on my thyroid. Surgery in January was imminent. I did not return to college that year. It was time for me to stay close to home and find a job in order to recover.

Working was so much more rewarding to me than sitting in a classroom learning things I would never use. After attempting several different jobs, I realized I needed to go back to school and learn a specific trade. Since I love math, accounting seemed like the way to go. It did not take me long to realize, with my transposing of numbers, that accounting was going to drive me crazy. It was while I was working as an account tech that I became interested in computers. So I went back to school again to get a programming degree. I started my programming career in 1980 and remained in that field for twenty-eight years, moving from computer programmer to systems analyst, senior systems analyst, project manager, and programming supervisor. Then I wanted to start my own consulting company. I loved the field and moved into being a comptroller and then director of information systems for Montgomery County government.

I realized about halfway through my technology career that God gifted me with people skills and problem-solving skills. In order to overcome my self-esteem problems, I read constantly. The first book I ever read was *I'm OK, You're OK*. I was hooked on self-improvement leadership books.

I had a pretty impressive career for a girl who hated school and was awarded the superlative in her senior class for the one that would marry first and live in a country home with a white picket fence. While I probably was the one that married first, there were no country homes and no white picket fences. As a matter of fact, my first marriage was a nightmare and ended in a divorce just two years later. I married at twenty years of age while I was recovering from thyroid surgery. I dated my husband sometime in high school and then ran into him again during English class in my freshman year in college. Now I know I married someone I did not love because of my low self-esteem at the time. I realize that so many times, women marry because they fear no one else will ask. Sometimes marriage is a way out of their current situation. So instead of waiting for the soul mate that God has planned for them, they rush ahead of God's plan.

At that point, my decision was to throw myself into work and school so I did not have to deal with the feelings of worthlessness and disgrace for being the only family member to ever go through divorce. Working was always an outlet for me to keep from having to deal with my feelings and emotions.

For years I struggled with relationships. The Lord finally showed me that my jumping in and out of relationships was nothing more than looking for love in all the wrong ways. I finally stopped and asked God to reveal to me the traits I needed in the man destined to be my husband. That list was kept in my Bible for years. In 1985, at the age of twenty-nine, I married my soul mate, and life was complete. The Lord had blessed me with a great husband and a moving career.

Robert and I were soon blessed with two beautiful children. Our first was a boy who struggled in school just like his mom. However, thirty years have passed, and now schools can test to see why students have problems in school. My son was diagnosed with attention deficit/hyperactivity disorder (ADHD). Could that have been inherited from me? He was just like me emotionally and intellectually. Just as I had made it through high school with lots of prayers, so did my son.

Then there was our daughter, Bracey. She was a beautiful girl with blue eyes that penetrated your soul when she smiled, but she was as strong willed as they come. I read every book I could find by James Dobson to help me in the journey.

After the death of Robert's mother and my children's grandmother, our troubles escalated. Bracey was in the seventh grade and was our straight A student who read constantly. Her grades began to fall. I never recognized the signs because I was busy trying to hold my own marriage together. My husband's self-esteem plunged after losing his mother, his adored grandmother, and his job all in the same year. We were emotionally and financially ruined, but my husband never stopped looking to God for strength. He read the Bible every day and continued to give to our church the money we needed to buy groceries. By the time he and I regained our commitment to each other, we had lost our daughter. The only emotional support she had for years was her grandmother who had died. Bracey had turned to drugs, alcohol, and sex. We dealt with everything from her totaling cars in accidents to dealing with the legal system for being caught with alcohol as a minor.

The turning point came when we walked out of the courthouse in January of 2006. Our daughter looked at me with fear in her eyes and said, "Mom, I need help." I instantly called Bracey's counselor who had been working with her. She referred us to Tennessee Christian. I called my husband on the way to Nashville to tell him where we were going. He could not believe it was so serious that I needed to take such drastic measures. However, I knew it was out of my hands. After talking with our daughter, the doctor came out to tell me they were admitting her and that I could not have contact with her until they called me. I left the office, went to my car, and wept. I released emotions as never before in my entire life. I could not drive, I could not talk, and I was paralyzed with emotion. I finally called my husband, who asked me to stay right where I was until he could come to get me.

In the hour it took for Robert to arrive, I was stricken with blame and shame for the horrible job I had done as a mother. However, my strong family upbringing quickly made me put on my big-girl panties and deal with the situation. Each day I would get a message from the counselor that Bracey wanted Bibles—several Bibles. I was happy to take those to Nashville and thanked God she was asking for them. She was witnessing to other patients while she was getting help for herself. After four days in the hellish situation, we received a call from Bracey's counselor asking for a family conference. Finally, we would see our baby girl again. We were not prepared for what we heard. It all seemed like a blur as we heard the words rape, cocaine, bad parenting.

My husband didn't speak a word on the way home. I was desperate for some help on how to deal with it all. I called our pastor, who was on a mission trip out of the country. I went downstairs to check on my husband, and he was cleaning his guns. I saw revenge in his eyes and desperation only a father feels when he believes he failed to protect his child.

There would be several more days before our daughter would be allowed to come home. When she did, what would we say since communication was never strong in our family if it went too deep or too long? Being an introvert and emotionally absent, I felt incapable of the task before me. I knew in my heart that God was building an awesome witness in our young daughter and that He had great plans for her. However, could I be the mother she needed during this pivotal point in her life?

There were still many difficult months to follow. We pulled Bracey out of the local public high school to homeschool her as part of a new start. With many days of prayer and a suggestion from a mother in our community Bible-study group, we presented Bracey with information about the Honor Academy in Tyler, Texas. The Honor Academy was a place where young people committed only to reading and studying Christian books and listening to Christian music. It was an entire year of concentrating on one's relationship with Jesus Christ. At first she was not receptive. Then as she began to pray about it, she decided it was where she belonged. But there was one big obstacle.

It was actually too late to apply for the August term at the Honor Academy since it was already June. In addition, the academy would not accept youth until after they had graduated from high school. Bracey still had another year of school left before she was even eligible to graduate. She called the Honor Academy and told them her story. The representatives told her that if she could get her general equivalency diploma (GED) and complete an interview, she would be eligible for the August term. God again provided, and off she went to Tyler, Texas.

My relationship with Bracey was still a struggle. I was not the emotional support she needed. Satan continued to work on her and me. It was obvious she loved the Lord, but something was still tearing all of us apart. She returned from the Honor Academy due to a back injury that prevented her from doing her assigned job. After the academy sent her home without graduating, she experienced another blow to her self-esteem.

For months, Robert and I had numerous medical tests run to find out why Bracey always felt so bad. Nothing ever came back conclusive. Then Bracey began to find her calling for Christian counseling and started delving into books to try to understand why people act the way they do. This was a breakthrough that helped our family begin to heal from all the hurt.

Understanding that I had generational curses and sin patterns and accepting that I actually allowed some of those to pass on to my children was a reality that was hard to swallow. God graciously continued to provide the right people in our lives to help us understand and pray against those curses and stronghold patterns. Bracey's deep knowledge and relationship with God has provided a healing road for many of us in the family. Realizing that God made me Bracey's and Robert's mom for a reason has given me great comfort. God has wonderful plans for my children, and I feel so honored to be their mom.

I have learned that my children have different needs, and I cannot supply all those needs. Only God can. All I can do is love them unconditionally and never stop praying for them. It is okay that I am not emotionally needy, and it is okay that Bracey is. It is God's creative uniqueness that I do not need attention yet Bracey thrives on attention. Now I am okay with not being the perfect mom. However, two principles I will always have are to love and to forgive. These are important callings that God has for every human being.

As I write this, my father is dying. Yesterday was another incredible day where God provided for my family. Bracey realized that she was so much like my dad. She sensed that there was forgiveness that needed to be happening before he joined his Heavenly Father. As we drove to visit with my dad, our prayer was that God would bring reconciliation to everyone in our family before it was too late. God blessed us with a day filled with love, understanding, and forgiveness. It was a day that will impact our lives forever. We were given a gift of another lesson in success. Life is all about forgiveness. Sometimes it is so hard to forgive when we hurt so badly. At times we do not think we can ever forgive. However, God never gives us a command without providing the ability to obey.

I began my story talking about being born into a hardworking farming family. It was a Southern family stricken with prejudices. When my family found out my daughter was having a biracial baby, it became a wound that I thought would never go away. I had always taught my kids not to look at the color of skin but to look at the heart. However, some in my family were plagued with prejudice. Yesterday, my dad accepted his beautiful granddaughter for the first time. He touched her and loved her. What a blessing it was to me, to my daughter, and to sweet little Ellie. I serve the most incredible God, One who continues to give me gifts and blessings beyond words.

Success is not just about a successful career, a nice home, or fine possessions. Success as a parent is knowing in your heart that when you are gone, you have left behind a legacy that will change lives. I am proud of my children and now know that I will leave a wonderful legacy.

Success in business is making a positive influence each day in someone's life. John Maxwell wrote a book entitled *There's No Such Thing as Business Ethics*. The fact is each of us either has integrity and ethics or we do not. We cannot separate our personal ethics from business ethics. I have always made it a rule that when I lay my head on my pillow each night, I can answer yes to one simple question. That question is, "Did I make the right decisions today and did I make a positive impact?" When I can answer yes to that question, then I know I have made it a good day.

I often wondered how I could be so successful professionally and such a failure as a parent. Now I know that work was easy because it required little emotional energy. The hard work came with being a parent. God has seen our family through some incredible opportunities and always brought us through stronger and more committed than ever. Were there times of discouragement and frustration? Absolutely. But there was never a feeling of defeat. We are family, and we are blessed.

Contact Information
E-mail: bmburchett@montgomerycountytn.org

7

Elder Beverly A. Kirby

If I can help somebody as I pass along, then my living shall not be in vain. For I know it is only what I do for Christ that will last.

My name is Beverly Ann Kirby, affectionately called Mother Kirby by many. Married to the king of my life, Pastor Emeritus William B. Kirby, we have the blessed honor to parent nine children. They have given us twenty-two grandchildren and seven great-grandchildren.

Although my journey has many components along the way, I was gifted with organizational/ administrative skills. The Lord blessed me to organized the Bodacious Women Ministry. I am also an independent distributor for Ardyss International—"a healthier you inside out."

My hobbies include reading, traveling, and spending quality time with family. I am a Leading Lady.

You Can Make It

I can do all things through Christ who strengthens me.

—Philippians 4:13, New King James Version

"Who do you think you are? I don't know why you are trying to be somebody. You are ugly, fat, and four-eyed. You ain't nothing, and you will never be nothing. You are not smart enough. You didn't finish college. You don't dress good enough." Sounds familiar? These are hurting, spiteful words I have encountered on my journey. I know I am not the first, nor will I be the last.

I want to encourage you today. *You can make it!* Take a journey with me. The Lord blessed me with a praying mama! Attending Arkansas Baptist College, she married, then became a divorcee, mother of two children. It was her task to provide for the family. She took care not only of her children but also of her mother, her sister, her aunts, and any child that needed a home. Sometimes she worked two or three jobs (besides working in her own Ann & Emily Beauty Salon) to make sure the family was provided. She was determined her children would have a better life.

While the school system wanted to label me as a handicap or special-education student (I had a hearing/speech impediment), she held her ground and said no! Emily Lenora "Baby" Cooksey wasn't having it! She prayed, encouraged, and motivated my brother, my sister/cousin, and myself every step of the way. She pushed, encouraged, and motivated us to participate in many school and community activities along with that of the church.

Even in all that, I still grew up with low self-esteem, being shy, being very self-conscious about my insecurities. I quickly became friends with the elderly, knowing they would accept me just as I was, not judging me for my looks and/or lack of. Little did I know, this was part of my journey preparing me for portions of my journey.

You Can Make It.

Life journey took me on the road of being a single mom with four children, with one being a mentally challenged child. Listening and/or pantomiming so-called Christians, I copied their lifestyle. Dropping out of college, I was thrust into the throes of suddenly providing for my family. Having a mentally challenged child caused problems with daycare not equipped to take care of a mentally challenged child with frequent epileptic seizures; thus, I couldn't keep a job. I had skills and some training but no job. So I was forced to apply for welfare. Moving from the family home to the projects was not a likable option. But having no choice, we made the move. And the journey continued.

The journey propels me now to learn to walk on the brick path that is rocky, cracked, and rough. In order to do that, you must smooth those bricks by taking the ones that has self-consciousness, low self-esteem, molestation, lack of trust, etc., on them, one by one. "Now look to the hills from whence cometh your help; My help cometh from the Lord" (Ps. 122:1-2). Now, learn the attributes of the fruits of the spirits and take them on. When you learn to love God with all your heart, mind, and soul, you will obtain joy, peace, long-suffering, kindness, goodness, faithfulness, gentleness, self-control, and you will gain the attitude: I can make it! You can do all things through Christ who strengthens you. You will replace those old, broken, chipped, cracked bricks with strong mortar foundational bricks to live and walk a spirit-filled life. Focus on knowing the Word of God, and use it to speak to your spirit in every situation! Hide His Words in your heart that you may not sin against Him. You can believe He knows the plans He has for you (Jer. 29:11).

Like I stated before, I grew up with unresolved issues. Having a hearing loss can be quite stressful when trying to fit in. What you can't hear or understand, you make up, or you smile and go along with the flow. Adults as well as children can be cruel, so cruel. Children don't know better, but adults do. When you talk about God's children, you are talking about God. We were made by Him, of Him. Still I continued this journey, trying to make it.

With four children, one mentally challenged, came responsibilities that I was not adequately prepared for. Loving was not enough. Thus, the journey begins again to provide, educate them, and still live my life. As life progressed, there were issues after issues; health issues with my children, financial instability, trying to live up to the people's image, so on and so forth. It all became too much! Smiling all the time as if I had not a problem in the world trying to be a good mother, listening to everybody telling me how *I was supposed* to do it. Coming from a prestigious community family, expectations were pressed on to me. It was too much! Trying to live up to people's expectations, I made the decision one evening; my children would be better off with someone else that could provide for them in a more excellent way. Since I couldn't see myself giving them up while I yet lived, I decided to end my life. Loving them that much, wanting much for them, wanting them to have a better childhood life and to grow into healthy, capable human beings, I was ready to give my life so they could live. They wouldn't have to go to bed hungry, live in a roach-infested project, wear secondhand clothes. They would have a chance to live in a nice home with plenty of food, wear nice clothes, get the opportunity for the best education, and have a productive, successful life. But God had the final say-so. My only daughter at the time, Alnetta, who found me in an unresponsive state, called 911 and the church for the late Pastor L. L. Tisdale to tell him what was going on. Because he and Mama Tis were out of town, Pastor Weldon Tisdale came immediately to the children's assistance. After being taken to the hospital, stomach pumped, so-called counseled, I was returned back home. I found a dear Christian sister (and we weren't really close) with my children, cleaning my home. Now I was faced with shame, guilt, and still not knowing which way to go. Anita never condemned me nor questioned me as others did. She kept doing what she was doing, told me she loved me, gave me a hug, and continues today to love me unconditionally. Others questioned me. *Why? Don't you know God? What did you want? People lived in worse shape than you, but they don't or didn't do what you did?* See what I mean? *Pressure.*

As I journeyed on past that stop (thank God for a quick-thinking daughter), I progressed through life, going from crisis to crisis still trying to give to my children, give to family, give to friends, give to others, give to myself, wondering, *Lord, when will it be my time?* One night after worship, I was reading my Bible, which was on Malachi 3:11-12: "And I will rebuke the devourer for your sakes, and he shall not destroy the fruits of your ground; neither shall your vine cast her fruit before the time in the field, saith the Lord of host. And all nations shall call you blessed: for ye shall be a delightsome land, saith the Lord of host."

I fell on my knees and said, "Lord, I surrender all to you. I have tried it every way I know how and have not been able to push forward without getting pushed back. I know you said we would have trials and tribulations, but God, I can't do it by myself. Lord, I have listened, looked, patterned myself after everybody else, I stop it now. No longer will I live or imitate others, but I will live for you. Don't let them take my children, no matter how sick, troubled they may be. Give me an innovative way to provide for my family the sinless way. Lord, all I receive is this welfare and SSI check, but you will get yours. Not only my finances but also my time, my life, belongs to you. In the name of Jesus, I pray. Amen." I got up feeling ten pounds lighter.

My journey took another leap in leading me into my predestination. I received a phone call saying, "I will keep Robert while you work." Another call said, "We have a job for you. Are you interested?" Another said, "We have some Christmas presents for your family." Yes, you can make it!

Continuing to serve God, taking care of my children and others, the Lord began opening the doors. He always keeps his promises, but we have to do our part first. Even going through with sickness with myself, and two of my sons, the Lord was still blessing. My mama, whom I told you was a praying woman, introduced me to the love of my life, my king, my husband, Pastor William B. Kirby, and yet another leg of my journey continued.

It was years later as I sat listening to my husband preaching one Sunday morning; there is *no alternate plan*. My mind reflected back on my life. If I had really listened and known that then, some of the detours could have been saved. God's Word is true and means just what it says. You can't live by bread alone but by every word that proceeds from the mouth of God (paraphrase, Matt. 4:4). You can't straddle the fence and receive God's blessings. Matthew 6:24 says, "No one can serve two masters; for either he will hate the one and love the other, or else he will be loyal to the one and despise the other. You cannot serve God and mammon."

When you decide to do it God's way, you can make it! When you surrender your all to Him, you can make it. You can make it because you are who God says you are! Build your strength for the journey by digging deeper into His Word. Fortify yourself with ammunition, supplies for the journey. Surround yourself with positive-speaking individuals that have God's best interest in you. Build strong relationships with Bodacious Women and Leading Ladies in your area.

The present journey led me to be called and ordained by God to preach His Gospel to the poor, heal the brokenhearted, preach deliverance to the captives, recover sight to the blind, and set at liberty those who are oppressed. As I ministered beside my husband, the Lord showed me some hurting women, some struggling women, as well as some bound women who needed a motivation to really know God. (You can know of God, but the key is to really know God.) Formerly called the Hen Chat, Bodacious Women Ministry was organized. I invited young women to my home just to get into their heads, see where they were, and why they were struggling. How could I help them to get past the hurts and really see how God could deliver them from their pains to make the journey?

Bodacious Women Ministry was organized because we believe all women are important in God's eyes and is vital in His kingdom. We believe in unity and growth. Our goal is to provide resources for women to receive information to ensure spiritual and practical living. With the proper nutrition, you can make it! As the hymn said, "Time is filled with swift transition, naught of earth unmoved can stand, build your hopes on things eternal, hold to God's unchanging hand! Hold to His hand!" Another song writer says, "They said I wouldn't make it, they said I wouldn't be here today, they said I wouldn't amount to anything. But I am here today, I am to stay. I holding on to His Hand, and I will never let go of His hand."

On this journey, the roads may get rough and the hills may get hard to climb, but you started this race in Jesus, and He will provide. You must decide to make Him your choice! You will have trials and tribulations in this word, but be of good cheer, you will overcome if you just continue to trust him. Proverb 3:4-5 says, "Trust in the Lord with all your heart, and lean not to your own understanding. In all your ways acknowledge him, and He shall direct your path."

I thank God for my mother, Emily Lenora "Baby" Cooksey, for giving me my foundation. I thank God for surrounding me with godly men and women to pray with me, mentor me, support me to ensure that I would succeed as the woman I am today. Just to name a few, and there are many, thank you, Dimple Baldwin (deceased), for teaching me Baptist doctrine. Thank you, Papa (late D. C. Cooksey), for making me get up to go the office to train me as your administrative at the church. Thank you, Mama Tis, for always loving and praying for me. Thank you, Calevea McQuarters (deceased), for teaching me the Missionary Women's Ministry. Thank you, Mama Louise Coleman, Mama Mattie Lucy Long, Mama Odessa Eldridge (deceased), for adopting me upon moving to Tennessee. Your wise words of wisdom, your unmerited favor and love, your fervent prayers gave me provisions for my journey. Thanks to many prayer warriors, prayer partners that have crossed my path.

Thank you, Pastor Pearl Gray, for allowing the Lord to use you to pray for me despite my not wanting to hear what you, God, or anyone had to say to my confused mind. Thank you, Pastor Angela Jones, for answering my questions when trying to hear God's clear Words for this journey. Thank you, Pastor LaRita Horton, for sharing with me your calling, your struggles, your victory! Thank you, Bodacious Women, for allowing me to lead you on your journey. Yes, if I can make it, you can make it! Thank you, Bishop Calvin and Pastor Lynitta Lockett, for challenging me.

You can make it! I tell you, you can make it. Yes, we make some mistakes, some awful, dumb, stupid mistakes. Starting out on a journey not adequately prepared will make you have to detour. But do you know what the key is? Don't wallow in your downfall. Get up. Pick yourself up again, dust yourself off, and get back on the path. As Donald McClurkin sings, "We fall down, but we get back up again." The clue is learning from your mistake. We learn to ask God for wisdom.

If I, once a single mother of four, a suicidal woman, a very low self-esteemed individual, a self-conscious person, who now is a wife (a queen), strong praying woman, confidant warrior, mother of successful/professional children, an ordained elder, an entrepreneur, the founder of Bodacious Women Ministry, a musician, a woman of God pursing the Master's Will on this life journey! If I can, you can!

Dig deeper into His Words. Look to the hills from whence cometh your help. Have a personal encounter with the Lord, and know Him. Learn His Words, and speak His Words to your situation.

When you begin a long journey, you make sure you have enough fuel, resources for more, that you have enough nutrition to keep your stamina up; make sure you have a map or knowledge of where you are going. It's the same with everyday Christian living. You can make this journey from earth to heaven, even with stops along the way, if you put God first, family second, man third, and yourself last! I hear my youngest child, "Through Christ, I can do all things; through Christ, I can do all things; through Christ, I can do all things, through Christ that strengthens me." *You can make it.*

Contact Information:
Elder Beverly A. Kirby
E-mail: bodaciouswomen@aol.com
Facebook: Elder Bev Kirby
Twitter: @RevBWM
Website: ardysslife.com/revbev

8

Buena Montgomery

God Is on My Side

Study to show thyself approved unto God, a workman who needed not be ashamed, rightly dividing the word of truth.

—2 Timothy 2:15

Who I Am Is Because of the God in Me

I was born into and raised in the Church of Christ; I say this because I firmly believe that where you start in life will ultimately determine where you end up. I have what I consider a remarkable relationship with the Lord. Even as a young child, I wanted to know why, not that I was questioning God; I just wanted it all to make sense. In defense of this, as a young woman, I studied the seven major religions of the world; they are Christianity, Buddhism, Confucianism, Hinduism, Islam, Judaism, Sikhism, and Taoism, I must say that this search led me back to the Church Of Christ because that is the place where the why answers were given. I am reminded of a passage of the scripture in Matthew 15:8-9, and it reads, "This people draweth nigh unto me with their mouth, and honoureth me with their lips; but their heart is far from me. But in vain they do worship me, teaching for doctrines the commandments of men." I am a fifty-something-year-old wife, mother, and grandmother, aka Nana. I am married to a retired highway-patrol lieutenant, Benjamin Montgomery, and the mother of three children—Carmen, Chris, and Chase. My six grandchildren are Sharron, a senior in high school with a 3.85 GPA, very proud of her; Jaylen, my oldest grandson; Arai; Layla; Arlan; and Madison. My family is truly the second most important focus of my life, with God being first! I am a retired social worker for the state of Tennessee. I am a disabled veteran of the U.S. Army, retired after twenty-two years of service. I am a published poet, and I love writing as the Lord guides my thought process. In Romans 8:28, it reads, "And we know that all things work together for the good to them that love God, to them who are called according to His purpose."

All Things Happen for a Reason

I have suffered many things in my life, and I have many joys. In one of my favorite books, *The Prophet* by Kahlil Gibran, there is a passage that reads, "Your joy is your sorrow unmasked. The deeper that sorrow carves into your being, the more joy you can contain." This is indeed a true statement for my life. Seventeen years ago, my family suffered the loss of one of our three sons. No mother should ever have to bury her son, but I did. With God's love, I was able to go forward in my life after this tragedy.

These were words that I found to have comforted my heart during the loss of my child. I would not wish that anyone should suffer such a loss, but if it should happen, I would pray that they, too, might find peace as I did and comfort in a few words of wisdom.

> Your children are not your children.
> They are the sons and daughters of Life's longing for itself.
> They come through you but not from you,
> And though they are with you yet they belong not to you.
>
> You may give them your love but not your thoughts,
> For they have their own thoughts.
> You may house their bodies but not their souls,
> For their souls dwell in the house of tomorrow,
> which you cannot visit, not even in your dreams.
> You may strive to be like them,
> but seek not to make them like you.
> For life goes not backward nor tarries with yesterday.
>
> You are the bows from which your children
> as living arrows are sent forth.
> The archer sees the mark upon the path of the infinite,
> and He bends you with His might
> that His arrows may go swift and far.
> Let your bending in the archer's hand be for gladness;
> For even as He loves the arrow that flies,
> so He loves also the bow that is stable.

These words brought comfort to me and helped me understand just what I was dealing with in death, which is not to be feared.

When you understand that

> Your fear of death is but the trembling of the shepherd when he stands before the king whose hand is to be laid upon him in honor.
> For what is it to die but to stand naked in the wind and to melt into the sun?
> And what is it to cease breathing, but to free the breath from its restless tides, that it may rise, expand, and seek God unencumbered?
> Only when you drink from the river of silence shall you indeed sing.
> And when you have reached the mountaintop, then you shall begin to climb.
> And when the earth shall claim your limbs, then shall you truly dance.

Once I embraced these words and was able to separate life from death from true life, then and only then could I breathe again and go on living. I pray these words will one day help someone else the way they helped me.

You Can't Always Pick Your Battles
Just Make Sure You Win the War

Now I would like to tell you a little about going to war with your children. This was a time in my life that I was truly torn. It is also something that should never happen again. Now, there may be a difference in a father and son being sent to war together. I do not know, but what I do know is, putting a mother and her children in a war zone is not a good thing physically nor emotionally.

In February 2003, two of my surviving children, along with myself, were sent to war in Iraq. As a veteran soldier, I knew what we would be facing; the most frightening was knowing that we would be going with a unit that was ill prepared and a commander with not enough experience, so I prayed each and every day. It is one thing for a mother to send her children to a war zone and imagine what might be going on, but it is something else entirely to be there with them and know what is going on but still be helpless to prevent anything. Every time my children would go out on missions, I would be a ball of nervous energy until I saw their faces again. The constant roller coaster of emotions I suffered during this time made my faith unshakeable. I know people who say to me, "How have you gone through so much and still manage to smile every time I see you?" I have to say it is because I am carved out deeply!

While in Iraq, I witnessed many injustices, starting with the segregation of tents: one tent housing all-white, all-male soldiers, and another, housing all-black, all-male soldiers. This was because of the inexperience of our command. Later the tying of a noose by a white male soldier and the attempt to place it around the neck of a male black soldier was happening, and this was being accepted. One night, a lower-ranking soldier was beaten by two sergeants who were in the all-male, all-white tent because he came in, and they were using the word *nigger* like it was a part of their normal conversation. I imagine that it was in the confines of their tent; however, this young soldier had a sister who was married to a man of color, and he had nieces and nephews of mixed race. He asked that they refrain from using the *n* word and was rewarded with a brutal beating. The command was aware of this, and the young man had to be sent back to the states for the severity of his injuries; however, nothing was done to the soldiers who were responsible.

There was also an incident where a black soldier and white soldier were pulling guard duty together, and the black soldier was fatally shot in the head by the weapon of the white soldier. Now I must tell you that both soldiers had their own weapons. The white soldier never put his down, not even inside the camp. But he would have us believe that on this night, he left his weapon in the guard shack with the black soldier and went to the porta potty and the black soldier, while he was gone, took his weapon, an M16A1 rifle, and shot himself in the head. This soldier's death was ruled a suicide; the guard shack was torn down and burned before the investigation, so I cannot help but wonder just how the investigation was done.

As a result of all these things, I went to the Judge Advocate General's (JAG) Corps and made an official complaint of all the things that had been occurring in our unit; of course, this made me public-enemy number one. I was literally sleeping with the enemy; I felt safer with the Iraqi people than with my own unit. Because of my unwillingness to sit down and shut up, I was brought up on some trumped-up charges and held in Iraq after my unit was sent home for good and charged with a field grade article 15 because they said I did not adhere to an official command. I was in an argument with the white soldier, who admitted to tying the noose, when our squad leader told him to shut the hell up. My response was, "Who are you talking to?" He said, "Both of you," and I said, "Then why are you only looking at me, if you're talking to both of us, then look at both of us! Therefore, it seems that because I did not stop talking at what was termed an official command, I was officially charged. My question has always been when did "shut the hell up" become an official command? If he had said, "At ease soldier," I would have gone silent because that is an official command, but understand that I knew I was a target of my own unit because I caused the arrest of the soldiers who beat up another soldier that they outranked due to hate.

I've always had a problem with racism because it is the one thing we, as people, can fix. If we're willing, racism is taught, no one is born with racial hatred, it is taught. To me this is the worst form of child abuse imaginable, to take pure love and innocence and defile it in such a manner should be punishable by death, and I don't believe in the death penalty, but that's another book. But I'd like to share this with you. As I've grown and matured, I've learned that there are indeed terrible things that happen in life each and every day to different people everywhere, and how you handle these things will be a deciding factor in your life forever. My advice is to always turn to God because His infinite wisdom really is all that you'll need, and of course, you have to act. God gives the bird the ability to build a nest, but He does not build it for them! Some of the most soul-shaking things that have happened in my life after the loss of my child is racism. This age old sorrow has touched my life only a few times, but I must say that the profound effect it had left me with these words that I would like to share with you. This poem is entitled "RACE":

> I am part of a race you see
> Set apart by nationality
> The color of my skin
> The gentle curl of my hair.
>
> My race has many hues, skin color's so fair
> Some you can't know, know unto which race to bestow
> God created but one race you see,
> None set apart, all of the same heart.
>
> The human race is not apart, God created it whole
> But men with their seeing eyes,
> caused separation because of the hues
> What's on the outside can never reveal that on the inside
> That which is hidden from man is his true nature
> What if one could see man from the inside out
> Who, then, would want to separate from men?
>
> So why don't we, if just for a day, have the ability to say
> I will see all men for what they truly are
> I will see them first from the inside and then from the outside
> I know that if this we could do, then it wouldn't matter what the hue
> Because then we would be able to see, just what God intended to be.
>
> That we all be a part of the human race
> That we live together in harmony and grace
> That we see each other as we're supposed to see
> One nation under God *unconditionally*!

I've written many poems in my life and this is one of my favorites. I am reminded of the words of Martin Luther King Jr. when he said, "Injustice anywhere is a threat to justice everywhere!"

So you see, we really must act when we are faced with injustice even when the injustice is not directly focused on us, because I say not us today, but if we continue to fail to act, it will be us tomorrow!

My Wisdom Is Shaped by Years

My life has been touched by many women of wisdom, and I would be remiss if I didn't mention them. My late mother, Hilton White; Katie Robinson, aka Little Mama; Johnnie Arriba, aka Momma Johnnie; Pinky Dowell, aka Aunt Pinky; Cynthia Rawls Bond; Joyce Fannin; the late Helen Williams; and many others whom I have interacted with over the years.My mother had a saying that has served me well in my life. She would say, "It's a sad wind that never blows a change," and this simply means that we should not be doing in our fifties what we were doing in our twenties, nor should we continue to be judged in our fifties by the things we did in our twenties, especially if we have made strives to change our lives for the better.

Another true friend brought this to my attention. I must say that I really had never looked at this childhood quote like this, but it makes sense. Ms. Cynthia always says that words cannot hurt me is the craziest thing she has ever heard, and I must agree. As a child, I would often say that sticks and stones may break my bones, but words can never hurt me; but as I have grown up, I have found that words can destroy. In James 3:5-8, it reads, "Even so the tongue is a little member, and boasteth great things. Behold, how great a matter a little fire kindleth! And the tongue is a fire, a world of iniquity: so is the tongue among our members, that it defileth the whole body, and setteth on fire of hell. For every kind of beasts, and of birds, and of serpents, and of things in the sea, is tamed, and hath been tamed of mankind: But the tongue can no man tame; it is an unruly evil, full of deadly poison." Also in Matthew 12:36, it reads, "But I say unto you, that every idle word that men shall speak, they shall give account thereof in the day of judgement." I say that if this does not make you stop and think before you speak, well, I do not know what will! In all the things in life we seek, understanding and wisdom should be at the top of our list, for if we possess these things, then we are able to know just how great God is and always place Him at the front of our lives, and He will add everything else to us! Always seek ways to please God, for in doing so, you yourself shall find pleasure. I will offer another word from my favorite book, *The Prophet*, about love in the hopes that we will all seek it in like manner. "Love gives naught but itself and takes naught but from itself. Love possesses not nor would it be possessed; for love is sufficient unto love.

When you love you should not say, 'God is in my heart,' but rather, 'I am in the heart of God.'"

I have to say this: be women of excellence because that's what God intended you to be, the very best in representing Him and His Word. "Let us hear the conclusion of the whole matter: Fear God, and keep His commandments: for this is the whole duty of man," because that's your whole mission in life, serving God!

Love God, then love yourself!

For speaking engagements, contact:
Buena Montgomery
351 Friendship Rd.
Brownsville, TN 38012
Buena@att.net

9

C. Lynne Tate-Shakeenab

And we know that all things work together for good to them that love God, to them who are the called according to His purpose.

—Romans 8:28

Greetings! My name is Lynne Shakeenab. I was born in Bad Kreuznach, Germany. I have two adult children, and I am also a Formalwear business owner. I enjoy decorating and doing home makeovers. I truly love being a servant of the Lord. Be Blessed!

Use the Gifts That God Has Given You

Reflecting back upon the first year of my life, my father told me that during that period of time, I was near death twice! On both occasions, my small frame appeared lifeless, with barely a pulse, and my eyes had rolled back and had *set* in a fixed position. Physicians at the emergency room in Germany told my parents that they thought I was having *seizures*! In my early teens, there were times when I would experience the feeling of sharp fingernails moving across my eyelids. Once when I was twenty, I awoke with my pupils extending beyond my eyelids! Since that time, I have had two other episodes concerning my eyes. The devil comes to steal, kill, and destroy, to sabotage us from receiving our gifts. Yet some blessings may be delayed but not denied.

It wasn't until ten years ago that I had the understanding of a gift that God had given me. That is why it is so important to watch your children and see what gifts and direction God is leading them into. Knowledge is indeed powerful! God either speaks then moves or moves then speaks. With me He moved then he spoke. From teen years, I would *see* things in open visions. I did not understand it and had no one around who could tell me what was going on. For quite some time, I assumed everyone had them. Truly, God does work in mysterious ways. Prior to being told and receiving an understanding concerning this gift, I would have an open vision and share it with my prayer partner. Within seven to ten days, what I had shared with her would come across the pulpit. She would sit on the second row, and I sat on the third. Countless times over the next few years, she would turn around with a strange expression on her face. Finally, one day after service, she asked me, "Am I the only one you share this information with concerning these visions?" My reply was yes! My sister was puzzled why I had not shared this information with anyone else. At that time in church, *getting cut* was seemingly going on a lot, and I wasn't in a hurry to get cut! Being reprimanded for not following the correct move of God or acting like you had a gift and actually did not! I shared with her because I trusted her.

God being the gracious Abba Father that He is will not leave you in darkness. If you seek Him, you shall find Him! We have not because we ask not. The Lord wants a great relationship with us! He wants us to know Him, for He already knows us. He tells us that His eye is on the sparrow and He knows the work ethics of the tiny ant, so we know He watches over us. We are fearfully and wonderfully made! Just as we want to be the best friend, mother, sister, wife, employee, or employer that we can be for others as well as for our own self in our personal unique ways, well, we should *always* seek to please God and to first put then keep Him first. You can't truly *love* or have a relationship with someone that you don't know. God has given us an open invitation to be intimate with Him. I once heard an awesome explanation of the word *intimacy*: in-to-me-see, or reverse it, and it becomes see-in-to-me! Once you take the time to stop, look, listen to, and learn about someone, then you begin to know them. A lot of people know your name, where you work, but that doesn't mean that they know you. Most mothers *know* their child. Need more be said? Time has been spent, they have been observed, you are a part of them. God desires *no less from us*! We are His offspring once we say *yes* to His will and to His way. See into God. At that point, know and feel that you *are* a part of His family. Satan takes pleasure in tormenting our minds because it starts with the mind. Guard your heart, and keep your mind stayed on Him, Jesus, our Lord and Savior. He sacrificed His life to save us from our sins! There *is no greater love*!

In our righteousness, we offer up "filthy rags" unto the Lord. In the righteousness of Jesus Christ, we are accepted. The price has been paid, enter in! Let me interject this point, once you acknowledge your sins and repent, you are forgiven. Forgiveness is a gift, a powerful tool! As we were forgiven, don't neglect to forgive others. When you forgive those who have wronged you, rather intentionally or unintentionally, you also free yourself from holding grudges, resentment, and bitterness. When we come to Love God, we can trust Him, depend on Him, and *believe in Him and His Word* given to us in the Bible (B-believers, I-instructions, B-before, L-leaving, E-earth).

Seeing young people accepting Christ, following His statutes, and using the gifts God gave them is an awesome wonder! As for me, I always believed that Jesus was the Son of God, yet having that personal relationship with Him came later in life. God uses people to accomplish His work. His desire is to work through all of us, for we are helpers to one another. Once God clarified the gifts that He had given me, it seemed as the most gorgeous sunrise literally appeared. God opened up avenues that were once closed, brought greater insight and explanation of His will for my life and the power to be an overcomer, destroying the works of Satan. Just as a baby undergoes great physical transformations from birth to, let's say, thirty years, coming to Christ has a wonderful spiritual transformation, first natural then spiritual.

God will confirm His Word by three confirmations. Through confirmations, I knew that being a seer and a watchman on the wall were assignments from God for me. Nearly twenty years had passed before clarification was defined. God wants to pours His spirit upon all flesh. Wisdom is not exercised when someone's gift is coveted. The gifts God have for you are uniquely yours.

Once the Lord showed me in an open vision that our physical bodies (think of your body as a church, and starting at the top of your head, divide your body into equal vertical halves) are the doors to our temple. The doors open, and people enter into your temple, and they sit down. And here's what God said, "While the people are there, what do they see, what word will they hear, and what will they think once they leave?" This is a *real* self-examination, like a Holy-Ghost checkup! The real you is who God sees and knows. Many disguise the true person and exhibit the person that we want the world to see. Be true to yourself!

Continuing to share God—given revelations: Everything that is precious and valuable takes three major components: (1) time, (2) heat, (3) pressure. Over time, gold is well hidden deep in mountains and underground under great pressure; it takes dynamite, picks, and other abrasive methods to free it from the hard surface that contains it. It has to be heated and molded. Diamonds start out as coal. Under pressure and with time, these minerals undergo transformation. Like gold, it is violently dislodged from its source, then must be cut again and again into facets and take numerous polishing procedures! Finally, the pearl, beginning with a tiny irritating grain of sand falling into the oyster shell. The shell halves come together and seal. The oyster begins to secrete layers upon layers of a mucus type of material around the silicone granules. Under the pressure and heat of the closed shell once forced open, the pearl is found! Sometimes situations or people irritate you, and you can't seem to get away. Often God is showing you what He wants to change in you.

Gold, diamonds, and pearls, along with other valuable stones, are not just simply found lying on the ground in plain view. When you meet or see a man or woman of God possessing the anointing (yoke-breaking power), be assured that they have gone through tests and trials to obtain that gift! This statement coincides with a simple story that reminds me of short stories called parables. Jesus used these often to relay a message to the hearers. A simple short story that can be remembered easily is far better than a long lecture where you may only retain one out of ten points when you only have a short time to share a quick testimony.

What makes one glass more valuable than another? You have a glass from the dollar store, and it costs $1, and there is a glass from the department store, and this one glass costs $100! Both are made from silicone (sand), both are transparent, and you drink from both of them. The dollar-store brand goes through ten firings in the hot fire, and the Waterford-type expensive glass goes through seventy-five firings! The expensive glass is handled individually in the hand of the craftsman whereas the less expensive glass is mass-produced on a routine conveyor-belt process. This glass is thick, heavy, and has numerous visible flaws and many air bubbles. After going through the basic process of forming the drinking part of the expensive goblet, the stem is formed and then the base. The glass is given to the artesian, where in their hands the glass is thinned, made lighter, cut and etched over and over again into a unique design or pattern. The process that one undergoes determines the value of an individual. Unlike the making of a glass, when it comes to people, we can decide the process, we have a choice. To whom much is given, much is required! If you were to take your fingers and thump the inexpensive glass near the rim, the sound would go *thud*! To thump the expensive glass near the rim, the sound would go *ping*! So the question is this, do you prefer to be the Christian who goes *thud*? If so, you are that will-do Christian just going through the bare minimum. Now if you want to sound off and go *ping*, prepare to go through more tests and fiery trials; but when you come through, your value is tremendous! You will have been in the hands of the master! Being groomed for kingdom work requires giving God a *yes*!

It is such a blessing and comfort to know that God is with us in every situation. The Holy Ghost is our comforter. What a mighty God we serve! We are stronger than what we sometimes think we are. You can't identify with something that you don't know anything about. Whenever someone would have a parent to die, I couldn't say that I knew how they felt for I had not lost a parent. Returning to the onset of this chapter, approximately eight years ago while sitting in church listening to the preached Word of God, I had an open vision of a man lying in a casket. I watched closely as the figure of the man's face became clearer and closer. It was my father! I told God that my father could not go at this time; I was unsure of where he would spend eternity! No one wants a parent to leave them, yet I had come to terms to know that if the Lord had a place for my father in His kingdom, I could accept that. But being unsure of where my father was spending eternity, my quest was on! Once I reached home that Sunday, I began to seek the face of God for help. My father and I were already close. We became closer. Dad was diagnosed with dementia, then Alzheimer's. His memory, mood swings, and temperament varied for the first six years. Watching a loved one diminish before your eyes is like a travesty. You seemed rendered helpless but not hopeless. Four years after the vision of my dad in the casket, he came home one Wednesday evening stating that he had went to the altar and told God that in the days that he was given to remain in this life, he would live it for God and do whatever the Lord wanted him to do! Stay strong; never give up. God answers prayers according to His will. In January 2012, Dad's health began to rapidly decline. He was hospitalized for two weeks, and then he came home. Dad had bounced back many times before, and I thought he would again. A hospital bed, wheelchair, and other items to be used to assist him were set up upon his arrival via ambulance. I took pictures every day, not realizing that these were the last photos I would have of him, as if to be recording his departure. A male nurse was there to assist us with Dad. He was a hospice nurse and had many years of experience working with dementia patients. After examining Dad, he told me, "You do know he has only three to four weeks left to live." I looked at him in disbelief. He thought that the doctors at the hospital had informed me; they had just deluded me.

We had a big fish fry, and friends and family attended. Days passed, and Dad began to respond less. The body, before life begins, prepares for life in this world; and when death approaches, likewise the body prepares for departure. Dad began to sleep almost twenty hours a day, his appetite decreased, and he refused food. I bought him jars of baby food and Ensure, anything that I thought he might consume. The last two years, I was Dad's nurse and housekeeper. It was February 12, 2012. My mother called me at work and said that Dad told her he did not believe he would live to send the end of February. Mom asked why he thought that, and he said that He had a talk with Jesus and that the Lord said that His work was done. My dad was saved!

Friday, March 30, 2012, my mother, father, and I were all together downstairs. Dad kept his eyes closed all day. We had to turn him every four hours to prevent bedsores. Dad's breathing had become labored, and it was difficult for him to cough up phlegm, so a suction machine and oxygen were brought in. Friday evening was quite still. I was reading the last of St. Mark, and Mom began to sing hymns. She asked me to pray over some oil, and I did. Then I spontaneously got up and went over to my dad's bed, prayed, and anointed my beloved father from his head to the soles of his feet. During this time, he never moved.

Saturday, March 31, 2012, was a sunny day, and I felt quite energized. My mom wanted me to go run some errands for her, and I did. Upon returning home, I fed my mom, son, and a friend of the family. Looking upon my father, I observed he was not breathing. When I touched his hand and lifted it up, it was cold and stiff. I didn't alert Mom, who had been sitting with him all day. I called hospice, and the nurse came out and checked for a heartbeat or pulse. Upon the first check, there was no response; at the second check, a faint pulse remained. We had approximately one minute to say goodbye. While looking upon my dad, I smiled, kissed him, and told him that I loved him. The gifts of God are wonderful! God has *everything* that we need, and His love is everlasting!

Look to the Lord God for *everything*! There is nothing too hard for Him. The best gift God gave us was His Son, Jesus. The Lord wants us to activate the gifts He has given unto us! Walk by faith, and live in total victory!

Contact Information:
E-mail: lynnetate408@gmail.com
Facebook: Coraindia Lynne Shakeenab

10

Christine Jolie Littleton

Do not conform any longer to the pattern of this world, but be transformed by the renewing of your mind. Then you will be able to test and approve what God's will is—his good, pleasing and perfect will.

—Romans 12:2, New International Version

Introduction

My name is Christine Littleton, and I am originally from Jackson, Mississippi. However, I moved from Mississippi when I was eight years old due to my father being in the military. I have been a resident of Clarksville, Tennessee, for seventeen years, and I work at Gateway Medical Center. I am a member of Zeta Phi Beta Sorority, Incorporated, and I enjoy participating in community-service projects with my sorority's Clarksville chapter, Rho Mu Zeta. I also enjoy reading in my spare time. My wonderful parents are Dr. J. D. and Shirley Littleton.

Words of Sharing

For so many years, I had struggled with self-confidence. Although I had caring parents who were very accomplished in their educational and career endeavors, I personally felt I could not reach that level of success. Doubt and fear had gripped me so tightly that I had decided to settle and be content with having my associate degree and my credential as a registered health information technician. There were several goals I wanted to complete in my life, but I was afraid to pursue them. I had listened to the lies of the enemy for so long that I believed I could not achieve my goals. However, God had other plans, and He began to show me through His Word that I am fearfully and wonderfully made and that I could do all things through Christ. In addition to growing stronger spiritually, I had determined in my heart to accomplish my goal of obtaining my bachelor's and master's degrees, plus join an organization that could greatly benefit me and the community.

First, in 2002 I decided to apply in Austin Peay State University and start at the beginning of 2003. I remember talking to an advisor about the professional-studies program. This was the best route for me to take since I already had my two-year degree, which would take me less time. It was a blessing not to completely start over. I knew that God's hand was in the situation for me to go back to school because the process was going so smoothly. Now, I am starting classes after being out of school for six years. Let's just say, I had to study really hard a lot after being out for so long. Again, the enemy tried to tell me that I wouldn't make it and that it was a waste of time. Another issue was that the individuals who claimed to be my friends did not support my goal. Some people questioned why I would want to do this. They would criticize and wonder what continuing my education would do for me in the future. I was a little hurt and discouraged, but my God is awesome, and He was with me the whole time. After two years of hard work, I graduated in 2005 and was awarded a bachelor of science degree in professional studies.

Second, I wanted to complete my master's degree, but I didn't do it right away. I waited five more years to attempt to work on this degree. Again, I had settled and made excuses as to why I couldn't do it. But the Holy Spirit kept reminding me that if the Lord had gotten me through obtaining my bachelor's degree, He could definitely help me through this. Finally, in 2010, I decided to apply for the master of business administration program of Bethel University. I was accepted and attended the introductory seminar in Nashville, Tennessee. That first seminar was overwhelming, and after our first session, I decided that it was not for me. I was ready to give up. I thought I couldn't do as well as the other individuals in the program. It seemed that I was slow in understanding as I was listening to the details of the program. However, the Holy Spirit had to remind me who I belonged to. I am a daughter of King Jesus, and I could accomplish anything through Him. That was enough to keep me in the program. I had a good start in the program and was doing very well, until March 2011. After suffering strokelike symptoms, I had to be admitted to the hospital for about three days. I was bedridden for several days, which allowed me to assess my situation and make changes in my priorities. Praise God that I recovered and I was able to return to school. Although this situation set back my graduation about four months, I was able to finally graduate in 2012 with a master's degree in business administration.

Third, I wanted to join a sorority. This was something I had wanted to do ever since I was working on my undergraduate degree. I would see the ladies on campus wearing their letters proudly while serving their community at various events. I was in awe of those ladies. I wanted to be a part of an organization where women would set a higher level of achievement in their commitment to community and education. However, I was busy with my classes and didn't think I could do it. However, I let doubt and fear set in, and I didn't do it. Finally, in 2009, I had determined it would be the year for me to find the organization I could become a part of. God led me in the direction of Zeta Phi Beta Sorority, Incorporated, and I became a member along with my mother. God has allowed me to be around a group of ladies who will always speak life into my situation. They encouraged me to go forward in life and be my best.

Fourth, in accomplishing my goals, there have been so many people God has put in my life for constant encouragement and strength. First and foremost, my parents have been a blessing to me. Without them in my life, I don't know what I would do. There were times when I was ready to give up, and my parents would just tell me, "Keep going, you can make it." Simple words of encouragement can make a big difference. My parents were there to cheer me on when I achieved my degrees. With my parents by my side, I was able to make it. Next, there have been some great friends who have really been there for me as I was pursuing my dream: Tina Turner, LPN, Lucinda Head, Rommie McCatty, Melissa Argueta, and Barbara Ritz. When I had seemed discouraged, they always told me I could do it and that I could conquer any situation. Finally, the ladies of the Rho Mu Zeta of Zeta Phi Beta Sorority, Incorporated, have always been wonderful to me. God had placed these wonderful ladies in my life to show me that excellence is not just achieving educational goals but also giving back to my community by serving. These ladies do not complete their tasks with mediocre standards, but they give above and beyond.

Fifth, in between accomplishing these goals, my walk with the Lord has been very interesting. Let me be honest; it has been quite a challenge for me. I know that I am to be a doer of the Word, but there have been times when my flesh almost got the best of me. It was during those times that I really had to learn what true submission was. I had to learn that in order for me to accomplish something, I had to give everything to Him and talk to Him about my doubts, fears, worries, and so many other issues. As I stumbled along the way, there were always people that would question whether I truly walked with Christ or wonder why I was going through challenging times. I understand that although I stumble, I get back up, confess, and keep walking. Yes, trials would come, but I had to realize that those were times of testing for me. I admit, some of them I passed and on others I failed, but I had to accept it as a learning experience. During my time of being bedridden, I had to learn to put God first in everything I did. I had become so busy with trying to accomplish so many things; I did not realize how my priorities had gotten out of order. Looking at the situation now, I can say that I am thankful for what happened. If that did not happen, I do not know what would have happened. Learning to be content in all situations was another lesson I had to learn. I admit to many times of grumbling and complaining, asking God to take me out of this situation and make this a little easier for me. Again, the Holy Spirit had to remind me that grumbling and complaining was not pleasing to Him. Now, I am learning to praise and thank Him, no matter what goes on in my life.

Sixth, an area that has been challenging in my Christian walk is in the workplace. Being in the healthcare industry for a number of years, I have seen many changes. However, the change for me has been more spiritual. Before I became saved, I thought that just being a great employee would provide satisfaction. Believing that *being good* would be enough to make it through was satisfying to me. But in 1998, all that changed. While I was attending Faith Outreach Church, learning the Word from a wonderful teacher, Pastor William Luffman, I began to see that my faith had to affect my work ethic. For me, it meant that for whatever task I had to complete, I had to do it with the heart of Christ. Whatever job I had to do, whether big or small, there was to be no complaining or grumbling. That was definitely an area I had to work on. The other issue in the workplace that my faith had to affect was in how I interacted with people. Since my area is in customer service, this was something I had to come face-to-face with. Dealing with a variety of people and their attitudes affected me in so many ways. I would let my flesh get in the way and say what I felt. Again, I had to learn that I was not responsible for changing them. It was simply my responsibility to honor the Lord in how I reacted to certain situations and individuals. The next phase for me was in sharing my faith with people. I am going to be very clear on this: I was one scared person when it came to this. After all, I thought, *Who would even listen to someone like me?* Fear had gripped me, and I kept my mouth closed. But I had to learn that there are people out there who needed to know Jesus, and I was in a perfect position to talk to people about Him. Attending Grace Community Church and learning under Pastors Ron Edmonson and Chad Rowland, I learned to take that big step and just step out in boldness to share my faith. Being myself and telling my testimonies, I was able to share my faith with such freedom, it was truly amazing! As time progressed, I even began praying for people and their needs. This was an area I was scared to venture into. Yes, I prayed for people by myself, but with another person present, I would get too nervous. One particular day, a lady came in crying and began telling me all her problems and what she was going through. It was then that the Holy Spirit led me to pray. I fought long and hard on this one, but the Holy Spirit won, and I just asked the woman if she wanted me to pray for her and her family. Before I knew it, the words were just coming out of my mouth, and there was just such peace that was in the room. It was a feeling that I had never forgotten! Well, months later, the lady came in, and she wondered if I had remembered her and if I remembered her situation. I told her yes, I did. She reported to me that she was healed from her condition and that her family was fine. That was such a blessing to me! Meeting other Christians and receiving their encouragement is another aspect that is truly rewarding in the job. Let me keep it honest here; I know there are moments when I walk in the flesh and that situations get the best of me. But when that happens, God brings in one of His saints. I have met countless people and made wonderful friends during these times. One particular individual knew I needed to pray, and she prayed for and encouraged me, so I was almost speechless! To this day, we have remained great friends. This particular area has been such a growing experience for me; I can only sit back and just be in awe! The Lord places Himself in every area of your life, only if you let Him.

Finally, now that I have accomplished some goals, what is next? For now, this is a time of waiting. I am learning to listen carefully to what the Lord wants me to do right now. If He is not guiding me on my next move, I know I have to stay put. I had learned in the past that moving out of God's will can result in some serious consequences. My desire to know God has greatly increased. I am so hungry for Him now; there are no words to describe it. I am now learning to truly delight myself in the Lord. It is so amazing to be able to get to this point in my life. I am also learning that nothing else matters in my time of waiting but Him. For the longest time, I had cared about what others think and pleasing others. Now, I have learned to please only Him. Currently, I am looking to be more active in my sorority and to challenge myself to learn and accept new responsibilities within my organization. Plus, there are a few educational goals that I would like to accomplish, and I am currently looking into obtaining them, but I do know that when He closes a door, He will definitely open another one.

Closing

Although I had let the enemy rob me of my confidence and a healthy self-esteem for so many years, reading the Word of God and allowing Him to renew my mind kept my thinking on what He says about me. I know He wants the best for me. Also, another tactic of the enemy is procrastination. The devil wanted me to prolong my time in obtaining my degrees. This is where the enemy spoke to me and tried to get me to believe that what I was trying to accomplish would not be of great benefit. I chose to believe in what the Lord said. Another area the enemy attacked me in was through people who claimed to be my friend. They were never encouraging and always pointed out the negative side of a situation. Finally, when joining an organization, I knew that it was only God that lead me to Zeta Phi Beta Sorority, Incorporated. There were times when I looked to other organizations, but He lead me back to the sorority I needed to join. You may have it in your heart to do or join something else, but God definitely directs your steps. Through my struggles, God showed me how to step out on faith and just follow Him. It wasn't always easy because there were some areas in my life He had to prune. But I tell you, His pruning and disciplining me through my trials has made me a much better person. Although He has truly blessed me, He allowed the blessings so I could bless others. I thank my Heavenly Father for those wonderful opportunities. He is an *awesome God*!

Contact Information
E-mail: sufur_1@yahoo.com

11

Connie F. Booker

(Memphis, Tennessee)

Being confident of this very thing, that he which hath begun a good work in you will perform it until the day of Jesus Christ.

—Philippians 1:6

My name is Connie F. Booker. I was born in Memphis, Tennessee, where I still reside. I am the devoted wife of twenty-five years to my longtime love, best friend, and father of our children, Pastor Calvin L. Booker Sr., with whom I serve alongside as Co-Pastor at the Cathedral of Faith Community Church. Our marriage is successful these twenty-five years because God is at the head, and we could not have made it without the Lord on our side, because marriage takes three, as the poem states:

Marriage Takes Three

by Peter Tanksley

I once thought marriage took
Just two to make a go.
But now I'm convinced
It takes the Lord also

And not one marriage fails
Where Christ is asked to enter
As lovers come together
With Jesus at the center

In homes where Christ is first
It's obvious to see
Those unions really work
For marriage still takes three

I am a loving mother and grandmother, and I do not only share my love with my family, but I also spread my passion and love throughout the Memphis community and everywhere I go. I serve as the collaborate leader for Building Community Partnerships, chairperson for DCS Shelby County Community Advisory Board (CAB); I'm a member of Foster and Adoptive Families of Memphis (FAFM) and project manager for Teen Pregnancy and Parenting Support(TPPS) of Shelby County. My hobbies include cooking, traveling, and meeting new people. I consider myself truly blessed to be one of God's chosen Leading Ladies.

I am truly thankful to God and His goodness; I thank him for keeping me when I wasn't fit to be kept. At the age of six after watching the Easter story of Jesus being crucified, I knew at that moment not only did I want to know

God, but I also wanted to dedicate my life to Him. Ever since that day, I do everything I can to live a life that's pleasing in His sight.

Philippians 1:6 states, "Being confident of this very thing, that he which hath begun a good work in you will perform it until the day of Jesus Christ." It has not always been easy to see the *good work* being performed in me because *the beginning* of the good work required breaking up of soil, cutting out the weeds, and removing the rocks and stones. The process was not enjoyable, but I endured the hardships and pains of growth to become what God wanted me to be. I've been through a lot, had ups and downs, lost some things, gave up some things, but I've gained much through this journey called life. I've made some bad choices and decisions, but because I had a praying mother and grandmother, I came out victoriously. My grandmother taught me the true meaning of unconditional love. She was truly an inspiration to me. It didn't matter how you treated her; at the end of the day, she gave love. She would say, "Go, if you have to go by yourself. Stand, if you must stand alone," but realize at the same time that no man is an island, and you can get strength from those who have traveled this journey before you.

Weakness pulls you down, and strength lifts you up. You don't know real strength until strength is the only choice you have. God is being true to His Word, as in Isaiah 40:31: "But they that wait upon the Lord shall renew their strength; they shall mount up with wings as eagles; they shall run, and not be weary; and they shall walk, and not faint." As I sat idle one day, I thought about a movie I had seen some time ago, *Imitation of Life*. I saw myself as that young girl who could not be found until it was too late. Her mother passed away, and they could not locate her. When she was finally reached, it was too late to be reconciled with her. I thought about my grandmother, and I did not want it to be too late for me. She was my inspiration, and I gained the fortitude to change my direction and seek God with my whole heart.

My family's continuous support and faith in God would not allow them to give up or turn their backs on me. And so like the prodigal son, one day I looked in the mirror, and the person I saw was not the person my parents had raised or the person God intended me to be. I said to myself, *This is not you*. I sincerely prayed and asked God to save me and deliver me, and He did just what I knew He would do because He is able to do exceedingly and abundantly above all we can ask or think. But at the end of the day, it's according to your faith. I truly came to myself in that very moment. It happened suddenly!

Someone once said, "Love God, love yourself, and love others." I found that you cannot love God or others until you can love yourself. I decided to please God and not people. One of the hardest things for me was to know it was okay for me to be happy. I was so caught up in making others happy—doing what everybody wanted me to do or needed me to do—that I put everything else on hold. I was so busy making everybody happy that I was making myself miserable in the process. I had to literally give myself permission to be happy. I had to pray the prayer: "God, grant me the serenity to accept the things I cannot change, courage to change the things I can, and wisdom to know the difference." God to wants us to be happy and enjoy life; that's why Jesus declares in the Word, "The thief cometh not, but for to steal, and to kill, and to destroy: I am come that they might have life and that they might have it more abundantly." Don't be weary in well doing, for you shall reap if you faint not. God has restored my soul, and I am redeeming the time.

Now I see myself as fearless. I fear God, and when it comes to the storms in life I have to face, I resist the urge to worry, but instead I trust God. I'll admit, sometimes my flesh gets in the way; but in the end, I know that God has worked things out for me in the past and He will do it again.

I keep a little sticky note on my computer that says Stay Focused. It reminds me to focus on one thing at a time; because I've learned that if you try to do too much at once, one of those things will end up faltering. Whatever commitment or obligation is at hand—whether in a meeting, on a conference call, or whatever hat I'm wearing at the time—someone's life and well-being is depending on my ability to stay focused and pay attention to the work I do.

With everything I do, my overall purpose is to put God first and let His light, which is in me, shine through. The Word shall be a lamp unto my feet and a light unto my path. I don't mind sharing my testimony to encourage others; I strive to remain humble and let others know that my story is for God's glory, not my own. Reflecting once again on my mother and grandmother, I consider them two of the strongest women I know. I am strong because of what was instilled in me from them, and with faith in God, I know that I can do all things through Christ who strengthens me. As the storms of life rage, I don't ask God to move the mountain; I just ask Him for strength to climb it. I know the battle does not belong to me, but there's a quote that says, "God gives His hardest battles to His strongest warriors." When I reflect back on my life and all the things the Lord helped me through, I get immediate joy. I just know that He gave me His strength, which gives me the type of joy that the world cannot take away. When I would have failed or fallen weak, His strength was made perfect in me.

I don't try to be anyone else. I love who I am. I constantly remind my children that life is not about finding yourself; it is about creating yourself and being the person that God has created you to be. It's not an easy job. Many like to say "finding self" because it takes away personal responsibility. Who you are is not hidden from you. You don't play hide-and-seek with your character, goals, and principles. I've learned that all those things are within me, and it is up to me to mold my life and choices according to God's will, and that's what I do on a daily basis. I make choices. I also know that my choices do not just affect me, but they also affect everything and everyone around me, which is why I choose optimism and faith over pessimism and doubt. It is up to me to be a thermostat and not a thermometer. I have the power to change the atmosphere around me.

God said in His Word that we are not of this world, so I know I cannot just *go with the flow* of things. It is up to me to bring about a spiritual difference in the world around me and be that city set on top of a hill, which cannot be hidden. I am shy to the spotlight most times, but when I am called, I know God has a purpose for me in that given time. I do my best to let everything that He has given me and bestowed upon me shine bright. Often times I tell people, don't concern yourself with being recognized for what you do as long as what you do is pleasing in God's eyes. God knows all and sees all, and one day you will get the credit you deserve. Being looked over, looked past, looked around is not fun, but the last shall be first, and my day is coming. I do not look for glory in the eyes of man. I give God the glory, honor, and praise that He deserves because without Him I am nothing; therefore, I look for acceptance and to hear "job well done" from my Heavenly Father.

It was my family's belief that the Word of God was true when it said, "Train up a child in the way he should go, and when he is old he will not depart from it" (Prov. 6:1). In life, I have strayed away, but I couldn't stay away because the way was planted in me from the early beginning. It didn't matter how far down I went in life; Jesus's arms were not too short to reach me. Jesus could and would pick me up if he had to reach way down to get me, and that's exactly what He did. Now I use the examples from my life to inspire my family and help others and share the passion that I possess within me to create a lasting legacy. I've had to give up some things, and I've even lost some things—house, car, and even time—but I know that the weapons of our warfare are not carnal. And by putting on the whole armor of God, I am fully equipped to go into the enemy's camp to take back everything the enemy stole from me. As far as time, God will restore, and there's no need for me to be ashamed. Out of all the trials and tests I've gone through, I've never let it get the best of me. I knew the devil meant it for evil, but God meant it for my good, because the Word of God says, "For we know that all things work together for the good of them that love the Lord and are the called according to His purpose." According to Joel 2:25-26, God's Word says, "And I will restore to you the years that the locust hath eaten, the cankerworm, and the caterpillar, and the palmerworm, my great army which I sent among you. And ye shall eat in plenty, and be satisfied, and praise the name of the LORD your God, that hath dealt wondrously with you: and my people shall never be ashamed." The roads have been rough, and the hills hard to climb, but I didn't ask God to move my mountains but to give me strength to climb them. I stand on the foundation of God's Word; because it's not by power, nor by might, but by the Spirit of God that we stand. My house is built on a rock, and that foundation is the one laid in me by my mother and grandmother, who taught me to trust in God and stand on His Word. I thank God for all the people He placed in my life—too many to name here—who continuously encourage, inspire, motivate, and pray for me on this life's journey. God has been so good to me, and because of His Grace, I made it and will continue to make it. "Father God, I thank you for granting me the serenity to accept the things I cannot change, courage to change the things I can, and the wisdom to know the difference." This is what gives me the Peace of God, as I keep my heart and mind on Him. May God bless you as you read this, as He has blessed me as I wrote it.

Contact Information:
Connie F. Booker, Co-Pastor
Cathedral of Faith Community Church
2212 Jackson Avenue
Memphis, TN 38112
Website: cofccministries.org
E-mail: cofcc1@yahoo.com

12

Cynthia Pitts

Your Past is a Stepping-Stone to Your Future

The Lord bless you and keep you; the LORD make his face shine upon you and be gracious to you; the LORD turn his face toward you and give you peace.

Numbers 6:24-26 (NIV)

Introduction: My name is Cynthia Pitts. I am a native of Clarksville, Tennessee, a graduate of Clarksville High School and am completing my bachelor of arts degree in theology from Covenant Bible College. I surrendered to full-time ministry in 2008. My early career included more than ten years as a employee of the Clarksville-Montgomery County School System, were I served as an education support professional and retired as a vocational services testing coordinator. My career also includes a period working for the Clarksville Area Chamber of Commerce where I specialized in event coordination for the Chamber membership. During the past several years, I have devoted time to writing, authoring articles, devotional materials, and in 2007 I published my first novel entitled *Red*, the story of a young woman who overcomes the adversity of life to achieve her dreams and desires. Involved in many civic and community activities, I enjoy serving my community through organizations like Leadership Clarksville-Montgomery County School System (CMCSS) Class of 2012-13, and also serving as chairman of the board of directors for the Matthew Walker Comprehensive Health Center, Nashville. My time is also invested in leading a monthly Bible study at the Public Library. I am happily married to Joe Pitts, a banker and member of the Tennessee House of Representatives. I am immensely proud of five sons, three daughters-in-law, and four grandchildren.

My Story: Life, as they say, is a journey comprised of a series of steps, or stepping-stones, toward a future. As you take each step and begin to free your mind of past mistakes, God can begin to heal the wounds so you may see clearly who you are and know the purpose of your life. You are not what your past steps, or missteps, have caused you to be, which brings me to my story. Like that of many women, my life steps through a past littered with failings, all the while advancing toward a hope-filled future.

As a young girl, my life could best be described as active. I was always trying to keep up with everything my family was involved in, but outside the family, particularly in school, it was quite a different story. Painfully shy, withdrawn, and with little self-confidence, I would stay in a Walter Mitty daydream like state all day in class, imagining what it would be like being that pretty girl sitting across the room. Pretty, smart, and confident too. I always tried to find someone one I could use as my role model.

Many women in my life were hardworking women who loved their family. Substituting my reality for another, I would try to live my life like them. If I could be half the woman they were, I dreamed, I could do anything. My imagination was limited though due to my reality. I struggled with those thoughts all my life, trying to live up to an ideal self-image that was not real. So I followed the examples of many of the women in my family—married at eighteen, a mother soon after, raising a family, being the good wife, and going to church.

The dream of being a mother and having a family is a blessing and brings great fulfillment. As the years rolled on, living in another's shadow, I found myself in a place, not knowing me, who I was, or what my direction should be. I struggled. Expressing my thoughts to those around me yielded little in the way of comfort. How often did I hear "You remind me of your grandmother" or "You are such a good mother," but yearning to know who I am, I was dying inside. "Who am I?" became a familiar refrain. The pressure to overcome that inescapable sinking feeling brought me to the end of this life. The daydream abruptly came to an end.

The ensuing years after my divorce found me in a roller coaster of emotions, mostly guilt and failure. Time and an inner healing allowed me to move past that season in my life. The journey was one of humility. It took me back to where I started in my faith to what has become an even deeper relationship with God. That time of self-destruction and heartache, as I now know, were certainly stepping-stones to my future, and they can be for you.

Bring Healing to Your Life

The healing power of God delivered me from the destruction of life, and to know the word of God brings healing to every area of our lives. In Psalms 107:20, the psalmist speaks of the power of His word.

> He sent his word, and healed them, and delivered them from their destruction. Psalms 107:20 (KJV)

My self-destruction was caused by an inner conflict, the turmoil of struggling to believe God still loved me through a divorce, contrasted against the mind games as I struggled to get through each day. My identity changed from a family to something less. When children are involved, they, too, begin searching for their place. The family they once knew that brought security and happiness is now a family torn between two households. Instead of trusting God, leaning on my faith, all I could do was withdraw from life. A dark period ensued.

The healing came one morning when I came across evangelist Joyce Myers on television, talking about her failures in life and what she did to overcome her circumstances. Her story, even darker than my past, showed me a path to overcome. Joyce began to share how God brought her through some very dark seasons in her life.

Despite a life filled with church attendance, I never imagined the answers I was struggling to find could be found in the Bible. I took the first step. I began reading God's word while I fixed my faith on change. My heart desired to find myself through the verses I was reading. Overcoming the negative thoughts about me and the pain of divorce would not be easy.

My first step towards change was God's Word. I needed to reprogram my mind to begin thinking positive thoughts grounded in what I was reading in the Bible. You may be wondering, like I did, *How do I begin with this walk with God? Where do I start?* With me, I had to create the desire to change. If my thoughts and actions did not line up with the Word of God, it would be hard to see change in me.

The Bible offered me an instruction manual on how to change: "And be not conformed to this world: but be ye transformed by the renewing of your mind, that ye may prove, what is that good, and acceptable, and perfect, will of God" Romans 12:2 (KV).

Speaking negative words causes negative thoughts. I had to take my thoughts captive. As a child, I was captive or captivated by my thoughts in a daydreamer's world. I did not realize change can come by the words I speak. I began searching the Word of God for the answers I so desperately needed in life. Slowly, as I begin to speak differently, my situation began to turn around for the better. God created me to live in the spirit and not the flesh.

> You will keep in perfect peace, whose mind is steadfast because he trusts in you. Isaiah 26:3 (NIV).

The Word of God brought life to my situation. To know the Word is to know life and how to handle its emotional roller coaster. I stopped speaking negative words over my life, like "I'll never feel better again" or "No one loves me." I just decided to lay those words at the feet of Jesus and to see and know I was created for more.

> The Spirit gives life; the flesh counts for nothing. The words that I spoke to you are spirit and they are life. Yet there are some of you who do not believe. John 6:63-64 (NIV).

> The mind of sinful man is death, but the mind controlled by the Spirit is life and peace. Romans 8:6 (NIV)

I was like most people who trusted in the unseen hope of a new life in Christ. I started to dig deeper into every aspect of my life and to gain that fullness of God and to trust in that Word. I decided to speak God's Word and to believe in a change, not only for my life but also for my family. Whether anyone believes my story or not, I would proclaim it because of what God did for me.

Take the word of God as a seed, like those you plant in the ground. Your garden has different seeds—some producing vegetables, some fruit—and the same is true with the seeds of God. To believe in the incorruptible seed, and since God's Word will not return void, we should receive by faith the word of God on salvation. Once planted, the seed of salvation cannot be uprooted or taken away. The same holds true for the seed of healing, deliverance, prosperity, joy, and happiness. It all starts with a seed spoken by the individual for your life and your family.

> I am the Lord's servant, Mary answered. "May it be to me as you have said". Then the angel left her. Luke 1:38 (NIV).

Mary agrees with the Word of God to become pregnant. Mary received the Word in her heart, coming into agreement, or alignment, with the Word of God spoken over her life.

> You have been born again, not of perishable seed, but of imperishable, through the living and enduring word of God. 1 Peter 1:23 (NIV)

We are to believe the word of God by faith to be saved.

> In the beginning was the Word, and the Word was with God, and the Word was God. John 1:14, (NIV)

In Matthew 18:19 (KJV), it speaks of the prayer of agreement: "That if two of you shall agree on the earth as touching any thing that they shall ask, it shall be done for them of my Father which is in heaven." If you agree with someone on the negative, it will be negative, and the same is true when positive words are spoken. Nothing just happens; whatever seed you speak, good or bad, will produce that result.

To step out of the past mind-set into a future with God takes a step of faith, a step of belief in the seemingly impossible for your life when the heavy load of a burden weighs you down. At this moment you may feel hopeless and fearful not knowing what to do or where to turn, but begin to trust God and know He has a plan established just for you.

God's Plan

His divine plan starts with our obedience and submission to His will for our life. This scripture may shed some light on what God's thoughts are toward you.

For I know the thoughts that I think toward you, saith the Lord, thoughts of peace, and not of evil, to give you an expected end. Then shall ye call upon me, and ye shall go and pray unto me, and I will hearken unto you, and ye shall seek me, and find me, when ye shall search for me with all your heart. Jeremiah 29:11-13 (KJV)

What happens when you walk in obedience of the will of God, submitting to the plan and purpose for your life? God will lay out his designed plan just for you.

The Blueprint of Life

I call heaven and earth to record this day against you, that I have set before you life and death, blessings and cursing; therefore choose life, that both thou and thy seed may live. Deuteronomy. 30:19, (KJV)

This book of the law shall not depart out of thy mouth; but thou shall meditate therein day and night, that thou mayest observe to do according to all that to all that is written therein; for then thou shalt make thy way prosperous, and then thou shalt have good success. Joshua 1:8 (KJV).

The blueprint of your life is a map filled with choices and decisions. Whose blueprint will you follow: the plans established by man or by God?

Paul the apostle was speaking to the people about the choice to serve man or God. "For do I now persuade men, or God? Or do I seek to please men? for if I yet pleased men, I should not be the servant of Christ" Galatians 1:10, (KJV).

What a strong statement this is to think about and ponder on as we strive to serve God in all we do.

To some, success in life is measured by their plan according to the world's system. God's system requires us to meditate on His Word day and night. Many people follow others who have molded their success through their experiences or education or perhaps their talents to better society.

A question was once asked of me, "What do you want to do in life?" I would answer that question, professing that I wanted to help others. It took me years to see that before I could help others, I had to find my self-worth.

The revelation came one day as I was reading the Bible, and the following scripture came alive to me, that God made me in His image, His likeness, and could it be that I do have a purpose in life, that I do have meaning?

> And God said, Let us make man in our image, after our likeness . . . . Genesis 1:26 (KJV)

God made each of us unique, in the image of Him. Although life is full of decisions and choices controlled by everyday circumstances, it is time to step out in faith and rewrite the blueprint for your life that God has established from the foundation of time—that is to meditate by faith and imagine yourself free from the pressures of life you are living.

The change started for me when I stopped seeing myself in the image of others and saw myself in the image of God. Take the blueprint of life God has designed for you, and instruct the builder to follow the plan of God. If by faith you believe, then set your goals to get a vision and see the plan God has for your life and your family.

You can now see what must be done to reprogram your destiny by renewing your mind. You have to have a blueprint before you know who you are in Christ. Don't just imagine it. See it. Can you see yourself free from the burdens of the past to a future in Jesus Christ?

God took that situation of hopelessness in my life and turned it around with a fresh beginning. In its place, God restored my life and gave me double. He blessed me with a wonderful husband, a man who has the passion to serve God together with me. Through my failure, I found who I was created to be—a woman after God's own heart.

Plan of Salvation

For God so loved the world, that he gave his only begotten Son, that whosoever believeth in Him should not perish, but have everlasting life. John 3:16 (KJV)

For all have sinned, and come short of the glory of God. Romans 3:23 (KJV)

For the wages of sin is death; but the gift of God is eternal life through Jesus Christ our Lord. Romans 6:23 (KJV)

That if you confess with your mouth, "Jesus is Lord," and believe in your heart that God raised him from the dead, you will be saved. For it is with your heart that you believe and are justified, and it is with your mouth that you confess and are saved. Romans 10:9-10 (NIV)

If you do not know Jesus as your Lord and Savior, simply pray the following prayer in faith and receive Jesus as your Lord.

Prayer

Heavenly Father, I come to you in the name of Jesus. Your Word says, "Whosoever shall call on the name of the Lord shall be saved," and "if you confess with your mouth the Lord Jesus and believe in your heart that God raised him from the dead, you will be saved." I take You at Your Word. I confess that Jesus is the Lord, and I believe in my heart that You raised Him from the dead. Thank you for coming into my heart, for giving me Your Holy Spirit as You have promised, and for being Lord over my life. Amen.

If you have just prayed this prayer, every sin of your past has been washed away. Now walk in the newness of Jesus Christ. Your stony path of your past has become the stepping-stone of your future into a new beginning in Christ.

Contact Information:
E-mail: cynthiarpitts@gmail.com
Facebook: https://www.facebook.com/cynthia.haleypitts

13

Dara Smith

For God has not given us a spirit of fear, but of power and of love and of a sound mind.

—2 Timothy 1:7

My name is Dara Smith. I am a wife and homeschooling mother of two. In my spare time, I love to be outside, growing things in my garden. I have studied plants and herbs as medicine since I was seventeen years old.

I love sharing what I know with others, in hopes I can help them heal in the way God intended. My husband, Richard, and I founded and currently run the Lighthouse Community Outreach in Clarksville, Tennessee. At the Lighthouse, we minister to many, feed the hungry, set free the captive, and do anything else the Holy Spirit tells us to do!

One of our biggest projects is called Plant a Row for the Hungry. We have joined with Plant a Row to bring this to our community! First, we teach others to grow their own food, which gives them the skills they need to feed their family. Second, we encourage them to plant one extra row for the less fortunate!

We also visit shut-ins, widows, or those that are just in need. Below are a few pictures I took of one of our adventures with two of our young missionaries, Jordan and Dara Freeze, and my very good friend Pastor Faye Sanders.

My evangelistic ministry consists of speaking, ministering the Word, ministering in music, and deliverance, but it wasn't always this way.

I was raised in a Christian home in a Florida and taught the Word of God from the time I could understand it. I was filled with the Holy Spirit at the young age of five, and my mom would constantly cause me to "stir up the gifts" that had been imparted into me by praying with me. She was an excellent example and an amazing teacher during those precious training years. Proverbs 22:6 says, "Train up a child in the way he should go, and when he is old, he will not depart from it." My life is a witness of the power of the Word and that this scripture is true. My prayer is that my testimony will encourage not only those who have gone through what I have but also those parents whose children seem to have departed from the way.

My early life was very protected due to my mother's walk with the Lord and her knowledge of the spirit world. She kept things out of our home and taught us what would create open doors for evil spirits to enter. She was a true example with a powerful prayer life, always making time for the Lord. I continually thank God for a praying mother. We were always in church and couldn't wait to get there every time the doors were open. I was in a program called Missionettes from kindergarten until I graduated and was crowned at the age of fifteen. During that time, I grew tremendously in the Word and in the gifts of the Spirit. I attended a private Christian school, so I was always surrounded by people who loved the Lord. We saw constant miracles, which really was the foundation for the faith I now have. I was really blessed to have faithful teachers and mentors that truly loved the Lord. I must stress how important these developmental years are and how crucial they are to the later adult life.

In the middle of high school, my family moved from the town I had always known to a beach town where my grandmother had retired. Things in my life began to change; everything was so different. Public school, for one, was a major change; and unfortunately, this school was full of drugs, sex, and alcohol. I had the desire and goal to remain pure and to stand for what I believed. I had the reputation of the *good girl* and tried to find friends that held the same values. It was hard finding such friends, even in the church, for it seemed there was not the same fire and zeal that we had known in our previous church family.

As I neared college age, my friends began to change. They were doing things that I was taught were wrong, but I was sure that I could *hang out* and not conform. Boy, was I wrong! I began to make compromises in my walk with the Lord, and before I knew it, I was in a serious spiritual battle.

Shortly after I began to *give in* to the many peer pressures that surrounded me, a very strange thing happened. My best friend at the time called me one evening and wanted me to come over. She lived on the next street and asked me to start walking; she said we would meet halfway and walk back to her house together. I left the house and had not gone very far when I heard a loud voice say, "*I will* meet you halfway." I looked behind me for the person who said it, but no one was there, the street was empty. I was instantly struck with fear, and a *thought* came into my mind that said, *You could write good horror stories.* I shivered and began to run. I knew what had spoken was an evil spirit, but I believe to this day that because of my compromise, I did not discern the seriousness of what had just occurred. Little did I know, my choices would change my whole future.

I continued down the lukewarm road, which left me vulnerable to the subtle deception of the enemy. Due to my spiritual slumber, I had no clue that a spirit of fear was trying to gain entrance into my life. As fear slowly crept into my life, it seemed my faith quickly diminished.

Daily, unknown to me, the chains and bondage of fear grew heavier and heavier. As I married and had children, the fear only grew worse, affecting every aspect of my life. For some time, my husband's work kept him away from home during the week; and during this time, my fears grew greater. I was so afraid that while he was gone, someone would come and hurt us. Every night I would step outside my home and look in every window to make sure that no one could see in. I would not fall asleep until the sun came up each morning. I would sit up all night in fear of my life and my children's lives. The devil would so torment me in these dark hours that I was literally paralyzed with fear. In the same way that God shows me good spiritual pictures now, Satan would show me evil pictures that would send me deeper and deeper into fear and anguish. Due to lack of sleep and constant fearful thoughts, I didn't realize how depressed and sick I had become. Nothing was pleasant anymore; the world seemed ugly and dull. Satan would twist and give me horrid thoughts, even about things that used to be beautiful to me.

I remember one night, I was home alone with my baby daughter and was so tormented with fear. I kept hearing noises and loud bangs that I was sure someone was trying to get into my home. I grabbed up my daughter, ran out the door (leaving it wide open), jumped into my car, and drove off without looking back. Another time while home alone, a man knocked on my door after dark because he had broken down. This sent me into serious panic as the enemy bombarded me with lies of alarm and dread. This is how he would work on me; he would take the situation and lie through his teeth. Unfortunately, at this time, I believed him.

My relationship with Christ and time in the Word at this time was lacking. I would call out to Him when I was afraid, but really, that was it. No commitment, no time, no Word. I spiraled deeper and deeper into the depths of despair.

Still ignorant to the fact that this whole mess was spiritual, I begin to think that something was wrong with me. My doctor said I was having anxiety attacks and that I needed medication. I really did not know what to do. I knew that I could not go on like this and that what was happening to me was real. Unsure of what I should do, I refused the medication and headed home.

At home I turned on the TV. *The 700 Club* was on, and something compelled me to watch. Terry Meeuwsen was praying by the inspiration of the Holy Spirit and had a word of knowledge that someone watching was oppressed by a spirit of fear. She rebuked it and said, "You feel it coming off of you now," and I did! The presence of God came upon me, and my body began to shake. Just like Terry said, I could feel it lifting off me. It felt like a very dark, heavy cloak being lifted off my shoulders. I could not believe it! Instantly I was set free; everything was beautiful again! I felt so light and carefree. My faith that had seemed faint came rushing back now that its enemy, *fear*, was gone. I knew that the king of the universe had just taken time out of His day to speak to this woman regarding me! He loved me so much that even while I was living so unfaithfully, He broke the power Satan had over me! I began to praise the Lord like I had not done in a number of years. I was free! I mean instantly free!

The next days and weeks were amazing! I had a hunger for the Word like you would not believe. There were times I would study the Word all day long and not tire of it. I couldn't get enough! The more of God's Word I took in, the more power I walked in. Freedom never felt so good! I was so free I began looking for trouble, others in trouble, others who also needed freedom! It's awesome how often God will use you in the same areas that you have overcome, and that is exactly what He has done in much of our ministry. We are used by the Lord for deliverance of others in not only the area of fear, but often in that area.

What amazed me most was that the Lord did not make me start over. He is so faithful. He does not put us back to square one to return the spiritual soil that's already been broke. By that, I mean every gift that I flowed in before and every advance I had made in the kingdom, He did not take those away! He lets you start right where you left off!

I hope that my story is an encouragement to all who read it. I pray it touches you who have compromised your walk, because I am proof that it's never too late! I want it to encourage and uplift you, parents, who have been praying for your children! I am a living testament of a praying mother. I want it to speak to you who may be dealing with a spirit of fear. I want you to know you are not alone and that God knows exactly where you are and wants to set you free!

Contact Information:
dara.smith777@gmail.com

14

Darlene James-Runnels

I give you a new commandment; that you should love one another just as I have loved you, so you too should love one another.

—John 13:34

My name is Darlene James-Runnels. Out of all the decisions I've made in my life, the most important and meaningful one is being the mother of three boys—Daryl, Darius, and Dorian—and being the fiancé of my boyfriend,

Dennis, for seven years. Family means everything to me. I felt it was important to me to be a part of this book because I wanted to be able to inspire others to see that no matter what people think about you, no matter who people say you are, you are a child of God. You are who God says you are. And always remember: It's not what you're called. It's what you answer to! God is merciful enough to forgive us for all our sins, through the blood of Jesus Christ. Since He created us in His likeness, it is fair to say that He didn't make any mistakes. He didn't create any junk, just jewels! Many times, people let the pressures of life and what man's image of them weigh down their self-esteem. What's so beautiful about all of God's creations are that no two are the same. We all have our own unique qualities, our own faults, our own beauty. One of my missions in life is to develop an initiative for young women to build their self-esteem and let them know just how important it is to have a positive self-image. For the past eleven years, I have worked with young girls ranging in ages from five to eighteen. While some fit in easily and have high self-esteem, some of them have many negative images of themselves. The program that I want to create will be one to teach girls early on how beautiful, smart, and promising they are. One of the reasons I see many girls accept mediocrity in life is because, too often, they are not equipped with the Word of God, and their parents don't put in enough time and effort to show them all the good possibilities that life has to offer.

My Own Personal Testimony

I was an honor-roll student at Sabbath Elementary School in River Rouge, Michigan. Academics was very important to me, and I loved school. In fact, I hated it when I had to miss school. But in the years to come, those feelings drastically changed. When I began high school, I became very sickly and was ridiculed. I am hypoglycemic, which means I have low blood sugar and I used to faint. It took awhile for doctors to figure out what was wrong with me. I missed so much school that I ended up being removed from River Rouge High School's honors program called Able Learners'. This was devastating to me because I had no control over my sickness. It wasn't my fault. I didn't ask to be sick. I just was. Nevertheless, I was kicked out and had a hard time fitting in. On top of being sickly, I had people who made fun of the fact that I would faint. There were times when I wanted to give up. I was smart, but I wasn't popular. To a teenager, being popular is everything. Every morning, I struggled to get out of bed and go to school. There were days when I didn't want to go to school and my dad would make me. He would force me in the car and make me go. At the time, I was angry at him, but now I'm glad he did. Thank God I had a father in my life that was always there for me!

It was very hurtful to me. What really helped me through those hard times was my best friend, Andrea. She began inviting me to go to church with her and her family. (My mom had raised us in a Catholic church, but I didn't feel comfortable and needed a change.) They went to church faithfully every Sunday. It really made a big impact on my life. I began to see the blessings God had for me. I also had a special boyfriend whom I called and cried to, who would stay up with me and cheer me up. It meant the world to me at the time. He was there for me when I thought the whole world was against me. After my freshman and sophomore years, things got better, and I began to get back on track. I brought my grades up. Growing up in the eighties and early nineties, I watched *The Cosby Show* and *A Different World*; I think we all did! Those shows portrayed African-American families that had high socioeconomic statuses. I wanted to be just like them. I had my mind made up that I was going to college. I had a close family member tell me, though, that I wasn't goin' to college 'cause we didn't have the money to pay for it. I told her yes, I was, and that was the end of the conversation. I was steaming mad! How dare she try to crush my dreams like that? (Luckily I can be stubborn and hardheaded sometimes, which is actually one of my flaws, but God is not through with me yet!) Some of my classmates from River Rouge High School didn't expect for me to go to college, no less graduate! I was accepted into colleges such as Western Michigan University, Eastern Michigan University, Grambling State University, and Detroit College of Business (now known as Davenport University).

I recall catching the bus to Davenport University, and it was no easy thing! I would see on the corner some of the people I went to River Rouge with. They used to call me crazy for having a book bag on, walking to the bus stop after I had already graduated from high school. They laughed and taunted me every day I caught the bus. I didn't argue or say a word back. I just kept on going. Through rain, sleet, and those icy winter days at the bus stop, I kept going regardless of what they thought. (I still see these same people today on the corner.) I share this story to say that you can't let anyone get in the way of your dreams and aspirations. Whenever you are trying to do good, the devil will find a way to try to tear you down and call you everything but a child of GOD. It's your job not to listen or even respond to such negativity. It's designed by the devil to make you quit and fail!

I transferred from Davenport to University of Detroit Mercy (UDM) on my second-semester year. I received a bachelor of arts degree. I majored in communications, specializing in journalism. I also minored in business administration and am currently in a master of business administration program at UDM. Obtaining more education has always been important to me.

I am a substitute teacher and the owner of Blackberry Publications. I really enjoy teaching and writing. I had a job as a reading tutor at UDM, where we went to different schools in the Detroit area and taught children to read. I realized then that hmm . . . I really liked working with children and making a positive impact on a child's life. So in 2002, when my best friend, Andrea, told me they needed substitute teachers at River Rouge Public Schools, I applied. I've been substitute teaching ever since. I have been blessed to be able to sub for eight different school districts and work with students of various ethnic groups and cultural backgrounds.

Writing books is my life passion! I've been a writer all my life. In fifth grade, I let one of my teachers (now colleague Viveca Butler) read some of the stories I had written. She told me then and there that I would be a writer. Her enthusiasm sparked something deep in my soul. I began to write short stories and performed speeches for the River Rouge Optimist Club. It is my true passion and what I believe God has called me to do. I've been a member of the Motown Writers' Network since 2007 and have met many positive people along the way. I was able to meet Lee Thomas from WJBK Fox 2 News when he attended one of our events to promote his best-selling book *Turning White*, an account of his personal struggles with the disease vitiligo, in which there is a loss of brown color. This is the same condition the king of pop, Michael Jackson, suffered from.

I started writing professionally in 2004 when I was inspired to write a fiction book called *Catfight*, about the troubling ways that many African-American women, and women in general, treat each other. After going through a lot of drama in my personal life with women, I felt compelled to write about this problem. Even though it was fiction, it mirrored a lot of the problems women face on a day-to-day basis. There is so much competition among women that it negatively impacts the relationships we have with one another. I strive to not only entertain people through my characters but also shed light on the problems we face in society and search for answers to solve these problems. As women, we want to be the best moms, the best wives (or girlfriends), the best at our jobs, and basically be the best we can at everything! The problem, though, in our desire to be the best we can *be* is that sometimes we tend to compete with everyone else. As women (and men too), this is our biggest downfall. Instead of running our own race, we look at others and feel that we should measure up to what someone else has or has achieved. But since God made us all as different individuals, it is impossible to measure ourselves up to someone else. It is this that causes tensions among us. How did she get that man? Why does she have that house or car? It's these kinds of attitudes that cause division among us as women. It's really troubling to witness this, be a victim of this, or even be a part of this. If you witness it, you feel helpless. If you are perpetuating this attitude, you are wasting valuable time worrying about someone else's blessing and not seeing the value of your own; and if you are a victim of it, it can serve as a distraction to you and cause you a lot of problems in general. It is my goal that through my stories, I directly or indirectly shed light on these problems and hopefully come up with ways of solving them so that relationships among us women get better!

It shouldn't be our goal to tear down something that the next person has worked hard to build up. What glory does one get from that? Would God be pleased to see His children being jealous and envious of what someone else has when He has promised to supply our every need if we come to Him and ask for help? The answer is no, he wouldn't be pleased.

JOHN 13:35

By this shall all [men] know that you are my disciples, if you love one another [if you keep on showing love among yourselves].

It basically instructs us to love people and show our love by using our actions and not our words. I have been tested many times in my life in this area. When I was younger and didn't know God's word, I failed those tests. Now that I'm older and know the Word of God, I passed this particular test. I used to find it hard to show love to people who didn't show love back to me. What I didn't understand was that although it may feel natural to treat people the way they treat us, we must treat them in accordance with God's Word.

For example, I have neighbors who go out of their way to be mean to me—they don't speak, don't invite me to any of their functions, and mumble nasty things about me whenever we're outside at the same time. I'm the youngest person on my block, and from the things I've overheard them say, they don't feel like I should have the house I live in. They were also friends with the people who previously lived in my house. (They're shutting me out without even getting to know me. It may be their way of trying to get me to move.) One day I saw an ambulance pull up in front of their house. A family member of theirs had passed away. As I peered out the window, I saw hurt and sad people filling their home. Although I didn't know the person who passed away, I could feel their pain. I knew what it felt like to lose a loved one. It can be devastating. A few days later, my heart convicted to me to send one of my sons over to give them a card of condolences. I just wanted them to know that I was sorry for their loss. I didn't expect a thank-you or a response, nor did I get one. I was okay with it because I knew in my heart what I did was the right thing. Months later, I saw the card that I'd bought, lying in their grass. Years later, while their hatred and dislike of me is evident, my compassion and forgiveness is still prevalent. No one wants to live a life full of hatred, backbiting, and spitefulness. I know I don't! It's not what God wants for his obedient children. We must have the resilience to be able to show love even though the love may not be reciprocated. That's what God wants. When you love others, you will be rewarded with a place in God's kingdom. Vengeance is not ours; it's the Lord's.

Dedication

I want to dedicate my portion of this book to my parents, Jeanette and Ricardo, who always had *faith* in me and encouraged me to do my best. I am very fortunate to have both of my parents alive. It is because of them that I can remain humble and most appreciative. They have both been here for me through the rough times and celebrated the good times. I thank God for having great parents like them. (I talk to my mom every day and run my mouth for hours on end 'til my phone battery dies.) She has sacrificed and raised five children and gave her all to us. My dad has worked hard for Ford Motor Company for thirty-eight years, working swing shifts, doubles, and holidays to make sure he provided for the family. He is a great man, and I wouldn't trade him for the world!

He purchased a house for me and my own family to live in to make things easier for us. To them I say thank you and I love you so much. To my Heavenly Father, I let Him know every day just how much I appreciate His grace, mercy, and blessings. Without the presence of God and Jesus Christ in my life, I would have perished in sin a long time ago.

I want to leave you with this one piece of advice. I hope that it will be beneficial to you. Be thirsty to develop your own spiritual character and not who man says you should be. The word *thirsty* means "eager to get attention" or be "thrust into the limelight or sought out." Well, we all want to be known, right? There's nothing wrong with wanting to be *popular* or *famous*, but you should be more thirsty for God's attention than anything else in the world.

Don't live to have the worldly possessions. While God wants us to have the best and strive for the best, material things will not last. What you do for others and how you positively affect the lives of those around you is what really matters. (While my church home is Union Second Baptist in River Rouge, Michigan, I must say that I love Joel Osteen and Joyce Meyer. If my cable were to go off today, I would truly miss those two shows). Joel Osteen says, "Don't sink down your critics' level. Do what you believe God wants you to do." We must keep this in the back of our heads on a daily basis.

Peace, *love*, and *blessings*, and I hope you have a prosperous 2013 and many more years to come!

Darlene James Runnels
email: blackberrybooks@yahoo.com

15

DaShaunda L. Turner

Keep Fighting, Keep Pressing, Endure

The race is not to the swift, nor the battle to the strong, neither yet bread to the wise, nor yet riches to men of understanding, nor yet favour to men of skill; but time and chance happeneth to them all.

—Ecclesiastes 9:11, KJV

But he that shall endure unto the end, the same shall be saved.

—Matthew 24:13, KJV

I am Leading Lady Ms. DaShaunda L. Turner. I was born in the heart of Birmingham, Alabama, to Elder Henry D. and Mother Cynthia Y. Turner. I am the oldest of five children and the only one of my parents' children with no children. My father joined the armed forces, which caused my family to travel a great deal. Our traveling journey ended in Clarksville, Tennessee, where I have been established for more than twenty years. I attend All Nations House of Prayer (ANHOP), where Apostle Garfield Curlin, ThD, and Elect Lady Mary Curlin preside. Since I have attended ANHOP from the tender age of eleven, the teaching of my parents have afforded me a foundation that has provided me stability throughout my life and have led me to success at a very young age. Instilled in me was the unadulterated Word of God and sound wisdom from experiences of others who have had a tremendous effect on my life. It is no doubt that the great influences in my life have assisted me in blossoming into the leading lady I am today.

As a child, I was constantly reminded that I could do all things through Christ who strengthens me. Thus, I am somebody and can be anything I want to be with hard work and dedication. Faith, as taught to me, is not just hoping and looking for some magical appearance but working toward that hope until something manifest; regardless of what the situation at hand may appear to be for now, faith is the substance of things hoped for and the evidence of things not seen. James 2:26 states it perfectly: "for as the body without the spirit is dead, so faith without works is dead also." As a result, I grew up believing that I could be successful in every area in my life. In that belief, I focused on obtaining my education and developing myself physically, mentally, and spiritually to become all that God would have me to be. I have accomplished my educational goals by receiving my bachelor's degree in organizational management, master's in human resources management, and I am very close to the completion of my doctorate in international business. At the age of twenty-five, I started a very successful career as an executive-level human resources professional for a Fortune 500 company and also established a very successful career in teaching at the collegiate level for several colleges. Life was just grand! I was on my way to being one of the most successful women in my family!

But Then . . . The Process

You should know that nothing worth having comes without sacrifice. I believe through experience of my own and others that when there is success, there are failures in the process. I also believe that the depth of one's failure measures the height of one's success to those who do not stop in their failure. I stated above my great achievements, but a lot of times, we forget the importance of the process and only focus on the finished product. I watched my parents have their home built from the ground. When I look at their home today, it is difficult to believe that the same building over ten years ago was only a wooden frame on uneven ground. There was no color, no brick, not even a door—just a frame. My point is that as beautiful as my parents' home is, without the process of setting a solid foundation, putting the frame together, running the electrical and plumbing work, etc., the house would not be in existence today. It is the same with you and me. The process is vital to the finish product. Nothing comes overnight, and during the process, there will definitely be some challenges where you may feel like there is no reason to continue. Although the foundation is the lowest part of a building, it is the most critical. Without a solid foundation, the rest of the building cannot withstand. I talked about the foundation that was laid by my parents, my pastor and first lady, my grandmother, and others in my life. Thank God it was a very strong foundation created because I have had to work and rework my framework multiple times. Just like some weather conditions caused setbacks in the building process of my parents' home, I, too, have had some storms that have caused some setbacks in my life. In fact, I am still working on the frame! But you know what? I am still standing. Thank God for a firm foundation! I stated my educational accomplishments, but what you do not know is that in the very first year of college, I failed and had to return home. I pretty much had to start over. I talked about being this great human-resources executive of a Fortune 500 company and this great college professor, but guess what? I lost both jobs. Even better, I was reared up in holiness, learning and understanding the truth of God. I gave my life to God and lived a sanctified life, and yep, I backslid and left the church and was stuck in a world of sin and death. "For the wages of sin is death" (Rom. 6:23, KJV). I was deceived and ended up in a bad relationship that drove me to shame and almost nothing. Everything that I worked so hard for, I lost through bad decision making. Thankfully, although my frame was destroyed and storms caused me some setbacks, my foundation was still sure. I was able to start rebuilding.

Keep Fighting

Although I found myself in horrible situations, because of my foundation, I know that if I called on the name of Jesus, I shall be saved. If I humbled myself, turned from my wicked ways, prayed, and sought the face of God, I could hear from heaven, my sins would be forgiven, and God would heal my land. I got tired of my bad relationship, bad decisions, and I cried out unto the Lord. I turned, and I started to pray with humbleness. Neither my education nor my career status mattered. When I did not have the strength to make it, God came down and rescued me and delivered me from my enemy. The fighter in me stood up. Whatever I could not handle, I allowed God to handle; and today, I have been redeemed by the blood of the Lamb! I was restored back unto salvation, and although my physical situation did not change overnight, the deep set of peace entered, and I was able to stand and fight for what is right in my life. Am I perfect? Absolutely not! But I'll keep striving; building on my frame. Sometimes, I may have to delay my working progress until a storm passes over; and sometimes, I may have to continue to work in unfavorable weather conditions. Nevertheless, I keep fighting; and day by day, I see positive results. I keep building, and I see the manifestation of my life coming together.

Keep Pressing

I do heavy-bag boxing as my exercise remedy to stay in shape. One of my trainers recently told me that I motivate her because I don't stop in my boxing workout class. That really encouraged me because I know that as my one-hour training class progresses, I have gotten tired and not always put forth the same effort and strength as I have earlier in the class. However, she was so impressed with the fact that I do not stop. I do not quit. Sometimes in the fight, you get tired. Try putting on some boxing gloves, and just keep jabbing a heavy bag nonstop for sixty seconds. I promise you, you will get exhausted! But a boxing round is three minutes long! So what do you do? You definitely do not give up, but you press with everything in you to keep jabbing for 120 more seconds; and if you put forth the effort and make up in your mind that you will not give up, you will press until the entire three minutes have elapsed. It is the same with life. I have been so tired until I became depressed, but because I hate to lose and I am not a quitter, I made up in my mind, and I put forth that effort through prayer, reading my Word, attending church even when I did not feel like it, and hanging around people who are stronger than I, that I was not going to give up but keep pressing. I keep pressing because I know that if I endure, I will reap if I faint not. Now,

I would not be truthful if I say I put forth the exact same effort each and every day, but I can say that I refuse to quit, and because of that, I have seen God bring me through trials that I would not have been able to bring myself. When I am training, I motivate myself by thinking about how good I will look and feel and also the progress I have made. In my life, I motivate myself by recognizing how God has brought me and the progress I have made, and I look toward the prize of looking and feeling good in the end. Thus, in my life, "I press toward the mark for the prize of the high calling of God in Christ Jesus" (Phil. 3:14, KJV).

Endure

The fact is that you can make it. I know what it feels like to want to give up and to feel that there is no hope. I have made the bad decisions. I have been in that bad relationship. I have lost my job and home. I have lost a loved one. I have absolutely failed miserably! But I have endured, and I have seen the salvation of the Lord. So far, what I have learned in life is that as long as there is a sure foundation, there is certainly hope. The foundation is the Word of God. Standing on the Word of God is standing on a sure foundation. As you can conclude from my life, I have great parents and awesome leaders who have groomed me very well, but it was the Word of God that has brought me. When I could not get to Mom and Dad or Pastor, I had to look to God who is the author and the finisher of my faith. Although I have had moments where I felt like giving up and felt like even God was upset with me because of my failures and bad decisions, it was scriptures like Jeremiah 29:11 that states, "For I know the thoughts that I think toward you, saith the LORD, thoughts of peace, and not of evil, to give you an expected end." That lets me know that Jesus is my hope and that He loves me more than anyone, including myself, could ever love me. When my heart was overwhelmed, I learned in Psalms 61:2 to ask God to "lead me to the rock that is higher than I." I learned in Philippians 4:6-7 to "be careful for nothing; but in every thing by prayer and supplication with thanksgiving to let my request be made known unto God." And the peace of God which surpasses all understanding shall keep my heart and mind through Christ Jesus. It is indeed the Word of God that has sustained me and given me that firm foundation to endure and that will continue to give me what I need to endure even until the end.

I was afforded the honor to have in my life for over twenty-five years my great-grandmother Lucille Jones, who lost her sight in the last decade of her life. She taught Sunday school for several years. She would always talk about the importance of the Word of God, and not just quoting scriptures but letting the Word of God be in you so that you can sustain in this life. She used to always tell me, "Child, they call me the walking Bible, I may have lost my sight, but the Word of God still lives in me." She was ninety-four years old when she went on to be with the Lord and had endured great trials throughout her life. During her final moments, we, her family, all gathered around and prayed unto God for healing. She rose up with all of her strength and, still ministering the Word of God in her last breaths, said, "Children, I've been here a long time." She went on to minister, in her own words, to her family, "II Timothy 4:6-8, 'For I am now ready to be offered, and the time of my departure is at hand. I have fought a good fight, I have finished my course, I have kept the faith: Henceforth there is laid up for me a crown of righteousness, which the Lord, the righteous judge, shall give me at that day: and not to me only, but unto all them also that love his appearing.'" Man, she was only four feet ten inches in statue, but she was one of the strongest, the most powerful women I ever encountered, and in my world, the leading lady of all time.

Physically, I was an athlete in my high school and college days, and even though I was never the swiftest neither was I the strongest, I succeeded because I had endurance. I had heart not to give up. I even received an award for being the most dedicated from my basketball team. I choose that same approach as I walk this life. I never quit. Because I didn't quit, I obtained multiple educational degrees and have established great success in my career. Because I reached for God and did not give up, God saved me and put me back on the right track after I have gotten off so far. Thanks to God that He has given me the same endurance attitude in my life because in His word, as long as I endure until the end, I shall be saved. I am encouraged to keep going. As I have stated, I have not perfected all things in my life. I am far from being perfect in anyway, but I am so glad that the race is not given to the swift or the battle to the strong. I realize that I have gotten to this point in my life only because of my Creator, the Almighty God who created the heavens and the earth. If it had not been for the process, I certainly would not be writing these words. I am blessed, I am highly favored by God, and because of God, I am a leading lady. So I say to you, keep fighting, keep pressing, and endure!

Beloved, it is my prayer that you prosper and be in health, even as your soul prospers. Realize that you are somebody. You are fearfully and wonderfully made. You can make it through, and you can win. Jesus loves you, and it is the will of the Lord that you make it in this life. In a recent message preached by my pastor, Apostle Garfield Curlin, Th.D., he stated, "God is not mad at you,

He's madly in love with you. You are God's masterpiece." May the blessings of God be upon you, and may you reach your full potential in Jesus's name. I leave this last scripture with you from Acts 20:32, KJV: "And now, brethren, I commend you to God, and to the word of his grace, which is able to build you up, and to give you an inheritance among all them which are sanctified." I say again to you, keep fighting, keep pressing, and endure! Blessing and peace be unto you.

Special Thanks

Special thanks to my Lord and Savior, Jesus Christ. To my wonderful parents, Elder Henry D. and Mother Cynthia Turner and to my Pastor and First Lady, Apostle Garfield Curlin, Th.D, and Elect Lady Mary Curlin. Thank you so much for training me up as a child in the direction that I may go, for as I have gotten older, my training has not departed and have allowed me to blossom into who I am today. I love you more than you may ever know! I also want to thank the members of All Nations House of Prayer. Thank you so much for your love and prayers. You are simply the best.

In Loving Memory

In honor of my grandmother Katie Mae Jackson and my great grandmothers Lucille Jones and Armada Rogers, I am so thankful for the love and wisdom that has been imparted into me from these great women now resting in the arms of Jesus. Their legacy still lives with me.

DaShaunda L. Turner
Human Resources Executive, Career Coach and Educator
I would love to be of assistance in any way possible. Please contact me.
E-mail: dashaunda.turner@gmail.com
LinkedIn: www.linkedin.com/pub/dashaunda-turner/18/31b/469/
Facebook: www.facebook.com/dashaundat

16

Demeshia

From Oppression to Opportunity

Many are the afflictions of the righteous: but the LORD delivereth him out of them all.

—Psalms 34:19

My name is Demeshia. I was born in Wichita Falls, Texas. I consider myself an old-fashion Southern belle that loves the fast moving city life and has dreams of making it big in the world! I have gone through enough trials and tribulations for a lifetime, where I could have given up, but the fact that I wouldn't allow myself to stay down always gets me back up to live and not die. In my journey, I have discovered to be optimistic and build up my faith in God. Although life has had its ups and many downs, "I AM A SURVIVOR!" I pray that this brief manuscript be a blessing to the reader as I take you on the journey that life has revealed to me.

My journey begins in Texas surrounded by my mother's and father's families. My mother, who was a virgin, dated my father during high school. I was a prom-night baby. I lived in the projects under the same roof with my mother, grandmother, auntie, uncle, and my cousin. My cousin is only two months older than I am. You see, my mother got pregnant right after her younger sister did. My cousin and I were like sisters from the start, but opposites. We shared many memories growing up together. We have a very close and loving bond. Even when it was time for me to go visit my grandparents on my dad's side, I would beg for her to come along. By the age of two, my mother married a soldier. I was not happy about it. Something about this new man was alarming. I didn't understand the level of discernment God had given me as a child. Suddenly, I was forced to leave the only place I had ever known and loved. Some people said I was lucky and that I would get to travel around the world because he was in the military. A part of me was ready to explore.

Luckily, where we moved to was only thirty minutes away. It did not take long before my suspicions about my stepfather became known. He was very strict and direct. The family explained it was because he was a soldier. I had very strict day-to-day restrictions and was put on harsh month long restrictions at times. I missed the love I felt with my immediate family. I went from being outgoing to shy and introverted. I was always fearful I would upset him, but I still had my determination to win his love.

I remember when I was ten years old, going out for ice cream one day, and I asked my stepdad, "When my little brother is born, are you going to treat me different?" He replied, "Oh, no, sweetie." Well, it was a blessing to have a new playmate; after all, he was a miracle baby. My mother was diagnosed with Lupus after she had me. Due to her illness, she was always in and out of the hospital. Oftentimes after school, I played with my Barbie dolls on the dialysis-clinic floor or sometimes had to go over strange neighbors' homes to stay the night or week. Then there were many times she would not be home after school because she had to be admitted into the hospital again. I even witnessed my stepfather press a wooden spoon on my mother's tongue to keep her from swallowing her tongue. At the time, I did not know she was having a seizure. That particular incident scared me into thinking about her dying and leaving me. I became a worrier.

As our family grew from just my parents and me, to me having a little brother and then having a little sister, many things shifted by the age of twelve. I started to feel abandoned and acted out in school. Since I was a worrier, I would start to overanalyze or assume the worst outcome at school. Then because I had no one to talk to at home, I was always talking during class. Due to always being on punishment, I was always anxious and could not sit still for long in class. Eventually I became a bully at school, being violent and saying harsh things to peers because of the treatment I received at home. Thank God for teachers that really care about their student because those behaviors did not go unnoticed and some teachers did build me up and explain ways to channel my energy. I discovered my ability to write stories, draw, sing, and lead others. I started turning my negative into positive. I became the fastest runner for my age at various schools growing up. This made my mother proud because she also set track records at her high school. I soon became an anti-bully student and used my height and wisdom to stand up for other kids who were being bullied.

As time went on throughout my school years, I grew further away from my immediate family in Texas and my mother. I always got the impression I did not belong. I was the black sheep of the family. I really felt look "looked over," in my family. To me, my siblings were treated like royalty, and I was the child who did not have her own biological father to come home to. That absence of a father, who truly cared for me, was a major void in my life. One particular time hurt me to the core. I was sixteen and was racing home to make my 10:00 p.m. curfew, but when I got home, no one was there. By this time, I had a phone in my room and my mother called at 3:00 a.m. to tell me that they were on vacation in the cabins and that she felt bad and wanted to check to see if I was home. After this incident, something broke in me and I began to resent my mother. I cried all night and went to school with bags under my eyes. I became a loner at school. I knew my stepdad was going to treat me different when he had his own kids with my mom. As a matter of fact, he treated me even worse. By this time, he would go out his way to single me out with no remorse. The spirit of suicide had been chasing me since I was thirteen years old. My mother found my first suicide letter that I purposely wrote in red ink about why I was so depressed in my life. I had been crying out for help for years. Many issues of isolation and neglect kept me bond in suffering, pain and torment during my childhood. All I had left was hope in my heart that he would accept and love me, as I believed he could.

Many sad days weighed me down at school, but having no one to turn to led me to start reading the Bible. I read the Bible at night, before school, and during my lunch break in high school. Reading the Word of the Lord uplifted me, and I went on to suppress my pain and excel in school again. I now knew my worth and potential and shifted into being an over achiever! I became popular and loved to go to school because I was free for nine hours. Then I got involved with after-school activities to combat against going home and being hit or yelled at or even ignored. Eventually my stepfather stopped talking to me. He never said a word. Not hello or bye. This went on for about a year until I left home at seventeen. I couldn't take it anymore; I had to stand up for myself. To me it had been 15 years of abuse by now. I was tired of being broken down and neglected every single day. I believed I was beautiful, talented, and very strong, so I had to separate myself from the place that caused so much pain. My best friend's parents allowed me to stay with them until I graduated high school. I was always crying and breaking down at just the thoughts of brokenness and trying to still have a normal senior year. I was in pain, devastated that my mom would not take up for me and tell my stepdad he was wrong for mistreating me! The day I graduated, I cried and I remember a classmate on my row asking was I crying, because I was happy and explained that it was because no family came to my graduation. He sat back in his chair stunned because I was a popular student, and I had just revealed a very raw part of me. Well, as I walked across the stage, I became overjoyed that I accomplished getting my diploma and not having any babies. My boyfriend and his friend greeted me and gifted me to show their support. I looked up, and my mother was standing there. She handed me some used Christian books and wrote her hotel room and new address on my diploma envelope. She explained they were moving away to a different state the very next day. I asked her where was my sister and brother? She explained my stepdad said they could not come. I could not let that sorrowful news break me. I hugged her and told her I would come by their hotel, tomorrow. That night my boyfriend of a year proposed to me, and I said yes! We went to say our farewells the next day, but once my stepdad saw me at the hotel door, he became mad at my mom for talking to me and told my siblings I was the devil. I cried and yelled back reaching for my little brother and sister, but he forced me out the room. This was the last time I would ever see my mother alive and well.

She died a year later in Texas. She had actually gotten separated from my stepdad and moved to her own home near her mother. We talked a few times, and in our very last conversation, she apologized for what she had done to push me away and cause me pain. I eventually had to go home to Texas when the doctors said she didn't have long to live. The supernatural wind of God strengthened me to call all her friends and family about her death and prepare her obituary. I found joy in the mist because I was able to see family I had not seen in years. I had to be strong for my siblings. After all the time that was lost, I loved and missed my brother and sister so much. My little sister stayed glued to my side from the time my plane arrived, throughout the funeral, and until I left to go home to my new husband. It was during this time when my stepdad began to start talking to me again. Everyone feared he would take my siblings and we would never hear from them. Thank God, he found the Lord and flew the kids to Texas often and kept in touch with everyone. He became pleasant.

Unfortunately, I started to see signs of destruction in my marriage. We were arguing about things we thought we had figured out while dating. He started lying a lot and staying out later and later. Eventually I fell into depression again, trying to figure out why everyone mistreats me so bad and turn on me. Thoughts of suicide entered my mind. I did not know this man, as I so adamantly believed I did. We discussed before marrying that drinking and cursing had no place in our marriage. We talked about going into ministry together because he came off so loving well versed in the Bible, and close to his family. This man cursed and drank alcohol like a fish, and after a few years, I could not get him to go to church, even on Easter.

Years later, our first child is coming and I was so worried, confused, and depressed. I did not know what each day held. I shed plenty of tears and had heartache, wanting him to turn from his wicked ways. I wanted so badly for him to want his wife and be into the birth of his son, but that day never came. It got worse when our son came. I eventually asked him to move out. He was also a soldier. After having tense conversations with his NCOs, we reached an agreement that I could get the car and he would have to pay the BAH from his paycheck to me. BAH is a housing-allowance income. I enrolled in cosmetology school with dreams of furthering my education and going to college to get my business degree. During this time, we only had answering machines; so when he would call, sometimes I would ignore him, but mostly I would be at school. I could not understand how he went from begging for a child to having to be forced by his leaders to take care of his son and me. This turmoil led up to a horrific time in my life. He broke into my home while we were separated. He was reeking of alcohol as he kicked me and punched me to the ground in the middle of the night. While he was beating me and choking me right before I began to lose consciousness, he threatened to kill our son and let go of my throat. I ran to the neighbors, and to my disappointment, he came in behind me and beat me some more as the neighbors watched. By this time, I was in survival mode, so I said anything I needed to say to deter him from driving off with our three-month-old son. I somehow ran back to my home when I realized the neighbors were paralyzed with fear, as my husband threatened them so they would not help me. I escaped and ran back to my home and dialed 911. The cops came so fast that night and arrested my husband. I was able to drive myself to the hospital. I know God was with me in the fire. I had been journaling and praying to God about my heartaches all the while. I even went to school the next day with blood clots in my eyes, determined to accomplish my goals. I ended up having to get a CAT scan of my brain because of injuries to my face, but that could not stop me from preparing for my future. You see, my now ex-husband is not all at fault. I was very headstrong but, still very naive when I met him. For example, I had to sneak to date; so every time we met, it was exciting, and he swept me off my feet. Since he paid for prom and graduation fees; something my parents wouldn't do, I feel in love. I thought he had a big heart. However, he knew enough about my home life to take advantage and act as if he wanted what I wanted knowing his intentions were not pure or revealed. Thank God for the Holy Ghost that comforted me and gave me wisdom throughout these trials in life. That is why I never would give in or give up. There was a spiritual force behind me pushing me in the right direction, even when I resisted. I had plenty of battles with myself and many regrets. Glory be to God who kept me alive and well to raise my son. I have gone on to accomplish every goal I have ever set in life. I continue to create more goals along the way of life. Knowing where my strength comes from.

As I build my relationship with God, he takes me down memory lane to reveal to me deep wonders in my mind about my existence. God amazes me with his wisdom and compassion. His grace does abound. I do love and worship God deeper each year of my life. He has brought me from a mighty long way. I now own my own salon. I am also an award-winning hairstylist and makeup artist and did go on to get my business degree. My work is featured in many magazines and on the cover. I love being a mother and singing in the choir at my church, Christ the Healer Church whom Bishop Calvin B. Lockett and Pastor Lynnita Lockett are husband and wife pastors. They actually live the dream I had for me and my husband. That's Gods way of saying a marriage that I've always desired does exist! God never ceases to amaze me. Just to know who He says I am in His kingdom gives me zeal. I can do all things through Christ Jesus!

Currently I am in pursuit of all that God has for me. I have seen in my life how I got ahead of God, for example, marrying my ex-husband; I was in such a rush. I have seen how choices can make or break you, but you must get back up to live again because joy does come in the morning. I am just beginning to understand the anointing God has placed over my life before I was born. I have beaten so many odds, especially when trials were stack up against me, but God would not let me fail or die. I now realize I am a conqueror! I am grateful that I can minister to broken vessels that sit on my styling chair day after day and pour into them spiritual advice that I have encountered from the storms I have sailed through. I am learning to sleep peacefully like Jesus did during the storms of life and not to worry and give it over to God. I thank God that I'm learning not to allow my old baggage to take up residence in my new life.

Contact me at

http://www.facebook.com/demeshia.hyman
www.demeshia_hyman@yahoo.com
platinumtouchcompany@gmail.com
Instagram page: SwagFabDiva

17

Dionne Jermeia

The Lord called me from the womb; from the body of my mother he named my name. He made my mouth like a sharp sword; in the shadow of his hand he hid me; he made me a polished arrow; in his quiver he hid me away. And he said to me, "You are my servant, Israel, in whom I will be glorified."

—Isaiah 49:1-3

Most mothers become excited upon the arrival of their child's birth. They are anxious to see who they will look like and what their newborn will wear home from the hospital. There are so many things about having a baby that give women an adrenaline rush in becoming a caregiver, a comforter, a mother. Under many circumstances, some women don't share these same excitements; their world of pregnancy is one of doubt and shame. Feeling some kind of a way in trying to figure out life, my birth mother was one of the women whose circumstance had taken her victim. She had many mixed emotions of my coming into this world; however, they all narrowed down to "Should I keep her or give her away to someone who can take better care of her than I can?" Upon trying to make a decision, my birth mother met a family at her home church whom she thought would be great for the job. Being pregnant at a young age was not the best thing in the world to my mother, but all in all, it was God's will. After meeting with the family that she had her eyes on, she felt even more that this was where her daughter needed to be. Her mind was made up that she couldn't give me the needed things I deserved out of life and that this choice would be one that she'd have to live with for the rest of her life.

At just four weeks old, my mother sent me to live with the family she met and knew, but she didn't know if we would meet again. Around the age of three, my mother felt that she was prepared enough in her personal life to have me come and live with her, so my godparents allowed it, and off I went. I moved to New York where my mother was staying, and I can actually remember till this day meeting my biological father at the age of three. He and my mom met while he was in the military and fell in love. My biological father had received orders to be stationed elsewhere and lost contact with my mother. He knew she was pregnant but had no idea she had second thoughts about it. My mother heard my father was in New York, and that's what prompted her move. While there, she realized that they weren't the same young kids in love they used to be. She was overwhelmed to find him dating another woman, and without telling him, she had plans of her own. There were so many memories I held on to from that time I spent with her, some good and some bad. My mother's life was not all put together as she thought it was, so she called my godparents to step in and take care of me. They informed her that they would soon be making a permanent move from Oklahoma to Tennessee and that they would take me with them. With a busy lifestyle and another baby on the way, she felt that giving me away a second time was truly the best thing for me and her.

Imagine being a young child and not understanding why your mother has handed you off to live with other people when all you want is to be with her. By this time I was five years old and had the hardest time dealing with the pain of being separated from my mother. It became an even harder thing to integrate with eight children I didn't know. Now I had sisters and brothers; yes, this definitely was a lot to take in. I grew up with my godfamily, which later became my family, whether I wanted it or not. I had no voice, and if I did, no one heard, so I thought.

While trying to move on knowing things have changed in a big way, I began to discover things about myself. I began to see myself as different, not just at home but at school as well. There were kids in my class who drew pictures of their mommy and daddy or other children who spent the day talking about their parents. My family wasn't like theirs, and it hurt to know my life was different in that way. My godfather had asked that I do not call him by his name but to call him Dad because he was committed to being such for the sake of me being a part of their family. My mother had still communicated with me by telephone pretty often. Her calls were always the highlight of my day. I just knew this move was temporary because that was my mother's pattern; she would keep me for a while and give me back. So I couldn't wait for the day to hear her say that we would be together again. What was even more exciting was that she was going to come and get me; well, that's what she said. Days passed; even months had drifted by one by one. I soon began to realize that she wasn't coming and that this was where I was going to be for a while. I settled down in school and moved on without my mother being in my life. I would cry and cry until the point of hyperventilating over missing her; it hurt that bad. Eventually that longing feeling for her turned into a dislike for her. She was not there when I cried out to her, and I held her responsible.

Every child wants to find out what it is that makes them stand out in the crowd and what they have to offer the world; well, I didn't. I wasn't interested in knowing what I could or couldn't do. I mean, hey, my mother gave me away, so I was just nobody, right? While attending my father's church, I can remember us kids being made to sing in the choir. Boring! Who wants to sing? Not me. Until one day at choir rehearsal, I noticed people looking at me as if I did something wrong, not realizing they were shocked at the way I was singing. Somehow toward the end of the song, I got carried away and was oversinging everyone else; and in that moment, I heard my voice. One of my sisters told me I sang a lot as a baby, but I had no idea or memory of that. So to hear this sound come from me at an older age became something I wanted to do over and over again. I liked it, but I didn't, and since it was part of who I was, I learned to turn it on and turn it off, not understanding this was a gift from God Himself.

As I got older, I learned about who this God was and how He blessed us with His Son, Jesus. I learned that He came to die for our sins and give us life forevermore. So at the age of eight, I accepted Jesus Christ as my personal Lord and Savior and became a Christian. Even though I had moved on, I still was hurt on the inside, but I learned how to cover it up to please others. Attending church was a regular for me, and so was singing in the choir. I would sing at school and other church functions to show people I had this awesome gift. I had no idea how to use it; I just liked to hear myself. I was just thrilled to know there was something I was good at. During my teenage years, I began to hold on to more hurt because I wanted to reach out to my mother more than ever but couldn't. That caused me to become a problem child at home. My parents had become so disgusted with my attitude that they thought it would be best if I went to live with my mother. So I did, and I must say it felt great for a while. I had so many questions and needed so many answers. I loved her, but I was angry with her; I wanted her, but I didn't want to be around her. There were so many mixed emotions going on in my heart and mind I couldn't take living with her. So my maternal grandmother took me in, and I stayed with her for a while. She enrolled me in school and helped as much as she could to provide for me. My grandmother sang in her church's choir and played the piano as well. I began to see my ability to sing as a way to bond with my grandmother. While living in Oklahoma with my biological family, I discovered a lot about myself. I soon realized that I came from a group of people who could sing like me, and there were some of whom I resembled. This was great in a way, but I still had no relationship with my birth mother, and we were just houses from each other instead of hundreds of miles.

The time apart from my mother gave room to build up a wall of hurt and pain. A wall I was unwilling to tear down because it was rooted so deep. I had stopped doing things the way God desired and got caught up in too much while in Oklahoma. I wanted to go back to that life that was comfortable to me, so I called my sister in Tennessee and told her I wanted to come live with her. Somehow that request was not granted, and I moved back in with my parents. It wasn't that I did not love them; I was just more connected emotionally to one of my sisters because she was one I was attached to as a baby. In her is where I sought a motherly affection. After graduating high school, real life began for me. I longed for attention and affection so much that I forgot who I was and whose I was. I hung out at clubs looking for men to fulfill that void where love should be. I felt that God could care less about me and that I was in this thing called life alone. I begin to downgrade everything about myself, thinking I wasn't pretty or I wasn't going to amount to anything. Somehow I gave my past permission to control my present. I still loved singing but thought it sounded better at the club than it did at church. How wrong I was. I can remember going out to the club and people asking me, "Aren't you a preacher's kid? You're not supposed to be in here!" I ignored them for as long as I could until I realized they were right. I didn't belong there, and I had to come to the realization that I was lost.

I had spent so much of my time trying to replace my mother's love with things that did not even matter. I decided to rededicate my life back to Christ and told him to lead the way. God took me back, but things were different with my relationship with him, and I could feel it. He knew I had been hurt, and he knew I had experienced rejection. He would show me dreams of places I would go and people I would meet. God would even send people to confirm the dreams I dreamed to assure me that He had a plan and purpose for my life. He then began to replace my ashes for a crown of beauty, and my mourning for gladness. God also knew that the very gift He gave me would be used to help heal the hurt while seeking Him during storms to come. A garment of praise was placed over me to thank him for who He was and where He brought me from. The Word of God spoke so true to me that I began to draw closer to Him and learned to see the woman that He sees in me. When I was younger, I learned about God; but at this time in my life, I began to fall in love with Him. I began to build a relationship with Him, and it felt great. I soon found myself a new church home and followed my pastor's advice to become planted in the body of Christ. This was a new place for me with new people to meet, but I knew that it was God's will. God allowed me to experience Him in song, and He opened my eyes to how people's lives were touched by His presence. The songs that God had placed in my heart became part of my worship toward Him. Worshipping the Lord in song is such a peaceful place to be. I enjoy the Holy Spirit wrapping me up and taking me higher in the things of God. I love telling Jesus who He is to me and how much I love Him for who He is. In that place of worship, I began to experience Him as the lover of my soul. The mornings He allows me to see are started off in a prayer, asking, "Help me be pleasing unto Your sight. Help me, O God, to stay humble before You and Your people. Give me the words to say to someone in despair. Give me a song to sing to the brokenhearted. Teach me to accept the things I can't change and trust in You to do the rest." I soon realized that everything I went through from birth to now was part of the process. It was a setup for a come up! I began to put the pieces together about how God orchestrated my life, and I now understood how it all worked together for my good. I found out through my new relationship with Him that I was chosen and that He had an anointing upon me to bless His people. I learned I had to forgive my mother and father for their mistakes, and in order to receive what He had for me, I needed to let the pain go.

God blessed me with four children of my own, and I must say it's not the easiest job, but it's helped my heart to grow. They have taught me how to love hard and how to endure and persevere for their future. Thinking back, I thought I never had a voice while I was going through, but the whole time I did. No matter how hard the enemy tried to use my past to gag my future, it did not work. God predestined me before time to be great, He thought of me to be a blessing while in my mother's womb, and He restored me from my journey to be a testimony for His glory. Till this day, I really do not communicate with my biological parents, nor do I have the best communicating relationship with my parents. But I love them, and I am so grateful for them. I am even more grateful that God trusted me enough to bless me with such an awesome anointing, that I am able to give Him glory and minister to His people. Two years ago was the first time I had spoken to my biological father since the age of four. It was a very emotional moment, but I had no tears left to cry during our conversation. I enjoyed hearing his voice and him saying that he loved me, but the way I felt about my mom as a teenager was how I was beginning to feel about him. I quickly had to dismiss those feeling and realize that I am no longer that person and I am no longer in that place to waste my time holding grudges. So I talked with him and told him I loved him and that I didn't want anything from him but to stay in touch. And even though it's not the best right now, I trust God that it will get better.

I must say I am excited about what God has in store for my family and me. Last year, 2012, was one of the best years of my life. I released my first album entitled *All That I Am*, and it was a project that I could not have been more proud of. I have learned not to box God in because I will miss out on the blessings He has for me. With that in mind, I let God have his way in my life, and I was blessed to grace the stage and presence of many great gospel artists, not to mention have an article about my project placed in the *Convenient Shopper Magazine*. It is just February, and God has already unleashed some great things my way. I pray that you will all continue to pray for me as I enter a very emotional part of my personal life. I know that God has His hands on me and that He will protect me. If God be for me, then who can stand against me? I thought no one heard my cry, but God did; and even though I was tossed to and fro in the storm, God never abandoned me. He was always there so I could be here today.

Contact Information:
DionneJermeia@facebook.com
Dionnenewton@ymail.com
Artistecard.com/dionnejermeia

18

Evangelist Eva Bronaugh Barnes

Trust in the LORD with all thine heart; and lean not unto thine own understanding. In all thy ways acknowledge him, and he shall direct thy paths.

—Proverbs 3:5-6, KJV

The above verse is my *life* scripture, and the following testimonies are based on this verse.

Introduction

Hello, my name is Evangelist Eva Bronaugh Barnes; and as I have stated, the above scripture is my life verse. It is what has gotten me through every good and not-so-good test, trial, and triumph of my life. There have been so many testimonies during these fifty-four years of my life (all ending in great victories) that I cannot even attempt to share them all in these few pages, but I pray that what I do share will give someone hope and encouragement to trust in the Lord in all that you may be going through, knowing that He has a plan for your life and He is the director of your destiny. Even when we don't understand, we can trust Him with our future.

Scene 1: New Shoes

It seems as if I was always a loner. And my first memory of an encounter with my life scripture of *trusting in the Lord* was when I was six years old. Although it seemed as if I was alone, I was truly never alone, for the Holy Spirit was always with me.

My testimony of New Shoes began like this: I was six years old and in the first grade.

I was on the playground at school during recess and all alone, just lying in the grass, looking up at the clouds. Oh, how I loved looking at the clouds and the blue sky that my Heavenly Father had created. So it did not matter that we were a very poor family. And on that day, I was wearing a pair of little crooked-over, raggedy white shoes. All the kids would make fun of me. So I just went out to the playground and lay admiring the clouds and began praying, or should I say, began talking to my Heavenly Father. I said, "Lord, I need some new shoes." Notice I said *new* shoes. For me and my family, new shoes would be bought at what was called a secondhand store; today it would be like the Goodwill store. But when I got home from school that day, my daddy came to me and said, "Baby girl, we are going to the store to get you some shoes." That day my daddy took me to a *real* department store and bought me *brand-new* shoes. My Heavenly Father had answered my prayer in an instant. That may not seem like much, but to a six-year-old, that is major faith and trust in the Lord. Oh, how excited I was to get exactly what I had asked God for, and He answer so quickly. I still get tears of joy every time I think of this story.

From that day on, I believe that everything I have asked my Heavenly Father, I have received (maybe not when or how I may have wanted, but always on time.).

Scene 2: The Financial Helper

From the age of eighteen years old and even until this very day, I have always hated debt. And for this reason, I believed that I have been called to help the body of Christ learn how to get out of debt and to know that we can live, and I mean *live*, *debt free* by trusting in the Lord and living by His Biblical principles on finances.

I do not claim to be a *financial counselor* but a helper or a coach on how to manage your money God's way.

I believe that God wants His children to be debt free, spiritually, physically, mentally, emotionally, and financially.

Spiritually, we are debt free when we trust in what Jesus had done for us on the cross. "For the wages of sin is death, but the gift [free gift] of God is eternal life through Jesus Christ our Lord" (Rom. 6:23). We are debt free from sin. We no longer have to be a servant to sin.

Physically, mentally, and emotionally, we are debt free when we trust in God's Word. According to Luke 4:18, Jesus said, "The Spirit of the Lord is upon me, because he hath anointed me to preach the gospel to the poor; he hath sent me to heal the brokenhearted, to preach deliverance to the captive, and recovering of sight to the blind, to set at liberty them that are bruised."

As you take these scriptures into your heart, you will see that Jesus has taken care of our spiritual, physical, mental, and emotional debt. We only have to trust and believe in what He has said and done. But when it comes to our financial debt, there are some steps and some biblical principles we must learn and follow. Did you know that there are over two thousand five hundred scriptures in the Word of God pertaining to finances and money? That is why I believe that God is concerned and wants His children to know how to manage the finances He as entrusted each of us with.

Notice:

> Owe no man any thing, but to love one another . . . (Rom. 13:8, KJV)
>
> And the borrower is servant to the lender . . . (Prov. 22:7b, KJV)
>
> For the Lord thy God blesseth thee, as he promised thee: thou shalt lend unto many nations, but thou shalt not borrow . . . (Deut. 15:6, KJV)

Over the past ten-plus years, the Lord has allowed me to learn from books, tapes, and classes by Larry Burkett, Howard Dayton, Crown Financial Ministries, Dave Ramsey, and also by personal revelation knowledge from God and personal experiences; and to share that knowledge with anyone who is willing to hear and believe that God wants you to *live debt free*.

I am a living witness that you do not have to live from paycheck to paycheck. You don't need credit cards. You can live paying cash. It is not easy, but it is worth it. By following and trusting God's Biblical principles and leaning not on our own understanding, we can live debt free. I have no debt except my mortgage, and it will be paid off in less than five years. TO GOD BE THE GLORY!

Scene 3: I Shall Live and Not Die and Declare the Word of the Lord

The final testimony that I am about to share is a test that I know without a shadow of doubt magnifies my life scripture of *trusting in the Lord with all my heart and leaning not on my own understanding*. I don't even understand at this very moment how I am still in my right mind, but I know it is only by the power of the Holy Spirit (Holy Ghost).

On July 27, 2011, my nineteen-year-old son, Aaron Phillip Barnes, went to heaven.

My youngest son, Joel, and I had gone on a mission trip, Cruise with a Cause, to Jamaica. Aaron was unable to go with us because he was attending college, studying to become a male nurse. While on the mission trip, Joel was singing on the ship, and a lady heard him and thought he was one of her artists, but she loved his voice and wanted him to make a demo when he got back home and come to Florida. We were back home for a few days and had a birthday party (July 17, 2011) for Aaron.

On July 27, 2011, when I came home from work, Joel and my older son, Johnathan, who is a songwriter, was working on a song for Joel's demo. Aaron is usually the first to come meet me at the door when I come home from work. So I asked, "Where is Aaron?" And Joel said, "He was off from school today, so we cleaned the house and played some video games (*Madden* is Aaron's favorite game) and Aaron said he was going to take a nap. "Then I said, "How long has he been asleep?" Joel said, "About three hours." And I gasp, "Three hours! Go check on him." Joel goes into Aaron's room, and he is lying on his bed, and the side of his face is gone by an old shotgun that he had found when we had cleaned out the garage. When Joel began to scream; Johnathan ran into the room and came out hysterical and began crying and hitting the floor. So as I ran into Aaron's room and saw my baby's face, I felt the Holy Spirit (Holy Ghost) just swoop my entire body and I began to speak in the Spirit the whole rest of the time. Even as the people from church came, the police, the mortician, the Lord just held me and kept in the Spirit through every entity of the planning, visitation, home-going service, and even the burial.

The newspaper stated that it was a self-inflected gunshot wound, but I know and will always believe that it was an accident, because when my sister, Mary Holland, who is also my senior pastor, came into Aaron's room (she was also in the Spirit). She laid her hand on Aaron's leg, and she heard him say, "Auntie, I didn't mean to do this."

Aaron was a genius, a young man full of life, and he loved everybody especially his family. He would give his very last to anyone in need. He loved babies and would help single mothers with food, diapers, clothes, toys, and rides to school. He wanted to work in the nursery at the church. So I know he is *living* in heaven, helping with the babies.

He shall live and not die and declare the Words of the LORD.

(The next page is a copy of a portion of a college paper written by my genius son Aaron, and the first verse of the lyrics to a song about Aaron by his brothers Joel Barnes and John K. Montoya.

Thoughts of Heaven
by
Aaron P. Barnes

English 101
May 19, 2011

Religion is a *huge* part of our lives and, for that matter, has been since the dawn of time. Most would think this lifestyle is generated and/or originated from an awareness of higher or reality of one seeking an ultimatum. Some are simply yearning for purpose and reason for living and maybe looking to and, in most cases, in doing so, grasp enlightenment *beyond*, even before death. But what is heaven? Imagine experiencing all the joys in life whether possibly or impossibly; the most joyous possibilities *possible* and experienced or lived *as good as godly possible.*

Imagine experiencing your life on the ultimate level or in the ultimate sense: your whole world or *eternity* rather spent shaped into what you've always wanted. Imagine experiencing everyone living the ultimate lifestyle in an unimaginably wonderful reality. Imagine experiencing life even without the thought of problems but instead dilemmas on whether or not to play Madden with Sean Taylor or write rhymes with 2Pac Shakur; life or our perception of time spent would be all new, exhilarating, and have and all new likeness to it.

Life, in this earthly sense, still seems meant to be lived though. Heaven can also be perceived as a basis or foundation for how to live in this life as well, whether one lives one's life to the fullest and/or lives their life in the best-possible fashion. I would describe this lifestyle as reserved or *godly*, not distinct in comparison still, but intriguing and fulfilling as a past time.

If you can help it, one shouldn't worry one's self or other's nerves with thoughts of *life beyond death*, but better yet enjoy the joys of this life and love that this world has to offer and later experience the enlightened, nearly impossibly perceivable, eternal *heaven*, or however one chooses to perceive it.

Altar

by Joel Barnes and John K Montoya

Momma calls my name and said, "It's Sunday morning"-
I just waking up getting ready for church-
got to pass your doorway just to get a shower-
then I hear your laugh and, man, it hurts-
seems this feeling in my chest won't let up-
just passing one year that feels like forever-
am I tripping or did you just call my name-
In a distance I hear a still voice say-
Don't worry, I got him-
He fell from earth, but I caught him-
He got his second chance-
and now he lives again-
so-
take my hand-
Let me give you inner peace-
just hear my voice-
listen when I speak-
At the altar

All thanks to Leading Lady Ms. Treva Gordon for an opportunity to share my story.

To my pastors, Sr. Pastors Will and Mary Holland and Pastor William J. Holland, thank you for all your prayers and support during all my test and triumphs.

To my son Joel Barnes, thank you for always being by my side (I love you, man).

TO GOD BE THE GLORY IN ALL I SAY AND DO IN MY LIFE. Amen.

Contact Information:
erbfree@yahoo.com

19

Evangelist Regina Relliford Spivey

Eye hath not seen, nor ear heard, neither have entered into the heart of man, the things which God hath prepared for them that love him.

—1 Corinthians 2:9, KJV

Writing this manuscript has been one of the most challenging tasks I have ever been charged with by the Lord. As I prepared to write, I was faced with several challenges: sickness of self and loved ones, financial hardships, spiritual rut, disappointments, and displacement of loved ones. The list goes on and on. However, I know challenges are only my transportation to my triumph. The battle is already won. The completion of this manuscript is confirmation that someone is waiting to be blessed by reading what says the Lord. It is a testament of the goodness of God and all that He is! It's also part of my test, which later becomes my testimony. Despite it all, I continue to press toward the mark knowing the purpose for my being is already defined. I am victorious. I've committed myself to carry out God's plans for my life.

The Lord's assignments and appointments are never to be taken for grant or viewed as inconveniences. It's for a divine purpose. It is a testimony for you and hope for someone else. There is a reason He has chosen me for this task at this appointed time. There is a reason He has chosen you for whatever He has assigned to you as this time. I know in part it is my destiny and where He is taking me. I see this as one of God's assignments bestowed upon me in such a time as this. He has charged me with the task of witnessing in the form of a manuscript. To Him I give all the glory, all the praise and the honor. Blessed You Lord for giving me the words to spread the Gospel, to bring souls to Christ, and to tell of Your goodness. Through this manuscript, I pray souls will be drawn to You, people will be healed, delivered, miracles will happen, yokes will be broken, and burdens will be removed. I ask that supernatural blessings will happen instantly for anyone who reads this book. This is my prayer for the readers of this book!

What I thought would have been a simple and easy task, turned out to be one of the most difficult task in an awkward way. Me, finding myself speechless, unheard of, Lady Spivey, a woman of many words, sometimes too many words (laughing out loud)!.

I have been led to share with you three key principles that will bless you in any area of your life. These three principles have taken me through the good, the bad, and the ugly. They are "B*elieve*", "F*aith*", and "*Trust*", Bookmark for now. It will start to make sense as you continue reading.

Here's my story . . .

Hi, my name is Regina, aka Gina, born to Perry and Rosa Relliford (roots: Holly Springs, Mississippi, and Memphis, Tennessee). Born in Chicago, Illinois but raised in the South. Born the fourth child of six, (middle child syndrome). Type A personality, full of adventure, curiosity, and destined for successful at *any cost*. I have a master's degree in Education and a bachelor's degree in Business Administration. I was a pretty smart kid. I graduated from high school at age sixteen, and completed undergraduate school by age twenty, again determined to be successful at *any cost*.

My mother an anointed woman of God, former pastor and evangelist for over fifty years, educated, compassionate, and loving.

My father (deceased), on the other hand, was a blue-collar worker, womanizer, and alcoholic, WOW what a combination. Our household was what we perceived to be normal. Dad was in charge; he made the money and called the shots. Mom was a yes-sir, humble, meek, housewife and full-time praise and worshipper. The neighborhood kids would often make fun of my drunken father. He was the best dad ever when he wasn't drinking. But thank God he was delivered of his illness, drinking.

My sisters and brothers are from two separate fathers of two different age groups and two different generations. When we were teenagers, my older brothers and sister were old enough to be my parents. I never lived with my two older sisters and my older brother. I grew up with a sister eleven months younger and a brother eight years younger than me. My younger sister and I are as opposite as day is to night, and my younger brother and I never really bonded. There is an eight-year age difference, but I love him dearly.

I often found myself trying to lead my own way, forcing myself to become independent and mature early. In a lot of instances, I loved all the wrong things and people and never really learned and loved me. I spent a lot of time at church, "following" my mom, and involved in a lot of after school extracurricular activities. I always felt like there was more to life, and I wanted to see the world. What I'm really saying is there was a *"void"* in my life that I couldn't seem to figure out until later in life.

I became an adult at an early age. I was in college with folks twice my age. I was dating guys ten years my senior and hanging out with folks of the world. At that time, I felt like that was what life was all about. I had fulfilled my parents' dreams; I graduated from college with two degrees. I was without a child and independent. Isn't that what most parents' want of their children? I had a good job, made great money, moved up the career ladder quickly, and traveled the world. I even had opportunities to marry many Mr. Rights. Who could ask for more?

What could possibly be wrong? I grew up in church, very active my mother an anointed woman of God (Preacher's kid—PK). I never missed a service, I "knew" the Lord, yet my life had fallen apart. What did I do wrong to deserve this?

I remember very distinctively having a conversation with my mom, who was trying to explain to me what was missing, what was wrong. She thought I needed the Lord. How could I need the Lord when I already had the Lord (so I thought)? What did she mean? I knew the Lord. The mothers in the church were pushing for me to become closer to Him. They wanted me to become this person called a "missionary" aka an "evangelist", something I had no desire to become. I was just fine where I was in my faith walk and in my spiritual journey. Life was good for me, so I thought. I asked my mom the question, "How can I be a missionary, I have nothing that I can witness to anyone about. I haven't gone through anything." Little did I know, Satan was listening; and from that very moment, my life began to turn around, spiral downward, and take a turn for the worst. Little did I know he was going to give me something to talk about (a witness)? He gave me more testimonies than I could ever imagine. Don't tell me there isn't life and death in the tongue! Proverbs 18:21 (KJV) says, "Death and life are in the power of the tongue: and they that love it shall eat the fruit thereof."

Fast-forward after a divorce, one stillborn birth, one natural birth, unemployment, riches to rags, bankruptcy, moving from state to state, becoming a single parent, being a caregiver to an elderly disabled mother, and my only son incarnated, I finally realized something there was something really wrong. I finally got it. I realized I really didn't have a personal relationship with God. I really did not know Him. *I knew of Him*, which is a big difference from knowing him personally. I had heard and seen of His goodness and glory, but I had never really experienced His Shekinah glory for myself. It wasn't until I was faced with all of these life challenges that I came to know Him.

I learned several things having gone through the many trials. One, I quickly learned I had to establish a personal relationship with Him. I had to rededicate myself to Him. I could no longer live on the prayers of my mother and others. I had to "Believe", I had to have "Faith", and I had to "Trust" him for myself.

Through the challenges, the trials, the storms, hardships, disappointments, failures, discouragements, bleakness, voids, fears, and burdens I realized the only way out, the only hope and comfort I had was through knowing by developing a personal relationship with Him.

It wasn't about what my family, my mom, or anyone else believed; it was what I believed. See, my story is simple. You have to know Him personally for yourself. Without Him, you can do nothing. It wasn't until I was in placed in situations wherein I had nothing or no one who could help me. Money couldn't buy what I needed, friends couldn't help me, Mom and Daddy couldn't help me, my husband and child couldn't help me. Jesus and His promises were my only way out!

I could call on Him in the midnight hour, and He was right there. He promised he would never leave me nor forsake. He was omniscient (all knowing), He was omnipresent (always present) and He was omnipotent (all powerful).

> He never left me alone. John 14:3 (NIV, 2004) says, "And if I go and prepare A place for you, I will come back and take you to be with me that you also may be where I am."

Through building my personal relationship with Him, I learned very quickly that *I could do anything through Christ who strengthened me*

> Phil 4:13, KJV). I realized that all I had to do was apply three principles, "B*elieve*", have "F*aith*", and "T*rust*" him.

To "B*elieve*" simply means that whatever He has promised you, he is going to do it on His own timing. To "Believe" means whatever His Word says it will not return void To "Believe" means He is in control of whatever happens to you. Your life is predetermined and predestined. He has written the blueprint regardless of the twist and turns you take in life. It is up to you to Believe in what He says.

> He tells us in Jeremiah 29:11 (NIV, 2004), "For I know the plans I have for you," declares the LORD, "plans to prosper you and not to harm you, plans to give you hope and a future."

And this is his commandment, That we should believe on the name of his on Jesus Christ, and love one another, as he gave us commandment. (1 John 3:23, KJV)

"Faith" is knowing He will do just what He said He will do. "Faith" is giving it to Him and walking away in confidence. "Faith" is not worrying" "Faith" is not fear. "Faith" already knows the outcome.

> **Hebrews 11:1 tells us,** Now faith is the substance of things hoped for, the evidence of things not seen.

Are you exercising your faith? Is it on the shelf? What are you doing with it?

- o God doesn't look at your situations and circumstances, he knows them already
- o God doesn't isn't impressed by your gifts and natural abilities, he gave them to you
- o God looks at and is moved by your "Faith"

Hebrews 11:6 tells us,

> Without *faith* [emphasis added] it is impossible to please him: for he that cometh to God must believe that he is and that he is a rewarder of them that *diligently* seek him.

Your Faith is what pleases God!

"Faith" moves the hand of God.

Matthew 17:20 tells us,

> If ye have *faith* [italics added] as a grain of mustard seed, ye shall say unto this mountain, Remove hence to yonder place; and it shall remove, and nothing shall be impossible unto you.

- If you want to see God's miraculous hand in your life, pour out your "Faith"
    - o He's telling us to pour out our faith, not to hide it.
    - o Put it into action regardless of your circumstance or situation.
- As you pour out your faith, you can see the act of God, as did the widow with her son in 2 Kings 4.

"Trust" is believing in Him, knowing He has your back. As J. Moss says it best, "God's Got It." "Trust" is letting go and letting God do it. "Trust" is standing on God's promises. "Trust", it's the removal of fear, walking in the peace and resting in the knowledge that He is in control. Scripture tells us:

- **Micah 7:5 (NLT)**—Don't trust anyone—not your best friend or even your wife!
- **Psalms 91:2 (KJV)**—I will say of the LORD, He is my refuge and my fortress: my God; in him will I trust.
- **Psalms 37:5 (KJV)**—Commit thy way unto the LORD; trust also in him; and he shall bring it to pass.

If you believe God will take care of it, all you have to do is to apply the faith and allow Him to do it by trusting in Him. By applying these three basic principles, you will start to see the difference God will make in your day-to-day life. The burdens will become easier, the problems will seem less, and the heartaches and disappointments will not be as often. You'll learn to strategically manage life storms.

You have to start to recognize and understanding you are either going into a storm, you are in a storm, or you are coming out of a storm. It's not the storm; it's how you prepare for the storm. It's not how big the problem is but how you come through the problem that matters. In life there will always be peaks and valleys. The sooner you realize that, the sooner you can get a grip on managing your life and the things that come your way. It is inevitable you are going to go through struggles, trials, and situations what you want to call them; no one is exempt from them. He never gives you more than what you can bear. Think back to the last time you went through a struggle (for some of us, that wasn't too long ago). What happened? Are you still standing? Did you survive?

Not all struggles are ones you've created or caused yourself. Everything we go through is for His glory and for someone else. We use our struggles as a form of witness. We sometimes go struggles or problems that are created or caused by others, which unfortunately can be loved ones.

For example, a divorce, a bad marital choice I didn't go into the marriage expecting it to end in divorce. We sometimes suffer as a result of someone else's disobedience. Boy, it's hard when you have to go through because of something someone else's disobedience! But guess what? You can and will make it through. That, too, shall pass! Struggles, storms, trials and disappointments come from various sources—yourself working out of the will of God (rebellion), Satan, and God allowing you to go through for His glory. You have to remember our Father, The Lord is just like your natural father, and he has to chastise us sometimes. He has to reprimand and discipline us. He gives us those hard truths. He makes us face the mirror. Remember, with the help of God, you can manage your struggles. Choose the best route, one that will make things easier and peaceful for you. At the end, know He will never give you more than you can bear. He's always right there with you.

I encourage you, if you don't have a personal relationship with Him, that you get one right away. Get to know him personally before the storms come. You may be asking yourself, *how do I get to know him?* It's simple:

1. Accept him as your Savior; all you have to do is to repeat this prayer:

   Dear God, I come to You in the name of Jesus. I am a sinner, and I need Your forgiveness. I believe Jesus died on the cross for my sins so that I may have eternal life. You said if I would confess my sins, I shall be saved. Cover me in Your blood, wash away my sins. I confess with my mouth right now, and I accept You as my personal Savior. Transform my life so I may bring glory and honor to Your name. Thank you for saving me and giving me eternal life!

If you repeated this prayer, you have been saved and born again!

2. Join a Bible-based church that teaches the Word of God without compromise.
3. Read the Word daily.
4. Study the Word daily.
5. Learn scripture (this is your weapon for fighting Satan).
6. Mediate both day and night.
7. Pray often.
8. Incorporate praise and worship in your life.
9. Fast (some things only come by fastening and prayer).
10. Continue to seek Him; make it a lifestyle.

The more you get to know Him, the more you will thirst and hunger after him. Align yourself with others who have a love for Christ and whose light that shines. Be an example. In order to get someone else to change, you first have to change yourself and be that example.

My heart's desire is, if you don't know Him, that you will accept Him as your Savior, that you will spread the Good News and for you to know that you are not in this alone. I pray for those that read this book, restoration, healing, deliverance, set free, yolks are broken; and burdens are removed. Write me, and let me know how this manuscript changed your life. God Bless you!

Contact Information
Evangelist Regina R. Spivey
Facebook Evangelist Regina Spivey
evangelistreginaspivey@aol.com,
mpowermintinc@aol.com
#mpowermint global

20

Gloria Leavell

The LORD is my shepherd; I shall not want.

He maketh me to lie down in green pastures: he leadeth me beside the still waters.

He restoreth my soul: he leadeth me in the paths of righteousness for his name's sake.

Yea, though I walk through the valley of the shadow of death, I will fear no evil: for thou art with me; thy rod and thy staff they comfort me.

Thou preparest a table before me in the presence of mine enemies: thou anointest my head with oil; my cup runneth over.

Surely goodness and mercy shall follow me all the days of my life: and I will dwell in the house of the LORD for ever.

—Psalms 23, KJV

My name is Gloria Leavell. I was born on April 14, 1948, to the late Bill and Helen Cheatham of Cadiz, Kentucky. My father was a farmer, and as most farmers' children, my siblings and I were taught to work the land. Our father taught us to value ourselves, and our parents made sure to speak words of hope and encouragement into our lives. I know my parents had struggles just like everyone else, but they were hardworking people, and we grew up never knowing that we were poor. We were taught to take good care of what we had because it showed appreciation for the things we had been blessed with. My mother taught us girls to cook, clean, and store up things for winter. My father taught our brothers to work hard and to take good care of the land for the next crop. Both of my parents worked together, teaching us to become respectable men and women. Even though I grew up in a good, stable home, I still found myself pregnant at the age of sixteen.

I made the decision to drop out of school so that my sister could attend and not be ashamed. In April of 1964, I gave birth to my daughter. I wanted to make sure that while I was raising her, I would not be a burden on my parents, and so I helped my mother as much as I could. I helped others by babysitting for them while they pursued their careers. At age seventeen, I decided to marry my daughter's father. While married, I gave birth to another daughter and a son, but a few years after the birth of our son, we separated. We remained separated for a while before we were finally divorced.

I attended beauty school until my money ran out, forcing me to drop out. I then began looking for a job. Thomas Industries became my employer for several years until a layoff forced me to seek employment again. While working at Faultless, I became a born-again believer and was baptized in the Holy Ghost. I thought I was saved at the age of twelve because I joined church and was water baptized. I began to attend a holiness church, and there

I began to know who God really was. During this time, I asked God for a house and a husband who would be a good father to my children. I told God, "If You were to line all the men up, I couldn't pick the right one," so I asked God to pick him for me. During a church service one night, I was slain in the Holy Spirit and I heard God say, "I will give you a husband in My due time and season."

In October of 1976, I began to question God again as to when my husband was coming, and God said, "Soon." I called some ministers I knew to ask what does soon mean, because I thought it meant three days, but none of them knew what it meant either. During my waiting, I would have some lonely times, especially during the holidays. In December 1976, a friend of mine took me to see a woman of God who was of my same faith and who spoke of God in the same manner as I did. This woman asked me, "Are you marrying him?" I replied no. She asked, "Do you know someone who wears white to work every day? Because your husband wears white every day." See, the man whom I believed to be my husband was a veterinary doctor (who wore white) whom I broke up with when I became a born-again believer.

I was leaving work one Saturday in January 1977, heading to the Laundromat to wash clothes, when God told me, "Fix yourself up, you are going to meet your husband there." When I arrived, there was the doctor, and my heart fluttered. I continued to wait on God because he had not surrendered his life to Jesus Christ, and I knew I could not marry him. A few days passed, and the owner of the Laundromat asked me to stay with the laundry attendant while she closed because she was afraid at night. The extra money would help me purchase new furniture and a bigger television, I thought.

One evening a man was drying his clothes, and I said to myself, I wonder where his wife is? You do not find men doing laundry that often. He was dressed nice but was not attractive to me. On his way out, he spoke to me; I spoke and kept on talking to someone else. A week later when he was there and the attendant went out to read the gas pumps, I walked by, and he said, "Are you married?" I replied very sarcastically, "I'm divorced with three kids." He also said he was divorced with three kids. Then he asked if he could call me, and I said, "I'm waiting on the Lord." He said, "It's just nice to have someone to talk to." I do not know what happened, but his comment melted my heart.

Three weeks later, he called me on Valentine's Day and came by for a little while. He had to leave early to be home when his children arrived from school. That night, he came by the Laundromat with a box of candy and a card. Later that night, he called me. Still I did not know he was going to be my husband. It did not bother him that I talked about another man all the time because he knew I was his wife; he just let me talk. He went to work after the first night we met and told his coworker about me and said that he was going to marry me. I found him to be very nice, and I prayed God would give him a good wife. One night while talking, the Lord said, "Introduce him to Me." I replied, "How could I do that? He goes to church and sings with a quartet." One night I told him to turn to the channel I was watching, and I began to tell him about my relationship with Jesus Christ; he never said a word. He went to church with me and gave his life to Jesus. One day on his way to work, God filled and baptized him in the Holy Spirit. He said, "I always knew there was more than I had experienced." See, he would read his Bible and drink a beer every night. We later learned that two of his sisters were praying for him to have a saved wife. We continued to see each other; he was very nice and always on time. Right away, he asked if he could put a ring on my hand. I said, "I'm waiting on God," not yes or no because I did not want him to have to take the ring back, and I had not heard from God that he was the one. Meanwhile I begin to fall in love with him; he was the ideal man I wanted. I discussed this with my sisters, one thought he was the right one, one disagreed. So I began to tell her who he was and how I felt. He invited me to his home, and while sitting on the couch, the Lord said, "This is the one I have chosen for you." So one month and two days later, on March 16, 1977, we were married.

Now when I was younger, I wanted six kids. The awesome thing about God is that He knew I would have them. When I married, I had three children, and so did my husband, Major Leavell. There I was with my six kids and the husband that God had promised. We knew that since God had put us together, we were bound to have many great times ahead of us. Now, it was not always roses, trying to merge two different families together; but as time went on, it got better. My husband and I worked together to provide for our family; we shared many things together and grew closer to God. My husband loved to fish, and we often took the kids to the lake or go camping; spending family time together brought us great joy. One night during a church service, someone told my husband, "You are in the back right now, but soon you will be in the front." We assumed this meant a closer walk with God, but once again, God had something else in mind.

In the spring of 1981, Holiness Church of Deliverance was founded by the late Pastor Major Leavell and me, Pastor Gloria Leavell. I am currently the pastor now. The vision of the ministry is "to preach and teach the word of God with simplicity so that God's people can live totally free and be delivered from every walk of life. To equip and educate God's people to obtain and possess the kingdom of God. To build stronger families for every walk of life."

My husband and I were a true match made in heaven; my husband was a paint contractor, and I always loved to decorate. While raising our six children, we experienced many struggles as parents and pastors. However, we stood together in confidence that God would take us through every situation. Some struggles we encountered with our children included two of our daughters getting pregnant as teenagers, our son struggling with a drug addiction, one daughter facing a devastating divorce, a daughter desperately wanting to be married going through three engagements until she final decided to do it God's way, and one daughter leaving home unexpectedly during the night.

My Father in heaven saw me through when my husband's health took a turn for the worst; he gave me the strength I needed to take care of him. His legacy will always remain because he was a true man of God who loved and provided for his family. Remember that all things work for the good to those who love the Lord.

Over the years, I have reached out to countless women, men, and families who were struggling. Being led by his spirit enables me to give a sense of encouragement, renewal, and hope to others. Your home and appearance are an indication of how your mind is functioning. When things are cluttered, out of place, and disorganized, it tends to be that way in our minds. Once things have been organized and put in their place, the mind can be peaceful and creative, each thought in its proper place. Many times when I have a lot on my mind, I go home and do some things I have been meaning to do. Of course, I ask God about those things first, but He usually speaks while order is being set. Once I go home and begin to pull the weeds, dust furniture, organize closets, or do whatever needs to be done, I usually hear God give an answer to the questions I have asked or instruct me on an upcoming event I am planning to have. This is when we truly begin to see success take place, when the mind can be at peace to function properly and hear what the Lord has to say. I want people to understand that we all have problems and issues arise in our lives, but what we chose to do about them is what sets our future in motion. If you want success in your future, do not be afraid to let God arrange things for you, do not stop living or let problems over take you.

Instead of letting problems get the best of you, go before God and simply say, "Father, here is the problem, what should I do?" I know that this method will never fail you. Even if you feel you're not developed in God to know it is Him speaking to you, don't worry, He'll get the information to you. I have not always been able to hear from God, but he made sure to send someone or even a TV program to speak to me. God knows how to deliver and meet your needs.

I believe that if a person has a need, they should sow a seed. I continue blessing others with the skills I have acquired from my life experiences, the Word of God, and hearing from heaven. At one point, I made a decision to leave my job to help a young woman and her son get on their feet. After praying about this situation, I sat down with my family, explaining to them the need for us to do this to help someone else. I knew that to make it work, we would have to make some sacrifices and trust God. You would have thought that my godson was my own child. I took him everywhere, just as I did my own children; even they helped, treating him as if he was their brother. His mother was able to pursue a career, and God even brought her a husband. My godson is now a successful young lawyer. I thank God for all that He has done for my family, for me, and others that I have reached out to help. I know that the reason my husband was so successful in his business was because of all the seeds we sowed and the families that we helped along the way, and because I was faithful to carry out the things God laid on my heart to do, He provided and took good care of us.

I am the type of person who put my hands to the plow. Looking at the problems does not solve them; instead we have to seek God and put our hands toward solving them. The Word says that "faith without works is dead." You can believe all day, but you have to mix some work with it. If there was anything I could say to bring hope to someone, it would be to seek God for your answers today and wait to see him move on your behalf; you can only be defeated if you believe you are. Remember to always reach out to others, get involved in your community, and see what you can do to make a difference. God is and continuous to be that constant driving force in my life. Whenever things seemed to go in a different direction, I would always turn to the Word of God because I knew my God could not lie. The Word of God is alive and true if anyone is seeking hope, encouragement, a way out of a bad situation, or companionship. I encourage you to seek God and His guidance. I never would have thought that He would take a high school dropout who got pregnant to be a pastor. However, once healing takes place in your life, nothing can hold you back. Divorce could not stop me from remarrying because I allowed God to heal me. Jealousy could not grip me and prevent me from carrying out what I needed to do for others because I knew what God could do.

Therefore, thankfulness comes to mind when I look back over my life.

Psalms 91 (KJV)

He that dwelleth in the secret place of the most High shall abide under the shadow of the Almighty.

I will say of the LORD, He is my refuge and my fortress: my God; in him will I trust.

Surely he shall deliver thee from the snare of the fowler, and from the noisome pestilence.

He shall cover thee with his feathers, and under his wings shalt thou trust: his truth shall be thy shield and buckler.

Thou shalt not be afraid for the terror by night; nor for the arrow that flieth by day;

Nor for the pestilence that walketh in darkness; nor for the destruction that wasteth at noonday.

A thousand shall fall at thy side, and ten thousand at thy right hand; but it shall not come nigh thee.

Only with thine eyes shalt thou behold and see the reward of the wicked.

Because thou hast made the LORD, which is my refuge, even the most High, thy habitation;

There shall no evil befall thee, neither shall any plague come nigh thy dwelling.

For he shall give his angels charge over thee, to keep thee in all thy ways.

They shall bear thee up in their hands, lest thou dash thy foot against a stone.

Thou shalt tread upon the lion and adder: the young lion and the dragon shalt thou trample under feet.

Because he hath set his love upon me, therefore will I deliver him: I will set him on high, because he hath known my name.

He shall call upon me, and I will answer him: I will be with him in trouble; I will deliver him, and honour him.

With long life will I satisfy him, and shew him my salvation.

Contact Information:
Holiness Church of Deliverance
351 North Ridge Dr.
Hopkinsville, KY 42240

21

Jacqueline L. Knight

So Jesus said to them, *"Because of your unbelief; for assuredly, I say to you, if you have faith as a mustard seed, you will say to this mountain, 'Move from here to there,' and it will move; and nothing will be impossible for you."*

—Matthew 17:20

When I think about Leading Ladies, I think about success and the finish line and what it takes to get there. God showed me I can get to the finish line, but before getting there, I had to endure the race first, with prayer, balance, challenges in my life, obstacles I had to overcome, fear, and adversity. "Count it all joy, my brothers, when you meet trials of various kinds, for you know that the testing of your faith produces steadfastness. And let steadfastness have its full effect, that you may be perfect and complete, lacking in nothing" (James 1:2-4). The most important thing I realized was that I was not going to get there by blocking it all out. I had to surrender, walk it out, talk it out, go through some things, talk to God, yet the stretch still seemed to be miles away from getting to the finish line. The race was getting challenging, and I wanted to quit, but I could not; I kept pressing on. I realized that I did not want to live in depression forever and that I am somebody, a child of the Most High God. So ladies, you are somebody.

It took me a long time to realize that nothing would be impossible for me because it definitely was not impossible for God. I knew I had the potential to do anything, but I had to trust God first and realize that if I trusted and believed in Him and seek His face, He will direct my paths. If you want something in life, the time, and hours has to be put in. I pray my words will be an encouragement to someone today.

I was born in Union City, Tennessee, to my lovely parents, James and Loretta, along with five other siblings. We were raised in Jackson, Tennessee. Unfortunately, one of my siblings passed away in 1990 and my dad in 2010. I am so thankful for my sister and brothers.

I am so thankful for my mother, who showed me how to be a lady of strength and courage. She never forgot where she came from. Her mother passed away at an early age, and her foster parents raised her. She learned how to appreciate the little things in life and to never take a life for granted. "The Lord is my strength and my shield; my heart trusted in him, and I am helped: therefore my heart greatly rejoices; and with my song will I praise him" (Psalm 28:7).

Through my walks of everyday life, I learned nothing was impossible for me with the help of God who strengthens me. When I wake up every morning, I give God the glory; I think about how good God has been to me and how His grace and mercy has kept me. I managed to get through high school, and upon graduating, one of my teachers pulled me to the side and told me my smile would take me a long way. Without hesitation, I decided to join the military right after high school. I took the test, passed it, and had to wait approximately four months before going in. A couple of my brothers were against me going in the military. They told me I would get kicked on, spit on, treated like a dog, and everything else. Prior to going in the military, I had a setback and did not think I was going to make it in.

While waiting to leave for the Army, I and my cousin Regina, who had a full scholarship to Lane College, was in Jackson. She was waiting to start college. During this time, she and I decided to be brave and ride through my neighborhood on the hood of my high school friend's car. As he was driving, he accidentally hit the gas, causing the car to speed up, and Regina slid off the hood. In a matter of minutes, our whole life changed. Regina was trapped underneath the car. All I can remember was jumping off the hood and seeing the look of shock in her eyes before she started screaming. We couldn't believe what just happened. As she was rushed to the emergency room, all I could do was pray. Regina sustained life-threatening injuries. Our lives were forever changed. This is just a testimony of how quick life can change and that tomorrow is not guaranteed. Her dreams of being that basketball player were shattered; instead of going off to college, she was now going off to endure months of physical therapy. This could have happened to either one of us. At the age of seventeen, the pain I felt in my heart was very heavy knowing that I was still leaving for the Army and Regina was not able to pursue her dream. Regina's life is a true test of faith. I just want to thank her for the strength and courage she had while moving forward and how her actions encouraged me. "And we know that all things work together for good to those who love God, to those who are called according to His purpose" (Romans 8:28).

I joined the military in the fall of 1984, and during my tenure, it wasn't always easy. But as I progressed through the ranks, I got wiser. In the beginning I was reluctant to speak up for myself, but I learned how. When you join the military, it is mandatory to go through Basic Training and Advanced Individual Training (AIT). Basic Training was not a problem; however, when I got to my advanced training that was when things started changing. I started facing adversity and obstacles that I wasn't prepared for. If you noticed earlier, I spoke about getting to the finish line, but I had to endure the race before graduating. One of the privileges in AIT was for weekend passes. We were able to start receiving passes for the weekend after about three weeks into training. I was excited and looked forward to going out the gate to eat, shop, and relax. When the weekend came, everybody's name got called out except mine. I was trying to figure out what was going on. I knew my boots were shined, and I passed all my inspections. For reasons unknown to me at that time, my squad leader came up to me and said my pass had been pulled. Why was all I wanted to know? My squad leader pulled me to the side and told me the senior field had a big crush on me and that he talked about me constantly. The advice I received from my squad leader was to go in there and shake my butt in front of him and convince him to give me my pass. I couldn't believe he would say such a thing, and I told him I wasn't doing that because I did not do anything wrong. This was when I started to learn how to speak up for myself because at that moment, I realized that if I didn't take care of myself, no one else would. I requested permission to speak with the senior field. His excuse was my class A's were messed up; therefore, I did not receive a pass that weekend. My military career had barely started, and this was what I was facing. I said to myself, *Was it that smile that my teacher told me would take me a long way?* Regardless of what it was, the devil was a liar because *delays are not denials,* and I would succeed. I worked hard, and as the weeks passed, I *earned* my passes. The last word I heard from my senior field was after graduation when he said, "You be careful and take care." I did an about-face and walked away because I knew God had favor on me. "But those who wait on the Lord shall renew their strength; they shall mount up with wings like eagles, they shall run and not be weary, they shall walk and not faint" (Isaiah 40:31).

After a couple years in the military, I fell in love and was married to a *beautiful* man who initially said *he was attracted to my toes.* We were married for over twenty-five years, and unfortunately, we grew apart and decided to go our own separate ways. I was disappointed, but I knew God was in control. During my marriage, I was blessed with two beautiful children, my son, Eric Jr., and my daughter, Jasmine Tionne, who at an early age God called to His glory. Speaking from personal experience, I would like to encourage any of you that may have conflict in your marriage to just hold on to God's *unchanging hand*; learn how to *communicate,* and let God walk you through it. (Psalms 27:14) says, "Wait on the Lord; be of good courage, and He will direct your path; Wait, I say, on the Lord!"

As my military career continued, the challenges continued. I refused to waiver. I stayed and endured it because I was in the race for the long haul. After three deployments, I can proudly claim I was still standing. The military is not a bad place to be, however; it is a great place to be. What I found to be true is that the military didn't change, people did. Communication is not that complex; if you want to know something about a person, just ask. If you want to know something about me just ask. I can attest to all the ladies who are in the military: Run your race to the finish line. Claim your victory! If you are seeking that promotion, remember, nothing is impossible if you believe. All good and righteous gifts come from God. Be you, and be the *best you can be.* Allow competence and integrity to be your watchword. A career in the military is demanding all by itself, but so is having a family. I will never forget the look in my son's eyes when I had to leave for Iraq in 2003; it broke my heart. He wanted to know when I was coming home again. Several months after I hit the ground in Iraq, I was surrounded by the enemy. I was saying to myself, *Why is God taking me through this season?* It was bad enough I was away from my family. As a mother, bearing the thought of not knowing when or even if I would ever return home, I stayed on my knees constantly. I kept looking toward the finish line; I was still enduring the race. But God kept me. He brought me home safely, and my son was right there with open arms waiting for me when I returned. I would like to say to my son, Eric Jr., you can do it. Said who? *God said,* but you have to trust and believe in God for yourself. Thank you for being one of my biggest supporters. I don't care how old our children get; we still have to encourage them. "Trust in the LORD with all your heart and lean not on your own understanding; in all your ways acknowledge him, and he will direct your paths straight" (Proverbs 3:5-6).

After much prayer and consulting with my husband at the time, I decided to start the transition to get out of the military after returning from Iraq in 2004. Things changed. I was offered a job at the academy to be the chief of distance learning. I accepted the position and stayed in another four years. My challenges continued. Unknown to me on my third year in the position, my so-called right hand man and others were plotting against me, mainly because I was a female. I was firm, and I was fair. I could feel in my spirit something wasn't right. One Sunday it was confirmed when I was at the pulpit and a pastor by the name of Shamond Scales' prophesied over me. He told me I had a good spirit and to be aware that people were talking about me and trying to take me down. Don't tell me God isn't real. It all worked out. I did not waiver. God had favored me again. *"God will make your enemy your footstool."* Luke 20:43. A year later, I retired with twenty-three and a half years of service. Transitioning into the civilian sector was not a problem for me because God was directing my footstep.

My race is my race and mine alone. What God has for me is for me; what he has for you is for you. God made me just like he wanted me and not like anyone else. I am the original me. I am who I am. I had to take control of my life and my future; if not, who else is going to do it for me? *I can and I will.* I do not have all the answers, but I will accept the ones I have and practice serenity for the ones I do not have. I had to realize I could not do it all, but in God's season and timing, it will surely come to pass.

The only one responsible for my happiness is me. I have made some bad choices in my life, and I am so thankful that there is a God that sets high and looks low. Each day that I fall, He pulls me back up and gives me the strength to continue the race. I can recall certain situations when I wanted to look back for whatever reasons; God would lead me one way, and I wanted to go another. God is not an author of confusion. I had to press forward because I know God is God, and I didn't want to feel His wrath for being disobedient. My past is my past, and it will be connected to me in some form but it will not define my future. Said who? *God said.* God is telling me for this season to move *forward.* I was reminded of (Genesis 19:26): But his wife looked back behind him, and she became a pillar of salt.

Who am I? A child of God, a Leading Lady, business lady, CEO, Xceptional Lady, marketing consultant, entrepreneur, mother, and friend. I speak these things right now into existence. Some of these things have already come to *fruition.* I can get to the finish line. Said who? *God said.* I can be anything that God said I can be. I have endured some challenges, yet I stayed in the race, and this is how the story ends. I was blessed to achieve my master's degree, will be graduating with my doctoral degree in December and I must say, "it has been a challenge along the way but I am enduring the race; looking to start my own business in the near future to help write business plans for major corporations and small businesses. I am a University of Phoenix facilitator, served as the Regional Coordinator (Kentucky/Tennessee) for Xcellence Inc., recently named as the Corporate Compliance Analyst for Xcellence Inc. and received the Xceptional Lady Award, thanks to Angella Banks. Angella had *faith* in me. Thank you, Angella. I will continue to face challenges in my life and endure the race. I will remember that the finish line is moments away. So be encouraged, my brother or sister, the victory can be yours if you endure the race and get to the *finish line.* I give God all the praise and glory. He is my strength and refuge. He is my sun beneath the storm. Lord God, I just want to say Thank You!

"God makes His plans clear to those who genuinely and humbly seek His will. As this day unfolds, let us seek God's will and obey His Word. When we entrust our lives to Him completely and without reservation, He gives us the strength to meet any challenge, the courage to face trial, and the wisdom to live in His righteousness and in His peace." (Dr. Criswell Freeman, A Woman's Garden of Hope)

Closing

I want to give thanks to my family, friends, church family, and educators. I want to give a special thanks to Treva Gordon for giving me this opportunity. I am so very humbled.

Always Have Faith in Yourself

It is not easy to
Live life sometimes,
And face the world with a smile.
When you are crying inside,
It takes a lot of courage
To reach down inside yourself
Hold on to that strength
That is still there,
And know that tomorrow
Is a new day—
With new possibilities
But if you can just hold on
Long enough to see this through,
You will come out a new person—
    Stronger,
With more understanding,
And with a new pride in yourself
From knowing you made it.

—Unknown Author

Contact Information:
Website: jsuccess.worldventures.biz
Face book: Jacqueline Knight
LinkedIn: Jacqueline Knight
E-mail: jackiedba2013@gmail.com

Renee,

You have seen me go through. I am thankful for all your words. I love how you tell me what I need to hear, not what I want to hear. I love you.

Jamie Figueroa

Before I formed you in the womb I knew you, before you were born I set you apart; I appointed you as a prophet to the nations.

—Jeremiah 1:5

God Chose Me

As much as God knows us in our mother's womb, so does Satan. We are all born in this world as sinners. We don't get to pick our parents, our race, or even what class our upbringing will be. God will always set divine appointments in our life to choose Him.

Rejection began for me when I was in my mother's womb. My parents divorced before I was even born. As a child and young adult, I never knew who my biological father was. "A father to the fatherless; a defender of widows is God in His holy place" (Ps. 68:5). It wasn't until I turned twenty that I met my biological dad. To this day, my relationship with my real father is estranged.

But God shows me every day that I am in Him. He is my true Father.

At age five, my innocence was taken from me when I went to stay with a family member. The memory of being raped has been blocked from my mind. My mom and stepdad told me years later that I was tied to a bed while this man had sex with me. He told me that if I told my parents, he would kill my whole family. In my twenties, I called my stepfather asking him if I was really raped. He confirmed that it was true. My heart was broken because as a child, I was not protected by people that should have protected me.

By the time I was seven, my mom was married to her third husband. My mom and third husband would often leave us kids with different people to watch us. There was a man who moved into our home and watched my sister and me frequently. He would ask me to do sexual things for him. In return he would do chores that my mom had ordered me to do while she was gone. If I would tell him no, that I did not want to do anything sexual, he would tell me that he was going to tell my mom that I was bad while she was gone. I would do whatever it was sexually that he wanted me to do to not get in trouble with my mom.

One afternoon I went on a bus ride with my mom. I was having a conversation with my sister, asking her if we should tell my mom what this man was doing. My mom asked what we were talking about. I told her that this man would make us do sexual things to him while they were not home and come to our room at night. This man denied anything ever happening and continued to stay in our home. One day my mom and third husband walked in on him doing sexual things with my sister. He was kicked out without police involvement.

I was ten years old when my world got flipped upside down. The enemy had a field day with his plan of constant rejection in my life. *But God* always saw the bigger picture for the life he had for Jamie. That is why the enemy tried so hard to come and steal, kill, and destroy my life.

My mom and I were on our way home from a counseling appointment when we heard someone honking their horn like a crazy person. The closer the car got, the more we realized it was my mom's third husband. We got in the car, and he said to my mom, "Your daughter is at the police station." The rest of the car ride was silent. I was taken to my aunt and uncle's house. It seemed like my mom, sister, and third husband were gone for hours. I was sitting on the couch with my tray of food in front of me, eating dinner. The front door opened and in walked the third husband, saying, "They're taking the kids." That didn't register until my mom walked in the house. My mom walks in with tears streaming down her face, saying, "They are taking the kids." I knew at this point it was bad. A man and woman walked in behind my mom, and I went crazy. I jumped up screaming and crying, "I'm not going, I'm not going!" They had to carry me to the car. I remember looking out the back window, crying, "Mommy, Mommy, Mommy!" I looked out the back window until I couldn't see her anymore.

I remember being so angry. I was taken to this couple's house where my sister was placed. I was quiet the first night with the couple. I went to bed in the same room with my sister. I realized we got taken because she told her teacher that my mom's third husband was sexually abusing her. I was really mean to my sister that night, and I told her it did not happen. I cried myself to sleep, and so did my precious sister.

When we returned home, my mom became very unstable and abusive. We moved from place to place frequently. I recall times that she would get angry and start hitting my brother and sister. I would say or do something so she would hit me instead of them. I could not stand her hitting them. My mom was a very quick-tempered person. She would get angry if she dropped something on the floor. My mom screamed a lot, and I always knew when she got closer to me that I was going to be slammed up against the wall. My face would be slapped or punched often.

At the age of eleven, I was hit by a car. My mom was an hour in half away at a prison, visiting her fourth husband. I was knocked out and broke my left leg in half. This is another *but God* moment. I did not have a helmet on, and my head hit the concrete. God spared my life. I had to have surgery on my left leg and was in a cast for six months. During this time, I remember my mom getting angry about something silly. She stared smacking me anywhere she could hit. I got so angry that I screamed at her, "Why don't you just kill me?" My mom grabbed me by the throat and was choking me. My aunt walked in and yelled, "Let her go!" My mom tossed me across the room. I just sat in the kitchen and cried. I never understood why my mom always took out her anger on me.

My mom got turned into the Department of Children and Family Services (DCFS) by a couple of different people saying that there was abuse going on in the home. When an investigator came to the school, of course, I denied that any of it was true because as dysfunctional as my home was, I did not want to be away from my mom. I couldn't see or talk to my sister so we could tell the same story. I was asked if I was left alone with my sister and brother while my mom went to a different state. I could not lie about that because I had a family member that stayed at my house and had a seizure. I had to call EMT services to come take care of her. Also my mom was violating court orders that no man was to be living in the home with us girls. We got taken away from my mom again. I was eleven years old the last time I lived with my mother.

I was bounced around from foster home to foster home. The first foster home I went to was horrible. The foster dad was physically abusive. He took my little brother and slammed him on a footstool. I screamed at him, "Don't slam him down!" He said, "Shut up, you little *whore*." I didn't know what that word meant, but I knew it was not very nice. My sister got removed from the home. I began to act out like crazy. I did not know how to be away from my sister. I was the mother and protected her. It was ripped away from me. I did not know how to deal with the emotions of losing my mom and my sister within a couple of months. I was removed from this foster home and put in a group home. As the caseworker came that night, I just cried and cried.

I was placed in a group home that had 24-7 counseling. I ran away a couple of times, but for the most part, I did well in the program. I was out of the group home on good behavior within a year and a half. I was able to be placed in a foster home.

My next home was with Bob and Michelle. I mention their names because this couple loved Jesus like nobody I have ever met. I was fourteen, and I thought they were really weird. I remember Bob telling me his testimony on how he came to know God. They were faithful in prayer and went to church.

To this day my name is on a board that they have of all the foster kids placed in their home. They pray daily for each child that God placed in their home. I am a woman of God because they did not stop praying for me. They stood in the gap when I had no idea who Jesus really was at the time.

There was a couple that I met in church while living with Bob and Michelle. I became best friends with their oldest daughter, Melisa. Tony and Renee made a decision to get a foster license to have me in their home. I lived in a couple of foster homes before I was placed with Tony and Renee. By the time I moved in with this family, I had walls that I didn't know I had subconsciously built. I had dealt with so much rejection and mental and physical abuse from bouncing from foster home to foster home. I didn't know how to fit in with a family that loved me so much. I was sixteen dealing with normal teenage-girl hormones, teenage-girl issues, and my mom was signing away her rights over us kids to the state.

Tony and Renee also poured seeds of Jesus in me. I would not be able to write this testimony without thanking them for their prayers.

I found out six months before I was going to graduate high school that I was pregnant. I was in a bit of shock. As the days went on, everyone around me told me it would be better to have an abortion. This was not my first option, but ultimately I made the decision to follow through with aborting my child.

The following summer, I turned eighteen. I was a wild child, and nobody could tell me what to do because I was a legal adult. I ran into a boy that I dated in the eighth grade. I ended up pregnant with my second child. The father was in denial and wanted nothing to do with me. I decided to put her up for adoption when I was seven months pregnant.

I met what I thought was my first love when I was pregnant with my second child. I had his and his family's the support behind me. I lived with my boyfriend and his mother when I gave up my daughter for adoption. It wasn't five months later that I found out I was pregnant with my third child. I didn't care what the situation was; I was determined to be a good mom and keep this child.

I loved to dance. I got a job at the nightclub being a cage dancer (clothes on). The owner told me that they wanted me to do amateur night at the strip club downstairs. I gave in and was placed in the contest. From the age of twenty-one, I became a stripper for three years.

I quit dancing because I met a man whom I thought I was going to marry. I was head over heels for this guy. I was so in love that I would have done anything for this man. When we broke up, I was devastated. I moved back in with my foster parents Tony and Renee. I was in a pit of hell with my emotions. I tried to kill myself. I took half a bottle of Tylenol and a whole bunch of other pills in the home. I was in the intensive care unit for four days. My pastor and a bunch of people from the church came to pray over me. *But God* once again spared my life when I should have died a slow, painful death.

I became friends with a girl that glorified ecstasy. I had no desire to try it, but the more I hung out with her and the more she talked about it, the more curious I got about it. I started working at a club near Chicago with her. I went with her to a party one night and was introduced to ecstasy. I loved how it made me feel. I would try any drug once. During this time, I got pregnant. I flipped because I was heavy into drinking and doing drugs. I sadly made the choice to have another abortion. This sent me on a downward spiral. I self-medicated any way that I could. I had no boundaries to what I would try. I got fired from my job near Chicago. My uncle took my car. I had to do something, and fast. I did what Jamie did best and ran. I got a plane ticket to Nebraska to go and be with my family.

I was partying every day and night for three weeks. I was drinking by noon every day. I got involved in working for a couple of escort services. God protected me every step of the way because I never got into prostitution. *But God* covered me when I didn't deserve it!

On my last night in Nebraska, I was at a party with my two cousins and some friends when I realized something bad was about to go down. I had no idea that there were people at this party who had it out for one of my cousins. I could not get to my cousin in time when four girls and two men started beating my cousin like she was a man. One guy hit her in the head with a bottle, kicked her in the stomach so hard she was almost lifeless on the ground. He was punching her. I finally got to her and threw her in the car. We rushed to the hospital because she was covered in blood. I walked outside crying, looking up in the sky and saying, "There has to be a better life for me than this."

I went home on a train that morning. I surrounded myself with godly people who prayed for me. In 2001, I was lying in bed looking at the Bible. I went back to look up a scripture on pain. God led me to Jeremiah 15:15-21 (see). I said the prayer asking God to come into my heart. God has held his promise to me in spite of my choices.

In 2005 I married a solider. I completely stepped out of God's will for my life because we were unevenly yoked. It was a rough five years. I went through two deployments with this man. I did not always deal well with the rejection that happened in my marriage. I turned to alcohol to deal with the pain. I did not cover my husband with the blood of Jesus. I learned my lesson after being divorced in 2010.

I moved back to Tennessee. It has taken me two years to get my life back on track. I can boldly say God has done amazing things even though I turned my back on him. He never left or forsake me. On July 1, 2012, I went to Bethel Community Church. I had an attitude that I'm tired Lord of going to church and no one seeing my pain. I was going to go in and get the message and leave. God had a different agenda! I sat in the back row during worship and just balled my eyes out. (On June 29, my ex-husband's wife posted their marriage license on Facebook.) They got married at the same place we did and by the same guy. I was crushed! An amazing woman in my church came from behind and hugged me, saying, "I love you, I love you, I love you." Pastor Richard got up and said, "I feel heaviness in this service. I was supposed to speak on the tongue, but I feel God is taking this service in a different direction." He said, "I don't know whom this is for, but God hears your prayers and loves you." I lost it even more. I then realized that God had stopped this service, which I had an attitude about going to, for Him to tell me He sees my hurt, hears my prayers, and loves me. This was just the beginning of my healing. Pastor Richard had us come to the front, and Pastor Ron said, "Jamie, God knows the desires of your heart. He just wants you to give Him all of your heart. He will bring that husband you long for. He said the devil almost had you, the key word, Jamie, is *almost*. I see you bound up in condemnation and guilt, and you are set free from that today." I walked out of that church a free woman.

It doesn't matter where you come from in life. God can heal you in all areas of your life. I come from a long line of complete destruction, but God kept his promise from Jeremiah 1:5 to me. He knew me in my mother's womb. I can tell my story because God gave His Son and died for everything that I have been through. If you struggle with anything, just know that God can heal every area of your life.

Contact Information:
Jamie Figueroa
Jamiefigueroa15@yahoo.com

23

Janine Folks Edwards

Being confident of this very thing, that he who began a good work in you will complete it until the day of Jesus Christ.

—Philippians 1:6

Now to him who is able to do exceedingly abundantly above all that we ask or think, according to the power that works in us.

—Ephesians 3:20

During the second quarter of 2012, my life changed pretty dramatically. In April, I got a phone call from my childhood friend Treva. She talked about putting together a five-star luncheon to honor some amazing women. She would call it *Michigan Leading Ladies* (MLL).

She knew who she had in mind for a speaker. A venue had not been chosen yet, nor had the date. She wanted to work it around the Women of Transition monthly prayer gatherings, which take place every first Saturday.

Treva and I began to select women who would be honored. We shared ideas about how to make her vision work. I was catching her vision for MLL. She threw out some figures for costs. It sounded like an amazing idea, and then I wondered how we would really pull it off. Treva was very confident and excited about this endeavor. It would take a couple of days of pondering for me to get on board. I knew that if this thing happened, then truly *God would have to do it*.

My plate was already full, nearly overflowing with a full-time job, a part-time job, three children, writing for several publications, ministry work, and a plethora of other miscellaneous chores and deeds. I was already feeling overwhelmed with life, and adding a new thing to my plate, at first, seemed unwise.

For me, it was like making a decision to get on a roller coaster. While some people love to ride roller coasters and love the thrill, roller-coaster rides make me nervous. The last time I rode a coaster, I remember the anxiety beginning to build as I stood in line. The closer we got to our turn to board, the more nervous I got.

When it was time to hop into the cart, we strapped in, and the safety bars were engaged and locked. Once you hear that click, you know there's no turning back. You're in it for the long haul. You're on the ride until it's over. There's no exiting once the ride begins.

This is what my commitment was like to Treva and Leading Ladies. Once I decided to be on board, I was in. No matter how rough the ride or how many unexpected and abrupt crescents and troughs, I would stay on. I was locked in like, "LET'S DO THIS!"

I knew I had to be a part of the Leading Ladies project. Something inside knew this would be a monumental experience. Some of the greatest and most successful things I've done in life were things that I initially felt reluctant about. But when God is in it, no amount of reluctance or reservations can overpower that desire that God puts inside you. God gives us to do His will (Phil. 2:13). That feeling that feeds faith trumps fear.

Once the Leading Ladies ball got rolling, I was ready to ride. Anticipation and excitement were high. I was zealous and happy to be a part of this great event. With the actual event being months away, I hoped that the feelings of excitement would remain consistent. Six months of anticipation seemed like a long time to maintain this great feeling.

Fully aware of my personality, I feared that my mood might fluctuate and that my feelings would change. I did not *want* this to happen, but I knew it was likely. So I was prepared to deal with my passionate emotions, even when they would go against me.

A few weeks in, just as I figured it would happen, I started to feel doubt and an overwhelming fear. "What have I gotten myself into?" Out of nowhere and for no reason, it seemed I started feeling like I made a big mistake. My mind raced, suspicious thoughts began to attack, and I felt like I would have a nervous breakdown.

Deep down, I knew this was an attack on my mind because I had embarked on something amazing. My biggest battles are fought in my mind. I could not sleep. My thoughts were frazzled, and I knew I had to pull it together somehow because I was in this thing until the end. Backing out was not an option. I had made a commitment to my friend and to my God, and I would not back out no matter what my emotions were doing. I am learning to not allow my emotions to rule my decision making.

I am a highly sensitive person emotionally. This is a gift and a curse. As a gift, it allows me to feel deeply, not only my own feelings, but I can also empathize deeply and pick up on the pain and feelings of others. This helps me in my ministry. Adversely, I have a tendency to feel too deeply, and I end up over reacting and getting worked up about things more than I should. It takes effort for me to remain balanced. I could feel myself getting off-balance.

God is faithful, and He knew I needed a diversion. I needed something else to focus on. I needed another cause, another challenge. I needed another trail to blaze. That sounds crazy because I already had plenty of causes, challenges, and blazing trails. God has given me this amazing capacity to keep multiple irons in the fire, big irons!

So what would this diversion be? A few weeks prior to my meltdown, I saw a flier about women's roller derby in Detroit. I didn't even know we had roller derby in Detroit. *How cool is that?* I thought.

As a child, I had watched roller derby on television on Saturday mornings. I saw that it was a rough and tough sport for women. What made me most interested in roller derby was that the women were on roller skates. I've been an avid roller skater since I was a year old. I was told that I skated before I walked well. "Your mom put you on skates, and when she took the skates off of you, you crawled," a cousin revealed to me.

Both of my parents were roller skaters. In fact, that's how they met. I was raised on roller skates, and needless to say, roller-skating had become a big part of my life. So any activity involving roller skates would naturally attract me. As far as the rough and tough part is concerned, as a child, I was anything but rough and tough. I was a sweet, gentle, quiet, and passive child who was bullied in elementary school. Being rough and tough was a secret desire and fantasy.

I knew I was strong and smart, but my strength was never apparent to others. What could be better than roller derby as a way to skate and show my strong side? What better way to reveal my inner warrior princess? Roller derby would allow me to show the world how strong I really am, and it would teach me to fight. I could learn the art of war.

On a flier I picked up at a coffee shop, I discovered that local tryouts were coming up. By the morning of tryouts, I had already convinced myself that trying out for roller derby was ridiculous. Tryouts were at 9:00 a.m., and when I awoke and glanced at my clock, I realized that my roller-derby dream was toast.

Seconds later, I got a text message. The message read: "Good morning, derby girl!" The text message was from my friend Ty, to whom I had mentioned the flier and my wild roller-derby dream. For some reason, he believed I could do it.

I hopped out of bed and scurried to get dressed. "I'm going!" I grabbed my skates and was out of the house by 9:20 a.m. I went to the tryouts. I was about thirty-five minutes late and figured I would take a chance.

When I arrived, they had not started yet. They were still waiting for women to arrive. The building was difficult to find, and they wanted to give women a chance to find it. Even though I was late, I was really on time.

I had skates, but no gear. Unfamiliar with the sport currently, I had no idea what to expect or what I should bring. I just showed up with skates. As a result, I could not participate in many of the drills due to safety requirements for equipment. So I watched and listened. On day number two of tryouts, I had gear and was able to participate.

At age forty-two, I survived two days of rigorous tryouts and physical training. Sore in my body, I questioned my sanity, wondering if I was too old for such an undertaking. I could barely walk and required assistance putting on my socks and pants. When I realized the younger women were sore too, I felt better. I was also comforted to know that there were other women close to my age playing roller derby. I wasn't so crazy after all.

Meanwhile, I was in touch with Treva several times a week as we planned for Michigan Leading Ladies! Plans for MLL continued to move forward. We promoted heavily on Facebook. We flooded social media and e-mail, and the word spread quickly. People wondered who was backing us and how we had the audacity to pursue such a huge endeavor. We literally stepped out on faith.

Treva provided the design for the first flier, which was a two-sided postcard. When those ran out, I decided to try a different layout. I got a graphic artist to design a new flier. I provided him with the information and told him to design however he felt led.

When the design was complete, the designer e-mailed it to me. After some very minor tweaking, the new flier was a *go*. One side of the flier promoted the MLL luncheon and a Friday evening service. The other side promoted the Women of Transition prayer gathering, featuring my photo. The backdrop of the flier was a checkered flag.

The checkered flag appeared to be taken from a car race. It blended well with the design, but I couldn't help but wonder: *why a checkered flag?* What did a race flag have to do with a prayer gathering? Maybe it indicates that we're winning the race? Loving the contrast of black and white, I felt the fliers looked good, and we proceeded to pass them out and continue to promote MLL.

After two days of Derby U, I was eligible to try out for roller-derby boot camp. I passed the skills test and moved to the next level. Upon completion of an eight-week boot camp, I then became eligible to try out for the league. I passed both the skills and written tests. The next step was to participate in a scrimmage.

The scrimmage was public, and it was a big deal. All the new players were excited about making this far. I played very well in the scrimmage and scored the first ten points. A write-up was done about me in the sports section of my local newspaper, *The Telegram*. I write for that newspaper and never imagined being written about, especially in the sports section at age forty-two!

After the scrimmage, I was drafted to a team. I had my eye on a couple of teams because I had gotten to know some of the players. Ten women were in the draft. I waited anxiously for my name to be called by a team. Seven women went before me. Finally, my name was called: Furious Fro Sheba, number 407, is drafted to the GRAND PRIX MADONNAS!

I skated over to my new team, my new sisters, and my new home. These women embraced me, and it felt like a really good fit. I was excited about my new team and just a tad heartbroken about not being a Dame or D-Funk All-star. However, when I got to know these ladies, I became certain that I was on the right team!

My new team, Grand Prix Madonnas, had cool uniforms. They wore bottoms made of the checker pattern to represent the flag waved at car races. Tops were purple, like royalty. The name Grand Prix Madonnas is a play on words, mixing the idea of Grand Prix car racing and prima donna. I learned that *prima donna* means "leading lady" in Italian!

I started making the connection. I'd been working on Leading Lady stuff for several months. Oh, and the checker flag on the flier matches our uniforms! Had God been involved in this the whole time?! Remember, I didn't choose the Grand Prix Madonnas; they chose me. I was drafted! There was not a more perfect team for me on the league than the Grand Prix Madonnas, also known as GPM!

My team had a reputation of being the *smart team*! One of my teammates is a lawyer. There is a presidential award-winning scientist who is a professor at the University of Michigan. We have an engineer, a couple of marketing specialists, and other professionals. These are not just wild women who hit each other on the derby track. These women are strong, athletic, determined, focused, intelligent, and successful in the real world.

Working on Michigan Leading Ladies helped to prepare me for this next step in my life. I learned to push myself beyond what I think are my limits by exercising my faith. Pressing beyond my limitations has crossed over from spiritual to physical. Playing roller derby has taught me to use my physical body in ways I never imagined. My physical endurance now is greater than it was in my twenties and thirties combined. I never thought I would be running, doing push-ups, skating hard, hitting hard, taking hits and falls the way I do now. My legs are strong, and my arms are building. This is happening because I learned to push myself even when everything in me is screaming "STOP!"

I have God confidence, and I can do what seems impossible. Working with Treva on MLL, I learned how to work as part of a team. I learned to collaborate with others and merge the use of my gifts and talents with others. Now, playing roller derby allows me to continue to develop my ability to be a team player. I learned to be sharpened by teammates, learn from them, disagree with them sometimes and still remain a team working together. It takes a team to work the dream.

The timing of all this could not have been more perfect. I spent months working with Treva across the country. MLL had begun to occupy a lot of my time. What would I do when it was over?

Well, as soon as MLL ended, the season for roller derby began! I had a short break in between. I smoothly transitioned from one to another. I began practicing with my team, Grand Prix Madonnas. I immediately began learning valuable lessons in roller derby for everyday life. The derby track is a battleground. I learn to play offensively and defensively. I have to watch my boundaries and play by the rules. I learned to hit and take hits. I learned to play in pain, push when I'm tired, and face penalties when I break the rules. In a sense, I am learning the art of war. Life is a battle, and combat skills are essential for survival. Derby has taught me to be strong and courageous! There has not been a dull moment.

I am Janine Folks, known in roller derby as Furious Fro Sheba. *Furious* means "active with great energy and intensity." *Fro*, well, I love my natural Afro. *Sheba*, the Queen of Sheba, was very rich, a lover of wisdom and generous. And *407* for the day I was born. I am a proud mother of two beautiful daughters and one miraculous son. I am a licensed and ordained minister, a hospice chaplain, a contract chaplain at a children's hospital, and an author and writer for several periodicals, including a newspaper and a magazine. I am working on several more books, including one about life lessons I learned in derby. I am a Grand Prix Madonna. I am a prima donna. I am a Leading Lady who's excited about what God has in store for me next!

Contact Information:
E-mail: janinewritestoinspire@yahoo.com

24

Jennifer Kay Miller

BIO: I am Jennifer Kay Miller. I was born in Memphis, Tennessee. As a chosen Champion I have a masters of Arts in Teaching. Additionally I am a school teacher and college professor who believes in enriching the lives of all students. Success via faith is the destiny of a champion.

> **Jeremiah 1:4:** *"I knew you before you were formed in your mother's womb; before you were born I sanctified you and appointed you as my spokesman to this world."*

Destiny: I was created as an instrument for my beloved Father, Jehovah. Destined for greatness, I anticipate my life inside the sparrow's song; you are in the sunshine, the rain, and my tears of the days anguish. Chosen among the thorns, you found favor in me. Your love for me edifies the soul, your grace triumphs in my defeat because you are the awesome revelation of my elevation. Destined Journeys are symbolic and spiritual because it is the underlying depiction of one's purpose in life. In an attempt to explore every aspect of journey the notion is created that every journey is difficult and the specific path you travel in life prepares one for a spiritual revival.

Galatians 5:24 states that those who belong to Christ have nailed their natural evil desires to his cross and crucified them there. The transformation from death to a new life in Christ is similar to the passion of the apostle Paul who also sought to become one with Christ. There is a priceless gain of knowing Christ and that dying daily to the flesh is a mandate for a spiritual revival to remain constant in your life. Paul had a consuming passion "to know Him intimately, experientially, continuously." "That I may know Him, and the power of His resurrection, and the fellowship of His sufferings" (Phillipians3:10).

Essentially, if there is any question of a wasted life or miserable existence, remember that you were born specifically with a purpose that was ordained by God, you have the choice to maximize your potential and diligently seek the path in which God has bestowed before you. God in his sovereign loyalty to his creatures that he created always provides a way for you to reach him and we were all divinely elected by God, but we must work toward the will of God.

Shame: As a young child I questioned God and my existence. I hated the life that God had given me. I was born to drug addicted parents. I struggled as a child to make sense of life. When I was three years old I was molested by a relative and I contracted gonorrhea. The scars of molestation I buried deep in my soul because I longed for love. I pleaded with God to give me something tangible. It was a quest for love. What lies beneath the inner core of thought? The vast accounted incalculable layer of solitude, where thought captures you in a second of being alone. The soul craves love never balanced just proportioned. Love that is never pure, a fantasied imagined perfection that only the birds can feel makes you fly never touching the surface. There were times when I wondered what had happened to me. I forgot to look behind the walls, but I found no hope in me. Every corner I searched day and night, but still no me. I was fatigued and I remember that I wanted to quit.

I hate fighting me and this little enemy we call principalities, but I wanted to die because it seemed like no one understood the interior of me, a broken name, and an empty vessel.

As an empty vessel I carried the weight of depression and rejection. I would cling to the notion that no man would ever want me because I carried the sexual abuse inside my heart. The heart of a child was heavy and I experienced anxiety always looking over my shoulder wondering who would take my innocence. For most of my elementary school years I was mute at school. Furthermore, teachers and students alike thought that something was wrong with me mentally, but I decided that I was nothing because a piece of my existence was stolen. I decided that in the fifth grade that I would take my life and for several years after that I began to repeatedly try to commit suicide. In 1999, I decided that life was too much for me and the promised destiny that I thought I had been over. At the age of 16 I took over thirty lithium pills, but I woke up without a headache. At that moment I was amazed and overwhelmed by the presence of God, but I still was in denial of his love. I refused his presence, not realizing that he was sending his ministering angels to protect me. I thought it would be befitting to starve myself. I was filled with so much hate for myself I began to hate the very notion of people. There were times when I was unable to look in the mirror. The idea of being human seems to unveil a concept that identifies imperfection as a cognitive perception, a fictitious perception of perfection. Yet we live in this flesh, we breathe air, never perfect even though we create our own revelation of perfection. In our stubborn imperfection we kill people with our tongues that infect one's soul. The reminder of hate that was spoken lives in their heart as well as mine; a heart that hides under the flesh beneath the soul, a heart that does not breathe, veins have withered. I wonder how beauty, the object of my affection becomes the product of my infestation, infested with abuse, solitude, and that disease reciprocity, not a victim anymore, now I represent a new virus that will allow more souls to die with words from my mouth.

Attraction I:

God had given me a gift of subdued manifestations often revealed in dreams and visions. He offered healing in my hands and I could feel the pain of others as if I was wounded with their affliction. When I entered college, I was quite involved in my church ministry. I was affiliated with the college ministry that involved and retained college students to the church through various ministries. I thrived at this church in Chattanooga, Tennessee. The anointing of God showered this ministry like the dew of raindrops. My spirit became attracted to certain members in the church who had suffered with molestation. However, these people had never shared their experiences with me, but I was in an overwhelming fight, a diligence to know them. Nevertheless these people were men. Men of God. I began dating a mighty man of God, his name was an impression of God's gift. He carried the vile spirit of molestation and I attached myself to him and then one day all alone with him, often warned by the elders in the church, he raped me. I hated him. I blamed God. I was in a pit of despair, I cried out to my heavenly father, "you did not protect me." I walked around carrying this wound. I had to watch an anointed man of God minister the word of God. I wanted to kill him with my words. I wanted to expose him. At that moment, I began to see the favor of God in my life and the gift of healing. After the incident I never spoke to him, I would never allow my eyes at church to see him or watch his grim demeanor. God spoke to me at church. He said, "Go tell him that you forgive him because you must release him so that he can continue his ministry, you have healing in your hands." I was furious with God. I told God, this man hurt me and you want me to tell him I forgive him so that he can go forth. I argued, but before church service was over, the Holy Spirit came over me as if I was in a daze, a sense of mesmerizing power. I offered forgiveness to that mighty man of God and he began to weep at church and I wept. At that very moment I began to see my life in Christ.

Attraction II: I had an over powering zeal for love. At the age of twelve years old I began to pray for my husband. I often told my father, a minister that I was praying for him. There were times at a young child that I oftened awed my friends with this alarming quest for marriage. I always believe that my marriage would be a ministry. In 2003, I wrote a journal entry about my future husband and I knew him in the spirit and I wanted to him to hold on to God because we were soon to be together. I dated about 3 people in college and I often thought at least one of them was my husband. A sense of internal obsession of marriage consumed me and I was not at peace. One day I decided that I would rest in God's presence about my husband. I was taken to a dream and in my dream I was walking down the aisle and every person that I ever considered or dated was in the audience. I was horrified. In my dream my friend was pushing me down the aisle and I kept saying "I don't know him," and she replied, "Yes, you know him." She continued to push me down the aisle and I thought to myself as she pushed me, God who is this man since all of my options are in the audience watching me. As I stood in front of the unknown groom, I was awakened never to see his face. Although I am married I am waiting for the fulfillment of my married destiny.

Melody of Christ: Jennifer, my flower, and my precious gem I created you to be unique. Inspired by holiness and grace. Live inside the sparrow arm. I hear you, but I am afraid. Scared to fail, although I know I am destined to be great because in spite of me you chose me among the thorns, you found favor in me. Your love goes beyond this human desire. I love my husband, but I desire to be in love with you.

Contact information:
jenniferperkinsk@yahoo.com

25

Jennifer Rawls

Bold Over

There's something I've learned from watching most people: we're all pretty confident. Except for those times when we're not.

I've had a very fun life, filled with successes and challenges. I've spent a lot of time working with people of all backgrounds and abilities. I've seen people at their worst and at their best—and I've worked with some, unfortunately, that didn't know the difference.

Through all of these experiences, I've learned that a key to success is spiritual confidence.

What is spiritual confidence, and how do you get it? Unlike self-confidence, which is based on your own abilities and accomplishments, spiritual confidence is based on the realization that your skills, abilities, experiences, challenges, and achievements are all gifts.

> Self-confidence is based on attitude.

> Spiritual confidence is based on gratitude.

Before we get ahead of ourselves, let me emphasize that I'm not talking about living a perfect life, never making a mistake, never getting angry, or laughing at really bad jokes. I'm not suggesting that you walk around in a continuous state of peace and joy with a blissful expression on your face. Sure, I could encourage you to live like that, but frankly, I can't suggest you do something that I'd never be able to pull off.

Let's face it. Most of us are dreamers; we're visionaries. If you've never thought of yourself as a visionary, stop reading and get comfortable with that idea. Because I firmly believe that there is something inside of you that dreams of the life you were created to live.

Close your eyes for a second. Well, finish reading this part first and then close your eyes. I want you to imagine that there are no obstacles to achieving your dreams. No one will laugh at what you want to be or do. Your education, or lack thereof, won't be a problem. Your bank account doesn't enter into the equation. It's just you and your vision.

Now, assuming that there are no obstacles in your way and you can accomplish anything you imagine, what would you do? (This is where you close your eyes.)

What's the first thing that comes to mind? Veterinarian? Business owner? Would you learn to knit? Would you be nicer to people? What was the first thing you envisioned when you asked yourself that all-important question: What would I do if I could do anything?

I read an article about Anne Beiler, the founder of the Auntie Anne's Pretzels chain. The company began at a very tough time for Mrs. Beiler and her husband. A few years before, their daughter was killed in a tragic accident. Their marriage suffered, and Mrs. Beiler considered suicide before agreeing to attend counseling with her husband. Not only was their marriage saved but also was born a vision: her husband wanted to start a free-counseling center to help the families in their community. To support her education, she began selling pretzels at local farmer's markets. Twenty years and over nine hundred locations worldwide later, she sold the business for more than two hundred million dollars.

Please don't let that number confuse the message. While we'd all like to have that kind of money, the vision was to open a free-counseling center—which they accomplished. The center has grown to respond to the needs of the community, and expansion continues. If you had asked Mrs. Beiler what she envisioned at the outset, I'm guessing that her response would be to help families through the pain of life. That was her dream, and her means for getting there was the baking she'd done all her life. She built this internationally successful company, by the way, having a ninth-grade education.

Would you like to know how to bring that kind of success to your vision? Would you really? I ask this because there are some of us that don't really want to know how to make it happen. I knew for a long time before I changed careers that I wasn't happy practicing law. It's a wonderful profession, and I had some great friends and terrific mentors when I was practicing law. But I wasn't happy. And it only took me fifteen years of trying to admit it.

Yep, fifteen years.

I initially wanted to be a lawyer, as hokey as it sounds, to make the world a better place. I had grand ideas of government-policy changes and tweaks in the system that could bring new common sense to endless bureaucracy. I wanted to pull differing sides together, to create a common good, to help make a world where everyone had a chance at success. Needless to say, those lofty goals often come to a grinding halt when there are student loans to repay, rent, car payments, and so on and so forth.

So after giving it my all for a decade and a half, I had to confess, at least to myself, that I wasn't happy. It was one of the hardest things I've ever done.

Why? Because admitting that I wasn't happy would mean I'd have to find the thing I love, the thing I wanted to do. When I first asked myself what I would do if I could do anything, my honest answer was "I don't know." And I didn't know for a long time. It took trying and searching. It took spiritual confidence.

Back to you and your vision. When you are ready to live, really live, there are a couple of easy steps to get you on your way. Best of all, they won't cost you a dime.

First, be grateful for your dream. It may be complex, requiring several steps before you arrive at your destination. Perhaps your vision is nursing, and you never graduated from high school. Chances are you won't be a nurse tomorrow. There are a few educational steps you have to make. Still, be grateful and say so—out loud. Be grateful for the vision, for every step you'll take to get there, for every teacher, mentor, librarian, study partner, textbook author, patient, director, school administrator, everyone you'll meet and every experience you'll have during the journey. The fact that you have no idea how to get there shouldn't stop you. You've seen it. Be grateful and continue to be grateful every day.

The next step is to plan your journey. (This is the part I wasn't crazy about.) Think of your vision as a place on a map. You know, when you're driving and you stop at a rest area? There's always a map with a big red arrow that says, "You are here." Well, imagine a life map that says that. You are *here*. You know where you're starting, and you know where you're going. The really good news is that you can make the trip as scenic as you'd like. Take your time; go down a side road every now and then. Don't just stop for junk food along the way. Talk to fellow travelers. Enjoy the trip, and of course, be grateful for every mile.

Taking stock means recognizing what you have to work with. If your vision is to start a new business, take an honest assessment of what you know about that business. What do you need to learn? Who do you need to meet?

Step three is to take action. A few years ago, I was in a training session geared toward business professionals. One of the pieces of advice I heard in that meeting is that what you do today affects your business in ninety days. I don't remember much else from that meeting, but I haven't forgotten that. It spurs me to take some action, no matter how big or small, each day toward reaching my dream.

If you want to own your own business but don't know where to start, you might go to the library and check out some books on business ownership. You might call a successful business owner in your area and offer to take them to lunch if they'll answer your questions. (By the way, everyone I've ever approached like this has been flattered to have been asked. Don't assume people don't have time to help you. They just don't know you need their help!) Go online and find sample business plans to get you started. The point is to do something to move you forward.

Spiritual confidence, like faith, is a thing. Like all things, it is either living and growing or dying. There's no in-between. Remember Newton's first law of motion: "an object at rest tends to stay at rest, and an object in motion tends to stay in motion with the same speed and in the same direction unless acted upon by an unbalanced force." Your spiritual confidence is the object, and you are the *unbalanced force*. Take that as you will, but I think I've made my point.

Another thing about following your plan one step at a time is that it's easier to overcome your fears. And rest assured, you'll have them. Chasing your dreams, or realizing your visions, if you prefer, necessarily involves stepping out of your comfort zone. You'll reach a point where you'll have to learn something new, ask a silly question, make a new commitment, or admit that you don't really know something. I could, by the way, gloss over this point because some of you would be much more excited about finding your vision if you didn't have to take any chances. It just doesn't work that way. Why? Remember, this is about growing and living. Whether it's the butterfly working herself out of the cocoon or a muscle you're working for the first time in a long time, change requires some discomfort. Success comes when you deal with that change.

When I was leaving home for college, my mother made a wall hanging for me that says, "Courage is fear that has said its prayers." Pray, meditate, acknowledge your fear. Then move ahead despite it.

The last major step is the fun one. Sit back and watch. Being in a state of gratitude along the journey means being grateful for the challenges and the opportunities. You'll be amazed at how quickly it all appears as opportunities. If you can, please stop using words like *luck*, *coincidence*, and *fluke*. Even if you don't believe that you are a spiritual being, act like you do for a while. Why? Because the frequency at which people and things appear that will assist you in realizing your vision will dramatically increase as you become spiritually confident. In order to recognize them for what they are, you must be aware: aware of your vision, aware of your needs, aware of the opportunities. Passing them off as nothing more than random chance means that you're not really seeing them as something to be grateful for. Remember, if your spiritual confidence isn't growing, it's dying.

So how do I know that this works in real life? Let me tell you a quick story.

Several years ago, I could no longer deny that my vision is to be a writer and motivational speaker. It took me much longer to be confident in that vision. Once I claimed it, things began to happen. Within a few weeks, I noticed that I was looking for opportunities to meet people who make a living doing either or both. Within days, I attended a conference and met a terrific woman who is a very talented motivational speaker and executive speech coach. After I heard her speak, I asked for a few minutes of her time and asked what I could do to move forward with a career in speaking. She told me to find a Toastmasters club.

I returned home, looked on the web, and discovered that there was a Toastmasters club in my office building that met at a very convenient time for me. I joined the next week. Within a few months, I had the honor of serving as president of that club.

A few months later, I had been asked to speak at several events. Over the course of the next five years, I would give more than fifty speeches to large crowds and written several published papers. Based on those experiences, and with the help of some terrific people I met in the interim, I wrote and published a work of historical fiction called *The Vote*, which tells the true story of the passage of the Nineteenth Amendment, giving women the right to vote. And now, I have the spiritual confidence and opportunity to be a part of this amazing project with an awe-inspiring group of ladies.

So you might ask, is spiritual confidence really important? Don't people realize their dreams without it? Of course, some people do. To me, however, it makes a huge difference.

You see, a lot of people go through feeling like life is a bowling game and they are the pins. They're standing there, doing their job, waiting for the next critical blow to be delivered, hoping they won't topple over. In short, they are bowled over.

I prefer to see myself as that sturdy bowling ball moving with direction, a goal in mind. I seek not to destroy, mind you, but to accomplish my goal. Yes, sometimes, I fall off the alley (*into the gutter* just sounds bad), and I'm never totally in control. But I know what I'm about, what my purpose is, where I'm going. I have the confidence to be *bold over* the things I'm doing and the things I want to do and have envisioned.

You may have heard of a woman named Dolly Parton. She's pretty well-known. Dolly began *making up her own songs* as a child to escape the hardships of her young life. She began singing on a local radio station at age eleven, but by the time she graduated from high school, she was dreaming of a much bigger stage and moved to Nashville. The rest, as they say, is history: syndicated television shows, Grand Ole Opry performer, too many recording-artist awards to count, Oscar nominations, movie actress, businesswoman, and philanthropist. One of the things Dolly has learned through a life of extraordinary success is that "we cannot direct the wind, but we can adjust the sails."

I am honest about my own vision and treat it as though there is nothing in the way of my getting there. I take stock, realizing what gifts and abilities I have and those I need to develop. I have always known there were people I would meet and information I would gain, and I remain open to the opportunities that develop. With determination, I began to make some effort every day to reach my goals. I spend time writing or reading something that motivates me. Some days I ask questions of people who are doing the things I dream of doing. Every day I find some way to move my vision forward.

And always, always, I'm grateful for every bit of it. That gratefulness has proven to me that what started as a vision or dream is really something bigger. It's what I'm created to do. Knowing that, how can I be anything other than confident?

How can you?

Contact Information:
jenniferlrawls@gmail.com

26

Kelly Gore

Blessed are the pure in heart for they shall see God.

—Matthew 5:8

My name is Kelly Marie, and I was born in Tacoma, Washington, but raised in Clarksville, Tennessee.

I am an entrepreneur. I am the owner and founder of my nanny business called Nanny Poppin's. I am a health coach and will soon open my facility called Knockout: Generations Transformed, which will reach many people. My passion is inspiring, encouraging, and empowering people to embrace the greatness God has placed within them. I am an artist releasing prophetic worship that draws many into the deeper, more intimate places of God's heart, reaching those that have gone through dark and painful storms and are hurting and need to be healed and strengthened in God's amazing love. I am a Leading Lady.

As a young thirty-four-year-old woman, I am so thankful and grateful for every painful storm and the great challenges I have had to face in my life because they have definitely made me the strong, brave, courageous woman of purpose I am today. Growing up, I battled a lot of abandonment and rejection, which stemmed from a mother who didn't want me and a father who didn't take the time to truly *see me* but only made fun of my struggles and shattered my dreams. I had a very lonely and painful childhood, but that painful childhood has served a great purpose in my life. I now have a great relationship with my father, and I'm working on developing one with my mother. I love them both very much and understand they were just wounded parents without a foundation of God's love for them. I suffered from severe separation anxiety, which kept me isolated and imprisoned for many years. I was hiding inside of myself, afraid to just be *me*, afraid to believe I could follow my dreams.

While I was growing up in a military home, my father used a lot of negative reinforcement. I was so afraid of making a mistake and disappointing my father that I completely shut down. Fear had truly gripped my heart as a child. I was made fun of a lot through my childhood, so I never knew how to let my light shine. I never unwrapped the gifts that were deep inside of me, until the day I met Jesus. When I was twenty-one, I had an encounter with Jesus that forever changed my life, and I was Sleeping Beauty awakened with God's true love for me. I never realized how deeply I was longing and starving for *true love* until I encountered the true love of God. It is the power of love that will set your heart on fire and give you wings to soar to greater heights! Who is the one who inspires, encourages, and empowers me? It is God Himself! It is God in the hearts of many amazing people that have continued to set my heart on fire to dare to dream the impossible dream! I am so truly blessed for each amazing man and woman that God has placed in my life to play such a critical role in helping me blossom and grow. I love how so many different mentors were sent into my life to help cultivate the seeds of greatness inside of me. I look back, and I see a beautiful harvest that has come forth through many that have planted the seeds completely influenced by the Holy Spirit. I became pregnant with an amazing dream that would impact so many on their life's journey. My identity, purpose, and destiny was awakened by the passionate, pure love God has for me, and the little broken wounded girl who stayed isolated in her bedroom with a huge dream in her heart finally emerged liberated with God's love and began to walk in her divine purpose and greatness that continues to impact, heal, and restore many lives. I was a Cinderella who finally believed she could live in the palace. Who finally believed she was born for so much more than a *common life*. Everyone was always telling me to *face reality*, to get my head out of the clouds and stop daydreaming, but it was the daydreams that kept my dreams alive! It was the way I could escape and find myself!

I spent many years listening to a mom that told me, "If it looks too good to be true, then it is." That is what my mom believed, but that was not truth. My mom was deeply hurting and angry at herself for not taking a chance to step out and follow her dreams. It was that pain that shut her down; it was easier to believe that dreams were just dreams for my mom because she didn't feel the pain of giving up anymore. Her heart became hardened and bitter, and when she saw a young girl full of dreams, it reminded her of her own, so it was easier to lie to me and tell me that I would never be able to follow my dreams. I developed a mind-set that dreams were unreachable, that the stars I would see on television, the amazing stories I would hear were not for me. I believed I would just be the one sitting on the couch, watching a different world that I could never be a part of. It was very painful for me, and it was my prison. I saw myself the way my mom saw herself. I saw myself small, trapped, worthless, a slave to everyone else's rules. I believed I could only do what I was told. I was lost, lonely, and heartbroken. Though it did not look like a storm but simply reality, it was the darkest storm that tried to keep me from seeing *who I am*. Unbelief, doubt, fear, and rejection all came to bully me. They were like a gang that came to put me in a cell so that I would never believe I was worth anything. As a child I was never given the opportunity to have a mentor that would help me blossom as the very gifted child I was. It took many years for me to heal from that heartache. I was very outraged at my parents for not supporting me, not believing in me. I felt like it was too late for me. I thought of the amazing schools I could have been a part of to follow my dreams. I wanted to sing, to be on stage performing, sharing my heart with the world. I felt very neglected and abandoned. God put amazing people in my life to help me walk through a journey of inner healing. Deep inside of me, I had a very angry child that was never heard, and I finally embraced that child as if she were my own. And with God's love, I loved her, I embraced her, and I listened to her heart. I saw a vision of holding myself as a child who felt left alone in the dark for many years. The pain I felt was almost unbearable, but Jesus was there with me and let me finally deal with and heal from my painful childhood memories. I began to weep so much because I began to see so many other neglected and abandoned children trapped in many adults, their voice and cry never heard, completely forgotten and alone. The heartache I felt in that moment took the pain inside of me and birthed my God-given purpose. I will never forget the year of 2007 when it all took place. Jesus showed me a vision of a woman in painful labor ready to give birth. In her womb was the word *pain*, and as she pushed with all the strength and determination she had in her heart to give birth, the word *pain* in her womb came out and turned into the word *purpose*. I am here to tell you that no matter how painful your experiences have been, no one could ever understand because they are not you. Your deepest pain will birth your purpose and propel you into your destiny with God's passionate love for you. The Lord spoke to me after I had that vision that was so real to my heart. I felt everything this pregnant woman felt, and the Lord said, "I know the very pain you will go through that will birth your purpose and propel you into the destiny that I, the Lord, placed inside of your heart before you were ever formed in your mother's womb." When the Lord spoke those words deep inside my heart, it was like I was resuscitated by the Lord and brought back to life. I was in a spiritual coma, barely alive, and God's true love for me awakened me from such a coma. He resuscitated my broken heart, my dreams, and awakened my true beauty and revealed the wonderful treasures deep inside of me. I began to see how valuable and gifted I truly was. The little girl inside of me just held on to my Papa and embraced all His love and the amazing plans He had for me.

The fiercest storms that come your way in life are the gifts that open the eyes of your heart to see and remind you of the warrior and gift you truly are from within! These storms that come cause the seed of divine purpose to break open from the words the Lord has spoken to you. Here is a picture I found on the Internet that really awakened this truth deep inside of my heart. As I looked at this picture, I heard the Lord speak these words to me, "It's the storms of life that lead you back to the Father's heart."

"IT'S THE STORMS IN LIFE THAT LEAD
US BACK TO THE FATHER'S HEART."

I know too well that it has always been the storms in my life that have drawn me so much closer to my Heavenly Father. With Him, I have developed a deeper, more intimate relationship that continues to make me a *woman of greatness*. It was in 2004 that I had an incredible encounter and visitation from Jesus. It is so alive in me to this very day. Jesus came to me and kissed me on my forehead, placed a crown on my head, filled each piece on my crown with precious gems of each color of the rainbow, and He placed a scepter in my right hand with the inscription in gold that said, "AUTHORITY." He took my hand and led me to a huge double door, and above the door, in gold letters, was the word *greatness*. Then He turned to me and said, "Kelly, in this walk of greatness that I have called you to, there is much responsibility, but I have given you all the ability you will ever need, and all you have to do is simply respond to what I have placed deep inside of you." I will never forget that moment because this was when Jesus broke open the seed of greatness He placed inside of me, by sending the storms. In each of us is this seed of greatness that the Lord has planted in the soil of our hearts, and He comes to break it open through the storms that cause that greatness to awaken within our hearts; it takes root and begins to arise to the surface, birthing our divine purpose! We were not just born to just get a job and pay bills; we were born to awaken the greatness inside of each other! I need the greatness that God has placed inside of you! We are all connected to help one another destroy the darkness that plagues our world. Many people make bad decisions that are so destructive not only to themselves but also to those around them. They do this because they do not see or know the greatness that lie dormant inside their hearts. The painful storms only hardened their hearts with lies of the evil one to imprison them and blind them of their beautiful purpose. It is then that we come to realize God's love and authority to rescue the POWs, the prisoners of war. The worst feeling in the world is to know you're imprisoned and you don't know how to get out. Every day you pass by many people, communicate with many people, and never know that they are silently suffering because they are locked away in a dark cell with so many negative lies that keep them there. Our purpose is to release compassion and true love that will unlock them from captivity, and to me there is nothing greater than that. I remember when I was the one locked in a dark prison silently suffering and my mission, and my mandate now is to *set the captives free* with the true love of Jesus. So remember, storms come to awaken your purpose by leading you back to the heart of the Father to discover what that purpose truly is.

> "Kelly, in this walk of greatness that I have called you to, there is much responsibility, but I have given you all the ability you will

ever need, and all you have to do is simply respond to what I have placed deep inside of you."

Many opportunities came across my path, like Mary Kay and Avon, Herbalife, etc. These were God's way of saying to me, "You are a woman of greatness that will have her own business, and I want to awaken the leader that I know you are deep inside of you where I, your Lord and Savior, abide in you." You know, even in those times, my heart was so wounded and hardened from the painful experiences and the disappointments that I didn't believe in myself anymore. It was only when I cried out to God, when I became real with Him, that He became real to me! When I opened my heart and showed Him all the pain and anger inside, His true love for me began to heal the pain and reveal His purpose inside of me. I finally believed I deserved to have my dreams come true. Instead of being enslaved to a job, to a system that tries to tell me what I am worth, I realized I could create a business that I am gifted and passionate about, that would not only bless me financially but also bring wholeness and joy to many others. My deepest pain has become my deepest passion, which keeps my heart ignited with purpose, and the greatness of God! Now here I am! Here I am with my *whole heart* wide open, fully and passionately pursuing my purpose, and with God's love in my heart igniting so many others to passionately pursue their purpose as well! It is just out of this world amazing! I would never have imagined God would take a simple girl like me, who just wanted to be married with a family of her own, and raise me up to be a great leader one day and help many birth their God-given dreams to impact, inspire, and empower so many others! Inspire and empower many hearts to change their community, their state, and their nation! There are no limits! Only the limits you place upon yourself. Nothing is impossible to those who truly believe! Though I didn't have a lot of great childhood memories, there is a memory and a picture that I have lost but still kept in my heart, and it really spoke volumes to me. I was in fourth grade, and I was going to run a race at a college campus track. I will never forget how big that track seemed to a young girl like me and the many that were in the race with me. I remember there was quite a crowd there that day, and I was very nervous! I wanted to win of course, but when that gun went off and I began to run, I heard the loudest voice cheering me on, and it was the voice of my dad! My dad was screaming my name, shouting, "Go, Kelly! Run, sweetie, you can do it!" When I heard my dad's voice cheering me on like that, my heart swelled with so much joy and determination that my body took off like a rocket, and I not only finished the race but also got third place. It didn't matter if I would have lost; the only thing that meant the world to me was hearing my dad shout and cheer his daughter on!

Everywhere I go, when things seem tough or difficult, I can hear my dad; I can hear my Heavenly Father shouting, "Go, Kelly! Run, sweetie, you can do it!" I continue to be brave, to be bold, to open my heart wide, and to be the great leader and servant I can be to serve my purpose in this world. This one statement changed my life: "You are selfish if you choose not to walk in your greatness to serve humanity." I choose to be selfless; I choose to serve humanity by reminding them of the treasure and gift they truly are to this broken world. I believe that if we truly celebrate and honor the gift we truly are to each other, we would not see so many falling victims to the darkness that destroys so many lives. I choose to celebrate and honor others so they, too, will continue leaving such a legacy. I am going to open up the *Knockout facility*; I am going to record many soaking CDs that will heal and restore many hearts, families, marriages; and I am going to leave the greatest legacy, because as a leading lady, I am going to do it all in God's *perfect love*.

Contact Information:
http://facebook.com/AWAKENEDANTRANSFORMED2012
learning2soar@yahoo.com
www.nannypoppins.org

27

LaTrina Renee' Alfred

(Clarksville, Tennessee)

Remember the LORD your God. He is the one who gives you power to be successful, in order to fulfill the covenant he confirmed to your ancestors with an oath.

—Deuteronomy 8:18, NLT

My name is LaTrina Renee' Alfred. I was born in Toledo, Ohio. My parents are Floyd and Peggie Perrin. I am married to the king of my life and my best friend, Anthony, and we have five children. I've served my country in the army and as a civil servant for almost seventeen years. I am the first lady of Family of Faith Worship Center and Healing Hurting Hearts Covenant Ministries. I enjoy reading, writing, and spending time with family. I am a Leading Lady.

What Are You Fighting For?

Do you really know? So fight the good fight of faith and keep running. In today's society, Christian women often find themselves in the midst of a fight: fights about how they look, whether they should go back to school, what they will wear, choosing the right man, or even holding on to the man in their lives. The pressure on women has increased greatly. We concern ourselves with who has the longest hair, the biggest house, the most expensive jewelry, or even the biggest breasts or butt. Pressure here, pressure there; and every time we turn around, more pressure comes from the cares of this life. But if you look around through your natural eyes, the question would pose to ask where God is in all this. From day to day, the devil seeks whom he can devour and preys on the most vulnerable of women by presenting their issues as total failures, a great loss. I once talked to a man who was looking for a woman, a wife. I told him to go to the church, and he would find a good woman there. He told me that Christian women were the worst. "The worst?" I asked. He said, "Yes, most of them just want to find a man, any type of man, because they were lonely and needed to be touched." "Touched by what?" I asked. They need to be touched by Jesus, I was thinking. He said that those types of Christian women were a complete turnoff. Ladies, what you need to know is that your body is not all you have to offer. It's sacred, a priceless jewel. But today's television shows, movies, and the clothes that are now being designed for women exploits women sexually. This stereotype extends all the way back to our baby girls. This is why Satan can easily manipulate women and seeks to destroy them by blinding them from the truth. This deception keeps them from believing that God has put greatness inside of them and not just a beautiful body for men to manipulate and abuse. My sister, my friend, God can and wants to bless you with a husband, a good man, one who loves Him and will love you as Christ loves the church (Eph. 5:25). I can attest to this because there are times in my home where my husband refers to me as church. So I say, yes, God does have good Christian men out here, and they need and want you.

Ladies, God has gifted women with the ability to replenish this earth and bring forth the glory for His great creation/nation. We have a gift hidden in this awesome earthen vessel called a womb with the ability to bring forth life. The womb carries many great and precious gifts in the form of future preachers, gospel singers, praise worshippers, evangelists, prophets, and many more to edify the kingdom of God. So I ask, ladies, what are you waiting for? Why continue to fight in the flesh when you know that you already have the victory. Think about it, why do you fight? Why do you remain on this Christian road? The answer is because you were bought with a price and you are priceless to God. Your sins have been blood washed. You are His, and He is yours, and no one can change the love He has for you.

> For you were bought with a price: therefore glorify God in your body, and in your spirit, which are God's. (1 Cor. 6:20)

My sisters, if you do this, you will suffer in the flesh, and you will cease from sinning. There was a time in my life when I was a single celibate woman. I woke up one Saturday morning, read my Bible, prayed, and began to relax. But as the day went on, my flesh began to yearn for companionship. I had a few errands to run, but based on how my body was feeling, I decided to stay home. Why? Because I felt that no matter how much I prayed, read my Bible, or talked to God, my flesh was flaming and was on a seek-and-satisfy mission. I knew in my heart that if I had gone out, Satan would have had the right man with the right looks and body waiting just for me. So I decided to suffer in my flesh by staying home. Does this sound like you today? Are you a single woman or a woman whose husband is away and you have encountered such a fight? I was reading the scriptures and praying, but the more I did, the more the flesh had gotten angry, and showers were not helping. So I relied on the scripture. "For he that hath suffered in the flesh hath ceased from sin" (1 Peter 4:1[c]). I had come a long way in God, and I was not going to fail Him now. I wanted to please God and not my flesh. So that day, I prevailed through the Holy Spirit and the Word of God. I'm sharing this because it was not easy. It was not by my own might but by the Spirit of God. God will send help in the time of any trouble, and I know that if I had left the house, I would have been in for some trouble.

Let's take a look at Hannah. Hannah was in a fight. She was fighting for every woman who has a husband and desired children. She encounters torment, taunting, and lack. She had the man, she had the money, but she did not have the seed of the man, her husband whom she loved. Women today in some way shape, form, or fashion deal with all these. Knowingly and unknowingly, we have been through this type of fight. Not only in our wombs by being barren but also in our relationships, jobs, school, or even our health. So I ask, what will you do, or what did you do when you felt the fight was unfair or one-sided? Did you continue to fight, or did you just leave and allow the other side to win? Did you find your spirit in anguish and begin to cry out from the very depths of your soul? Naturally she was teased and mocked, and yet with all this going on in her life, it does not really mean she had issues within her body. But it was just a test that the will of God withheld her seed for a particular time a season. Hannah had to sell out completely in her Spirit. For instance, if you were to reach out to God in the way Hannah did, you will receive a greater blessing. Sometimes we have to get to the state of total travail before the Lord to receive the completion of the promises of God in our lives because He knows our destiny.

So I ask again, what are you fighting for? What are you seeking to receive from God? Have you truly given God your all and all, or do you make excuses for what or why you do not do what He asks you to do? A lot of times, we focus on what's not true. The devil, although he is real, can only form the weapon, but it will not prosper. That is an assurance that God has your back and that the fight you are in is a fixed fight. God's word reassures us that we have the greater one on the inside and that the battle is not ours. So why do you continue in sin, continue to doubt God, and continue to live defeated lives when you don't have to? The truth is God is real and He loves us. He cares about us, our disappointments, and our hurts. Many women have come and have gone with hurts that only if they had allowed God to fix them, they would have been healed, conquered the enemy, or even moved forward on their journey with God's blessings. But instead they lived a defeated life by not forgiving, by not letting it all go, and by not moving past the mess that was dumped in their lives. Does this sound like you or someone you know? I know that as the years have come and gone, I can see clearer now. Not forgiving is like a cancer; it can spread from generation to generation or from relationship to relationship. So I say choose this day to fight the good fight of faith knowing that God has already ordained this battle as victorious in your life. Don't you realize that every mess can be made in a masterpiece? Think about this and have a flashback in time.

In a sermon my husband preached last year in 2012, he said that since the fight is fixed, all you have to do is have faith. Now this is something that you may catch now or later, but it is a fact. My sister, my friend, stop fighting and allow God to avenge your enemy. This is not a natural fight but a supernatural fight that God has control over. So give it to Him and leave it there. The

Bible says, "Great is our Lord, and abundant in power; his understanding is beyond measure." Yes, yes, and yes. God is our great and very powerful Father who definitely understands what we are going through, and He cares for us. He is mighty in battle. And He understands why we do the things we do, so don't look back any longer, but *now* is the time to change. Now is the time to come out from among them and be separate. Set the example, and fight the good fight of faith knowing that the single mother can make it being content that God loves her and that God has covered her as His bride. God can fill all your needs, and you will have such peace while you are waiting. Working women, you can make it work for you even though there are more men in the workforce. You can start your own business or go back to school and get the same degree they have and move forward in the favor and humility of God. For all my dating sisters, you can be a woman of integrity and character. You can save yourself for that awesome man God has for you. You can be an example to our younger girls. With all these women came two words: *God's GIRLS*—gorgeous, intelligent, real, lively, and sanctified. My sisters, depend totally on God and God alone. He is the only man who, no matter where you rate yourself, if you multiply your rating against, will never depreciate you, but your value will increase. So sisters, if you are single, looking for a husband, then make sure you can multiply yourself against him and see value. Single ladies don't compromise with a zero. Get out there, and find your hero.

Push past hurting hearts, low self-esteem, and low moral standards, and make a difference in this world. Give God praise no matter what's going on in your life because He is worthy at all times. When you think there is nothing to praise God for, take a flashback to where God brought you from, how He saved you from hell, death, and how He gave the best gift He had for us when we were not worthy. He gave His only begotten Son, Jesus Christ.

God's GIRLS, as you look back at all that has been shared in this chapter, hopefully you have realized your worth and why you continue to fight in this race. Remember, my single sisters, that you don't need a physical man to be whole. I'm not saying that you don't deserve to have a husband or can't desire one. I'm saying that godliness with contentment will bring great gain (1 Tim. 6:6). So hold on, my sister, and know that as you mature in God, you're heading toward perfection in Him. For my married sisters, revere and love your husband, the man God gave to you. Love him and push him to release the man you want him to be for you by submitting to him. My business sisters, you can do it! Through all that has been shared and spoken to you, remember that it is God who "giveth thee power to get wealth" (Deut. 8:18). God has given you the ideas; now walk therein and birth this baby! Don't be your own enemy by procrastinating and doubting, but trust God and push past the natural fight by sending your faith to the finish line. The Bible says that faith is believing that you have the things you hope for because you can see them clearly.

> Now faith is the substance of things hoped for, the evidence of things not seen. (Heb. 11:1)

Finally this is a race. Jesus has passed us the baton, and we shall continue toward the finish line because our eternal home depends on it. When God said for us to run this race, He took off before us and finished the race. One reason He finished the race is because He knew we would encounter distractions that would slow us down. He knew that we would incur some hurts, frustrations, and utter regrets as we travel through our lives for Him. He knew we would get weary and want to stop.

I'm sure you already know the story about the tortoise and the hare. The hare was overconfident in his abilities to beat the tortoise because of his body makeup. He was faster, smarter, and altogether in better shape. But the tortoise—although not faster, smarter, nor in better shape—had one thing, and that was perseverance. Perseverance is what God sees in us; distractions will come, but persistence and faith are what will get us through to the finish line. So I say fight the good fight of faith; know that we have this great crowd of witnesses cheering us on toward the finish line where Christ Jesus awaits our arrival (Heb. 12:1). "So what are you truly fighting for?" I asked this in the beginning of this chapter. Well, we are all fighting for that crown of righteousness and to fill the third of heaven that is empty. So keep fighting, keep shouting, and keep praising God like your life depends on it because it does. So I encourage you that no matter what the circumstances or how you feel, praise God in advance realizing that you are auditioning for the praise section of heaven. Don't allow Satan to rule in your life any longer. Pick up your cross and bear it because your Heavenly Father has given you all you need to make it. If you have fallen, get back up. If have doubted, get back up, and take back the baton that Jesus first gave you, and keep on running. Swing hard through prayer! Swing hard through praise! Swing hard through God's word because it is *God* who gives *you* strength!

Father, I pray for Your daughters everywhere. I pray for God's GIRLS, that You would heal, deliver, and set them free because they have been deceived by the enemy. Help them to not walk as man says to walk but as You have instructed them to walk through Your Word. Father God, I believe that You are the Alpha and Omega; and from start to finish, You will lead us into what is right, holy, and pleasing to You. Lord, cover my sisters as they make the change, the transformation to be all You have called them to be. Lord, lead Your people back to You so that we will honor, obey, and seek You, turning from our wicked ways. In Jesus's name, amen.

GOD'S GIRLS SHALL PREVAIL!

Contact Information:
Email: tonyrenee04@bellsouth.net

28

LaTosha Roberson

Hello, my name is LaTosha Roberson. I'm thirty-eight years old. I'm the oldest of eight kids; my mom has five, and my dad had three kids. Family has always been important to me, and I love them all. I'm also a mother of five beautiful kids; they all have a special anointing on them, and they keep me laughing at their unique personalities. My household stays busy, day in and day out. I can honestly say there's never been a dull moment in my life; however, life for me hasn't always been smooth sailing.

As a child, I struggled with who I was and why I existed. My mother and I have a very close relationship; she and I can talk about anything. I thank God for allowing us to have the bond that we now have because as I've stated earlier, family is important. My mom and I did not always have the connection that we now have. My mother gave birth to me when she was thirteen years old; my dad was also thirteen when I was born. Being the oldest brought about many responsibilities as a child, and since I had teen parents, I did not have the best role models to grow up with.

My mom was forced to quit school in the eighth grade. She made an attempt to go back to school after I was born; however, she did not have anyone to watch me, so she decided to take me to school with her. The principal called my mom to the office during third period and told her that she can't bring a baby to school; it was against school policies, and it was unsafe. They sent my mom home with me, and she never returned to school as she didn't have a reliable babysitter for me. I grew up in Hopkinsville, Kentucky. The population is about 31,577; and back when I was born, the population was 21,395. Hopkinsville is a small city where everyone is related, or we just call each other *cousin* because our families grew up together or live on the same block. Either way, my hometown is where my life began and where most of my memories still haunt me.

As far back as my memory takes me, I never felt loved or wanted as a child. I was always cursed out, cursed at, beaten, called out of my name, or molested. I didn't understand why my mom was so mean toward me and why she didn't love me the way a mother is supposed to love a child. I never knew what a hug from a mother felt like. I used to think it was because she had me at such a young age and it was my fault she couldn't finish school.

My mom was twenty-one years old by the time she had all five of us. I remember having to babysit my siblings most of the time; occasionally we would go to my grandmother's house, but for the most part, I was made to watch my brother and sisters. My siblings and I got along fairly well when we were younger, and we are even closer now that we are all grown and on our own. I have always been overly protective of my siblings. I thought I was obligated to protect them, as my instructions were, "Tosha, I'm going out, watch your brother and sisters, and don't let nothing happen to them, and don't leave this house." I felt like a teenage mom; my obligations became overwhelming to me, and I wasn't allowed to achieve much. It wasn't fair (I thought). I couldn't go visiting my friends or go walking or even go to the movies without having my siblings with me; needless to say, I didn't feel like babysitting. I was angry and felt like my childhood was being robbed. I thought sneaking out of the house or simply running away from home was the answer to my freedom. Instead, I made my situation worse. My mom would always find me, or she would leave a note telling me what she was going to do to me when she gets off work. She followed through with her threat as soon as she saw me. I was beaten just like she had promised.

I remember being mistreated often. One day I was beaten so badly that the bruises left on my body led to my mom's incareration. She wasn't afraid or remorseful. She put up a fight with the cops and told them to take me if they think they can raise me better than she could. My mom was an angry woman; I assumed it was because she was a young single mother of five kids, and she worked to take care of us the best she could and without help. Whatever the reason, I used to think my mother didn't love me at all. I never felt close to her as a child, and it was hard living with her. I was ready to move out on my own.

When I was a teen, I was sent to a girl's home. I got along with everyone for the most part, but I didn't like being there. I missed my family and friends back home, and even though I was making new friends, it wasn't the same. I decided to run away with one of the other girls. It was spring break, and I didn't want to be locked down in a girl's home. We slept outside of an old abandoned house the first night since I wasn't sure where we were going. The next morning, my friend and I proceeded walking. I remembered riding in the van one Sunday morning, and one of the girls from the girl's home pointed to her house as we passed it. I saw the house again as I was walking and went to the door. She allowed us to stay at her house for a few days, or at least until school started back. When spring break was over, I went to the police station in Owensboro, Kentucky, and turned myself in. I later realized, it wasn't worth all the trouble, and I was tired of not knowing what my next move was going to be.

My dad was always in and out of jail. I knew him, but I didn't have a close relationship with him. I was told he talked about me all the time, and everything was always positive, but he wasn't there in the physical aspect of my life. I remember staying with him in Princeton, Kentucky, a few times, but that didn't last long. I loved my dad with all my heart, and I needed my dad to be there when I was younger; I needed my dad's protection as a child. When I was fourteen years old, I stayed with my auntie; she was always so nice to me. One day, I wanted to go skating. My aunt got approval from my mom, and I was allowed to go. My aunt had this boyfriend who smiled at me all the time, but I didn't think much about it at first. When skating was over, my aunt's boyfriend came to pick me up. He didn't say much to me while I was in the car, but I noticed we were not going in the direction of my aunt's house. He took me on this dark road. I was scared and asked him what he was doing there. He smiled as usual, but this time his smile was not warm and inviting; it was creepy. I was molested that night; afterward, he took me back to my aunt's house. The ride home was very bleak. Tears rolled down my face as he looked at me and told me not to say anything to anyone. The look in his eyes seemed heartless, and his smile vanished completely.

I went into the house, lay on the bed, and cried myself to sleep. Meanwhile, he was in the other room. I was awakened out of my sleep by a wetness that I felt. I pulled the covers back, and I was soaked in blood. I got up and went to the bathroom. I was hemorrhaging. I called my mom and told her I was bleeding, and she thought my menstrual cycle was on. She told me to wake my aunt up. I was scared because I knew what had happened to me, and I thought he would do something to me if I told anyone. I knocked on my aunt's door and told her to come to the phone; my mom asked to speak to her. I remember being on the couch and feeling weak. While my mom and aunt were talking on the phone, I remember getting up and walking toward the room; but before I made it to the bed, I passed out. I faintly remember all the details, but I remember staying three days in the hospital and a nurse telling me that I made it to the hospital just in time. Her words exactly were, "You're a very lucky young lady."

I know that you're not supposed to question God, but when I was younger, I used to question Him all the time. I never understood; I wanted to know what purpose I had in life. Why did I have teenage parents, when I felt like neither one knew how to properly raise me? I also remember asking God why I wasn't born an animal, because at that time, I just wanted to be free from torture. I didn't get an answer immediately, but I felt a sense of peace for a while.

I've always desired to have a father figure in my life. I thought, since my real dad was in and out of my life, it would be a good idea to look for a dad in someone else, and I did just that. I was about eighteen years old; I went to stay with this family who welcomed me with open arms. I felt good being there, I went to church faithfully with them, and I never imagined anything could go wrong. It was perfect. I finally belonged and felt loved.

One day, as we all sat around in the living room to watch TV, my spiritual dad asked me if I knew how to get to Jus 4 Feet. I responded, "yes, I know exactly where that store is because my cousin and I went there several times when I used to live with her. He smiled and replied, "Okay, because I need to go there to get me some shoes, I heard the shoes there had a good deal." I agreed to go with him and show him where the store was. We continued sitting there as a family watching a movie. The rest of that night was normal and very peaceful.

A few weeks went past, and I loved my new life; I was staying with my spiritual mother and father, and I felt love and understanding from them. We got dressed for church one Sunday, and while I was sitting on the pew, I felt a headache coming on and needed to take some aspirin. I got the key from my spiritual mother and went back to the house. As I was looking for Tylenol, I heard the front door open; and as I was coming out of the bathroom, I was met by my spiritual dad. He asked if was I okay because he saw me leave the church. I told him I was fine, but my head was hurting. He stood in front of me with this look that I still can't get out of my head. He pulled me into him, and as I was pushing back, he leaned forward to kiss me. I couldn't believe this was happening to me again! He talked to me about Satan and how the enemy was trying to take him over. I wasn't focused on everything he was saying; I was baffled with what had just happened.

Later that day, I was still perplexed, and I thought to myself, *This is it!* Obviously, I was looking for fatherly love in all the wrong places. If I can't trust a spiritual man, who also happens to be a preacher, whom can I trust? I was ready to give up; I felt so violated. This is the same man who looked at me and told me that I can trust him; I would sit in his office crying and telling him some of the things that I went through. The look he gave me seemed sincere at first, but that was only because I was naive to what was really happening. How could I be so gullible?! I thought I had a father figure to love and protect me, but later I found out he was nothing more than a manipulator!

I went to my best friend's house, locked myself in the bathroom, looked in the mirror, and cried until my eyes were swollen. It was at that moment that I attempted suicide. I wasn't scared. I didn't think twice; I just wanted to be free. Thankfully my attempt failed. Two days later, I went to the park; and while I was on the swings, I started crying as I thought about everything that has ever happened in my life and what I almost did to myself. I looked up at the sky, and once again I asked God why I had to be human. Why couldn't I be a bird so that I could just fly away whenever there was danger? That's the day I heard God's voice. God spoke to me and told me that I was not a mistake and he's always with me. He said I was chosen for His divine purpose. Immediately I felt God's presence all around me. It took awhile, but I realized that even though I've been molested, physically and verbally abused, manipulated, and mistreated by the people, I know and trusted that I can still be used by God. In Romans 8:31, the Bible says, "If God is for us, who can be against us?" My faith in God has helped me overcome every hurt and obstacle that has come my way thus far. I was invited to join a gang, and I was offered drugs occasionally, but I decided not to turn toward the use of drugs, gangs, and alcohol as my way of escape. I didn't want to become just another statistic. I wanted better for myself, so I picked up my Bible, prayed, and made a vow; I was not going to allow the enemy to destroy me or my future.

My life changed forever on February 11, 1997. I gave birth to my firstborn, a beautiful baby girl. I took one look at her, and I couldn't hold back the tears. I was overwhelmed with joy. For the first time in twenty-two years, I finally felt the feeling of true love. She was my new reason to live. The love for a child is indescribable. I promised my child that I would love, protect, and care for her to the best of my ability because this world was not getting any better, and I didn't want her going through what I went through. It was time for a change.

I quit school in the eleventh grade, but after I had my firstborn, I knew I had to set a better example than I had set for me. I refused to be labeled a high school dropout. I was determined to do better, but I didn't want a GED. I decided to go back to school at the age of twenty-nine! I enrolled at James Madison High School, completed my courses, and was awarded my high school diploma and my class ring!

I earned a 3.4 GPA, and I graduated with honors. Shortly after that, I enrolled at Queen City Beauty College and graduated from there in 2007. I am now a college student, currently enrolled at Austin Peay State University.

Even though I'm currently in the process of a divorce, I still keep a smile on my face, and I keep pressing on because I know God did not bring me this far to leave me. I realize it's a struggle out there, but in life we have choices to make, and I made the choice not to let my circumstances destroy me. I wanted better for my life, so I had to make a change. My favorite gospel song that I listen to daily, as it ministers to me, is called "What's Coming Is Better" by Deon Kipping. I'm learning how to move past my past hurts, habits, and hang-ups simply because *I refuse to give up* (1 Cor. 15:58).

Contact Information:
Luvntylerperry@yahoo.com

29

Laura E. Payne

Honor your father and your mother, as the Lord your God has commanded you so that you may live long and it may go well with you in the land the Lord your God is giving you.

—Deuteronomy 5:16

I am the fourth child of six and born in Columbus, Ohio, on June 6, 1953. There were two older brothers and one older sister by the time I was born. I was a daddy's girl from birth.

I don't think in those days there was any such thing as postpartum depression, but I'm sure that is what my mother was experiencing after my birth. She lost a baby after my birth and eventually had another daughter and a son.

Growing up, I recall how beautiful I always thought my mother was. She never left the house without carefully applying her red lipstick, always pin curled her hair each night, and had a pair of rhinestone earrings that I thought were exquisite diamonds.

Although we were definitively lower middle class, I thought we were rich. I never remember doing without anything of importance. Looking back, I can see how much my parents did without. They worked second jobs and struggled to provide for us, but all of that was kept away from us.

We had very active lives. Besides school, the boys were kept busy with Boy Scouts (my parents were pack leaders); we girls were active in brownies and later Girl Scouts (Mother was a leader in this also). My parents always raised large vegetable gardens; mother loved her landscaping and flower gardens. I remember that in the summer, after finishing all the yard work, we would play badminton or croquet as a family. In the winter we would play games. Mother taught all of us kids (boys included) how to embroider and crochet; no TV for us!

Then there was church. We were members of the Grace United Methodist Church in Delaware, Ohio. Both of my parents taught Sunday-school classes when we were younger. Mother was a member of the women's circle; Dad was active in the men's ministry. Church and church activities were a part of our daily lives.

Even though I had a wonderful childhood, I always knew something was missing. Mom was a good mother and did everything she should to take care of us kids, but I always knew something wasn't right. There was coldness about her even as she would comfort me if I was hurt.

Dad, on the other hand, more than made up for her indifference. He showered all six of us kids with hugs, kisses, and lots of I love you's. The older I got, the more my mother changed; by the time I was fifteen, things were reaching a climax in our home. She was nice to me in front of my dad, but when he wasn't around, she was a totally different person. Lots of accusations, name-calling, etc. Dad begged me to ignore her outbursts, which is really hard for a teen to do. If not for lots of praying and my strong belief in God, I am not sure how things would have turned out for me. Ephesians 6:1-3 helped a lot. "Children, obey your parents in the Lord, for this is right. Honor your father and mother, which is the first commandment with a promise that it may go well with you and that you may enjoy long life on the earth."

I finally eloped and left home at the tender age of sixteen. It broke my dad's heart, but it did get me out of the abusive situation I had been living in for the last few years. After graduating from high school, my husband and I moved out of state. My faithful Daddy called me every week and never ended the conversations without an I love you.

I did talk to my mom through the years, and we visited each other at least once a year, friendly but never close. Then things began to change again.

I am now a grown woman with grown children and lots of grandchildren. Suddenly my parents are the ones who are growing old and needing a helping hand. Mother called to say Dad was sick and he wanted me home. I spent three weeks at a time in Ohio helping her care for him. He lasted four months before the cancer took him home to be with our Lord.

During this time, I began to really learn life lessons. My father believed in everlasting love, never walking away just because things weren't perfect between him and Mom. He truly loved her in all of her imperfections! Ephesians 5:25-28 describes my dad: "Husbands, love your wives, just as Christ loved the church and gave himself up for her to make her holy, cleansing her by the washing with water through the word, and to present her to himself as a radiant church, without stain or wrinkle or any other blemish, but holy and blameless. In this same way, husbands ought to love their wives as their own bodies. He who loves his wife loves himself."

Dad told me that mother was beginning to show signs of dementia, and he made me promise to look after her when he was gone. He said I was a very responsible person, and he knew that I would do the right thing. All I could think of was how unfair to ask this of me on his dying bed! God, please help me get through this. It was then that Proverbs 23:22 came to me. "Listen to your father, who gave you life, and do not despise your mother when she is old." Okay, God, I am willing to try!

The first few years were pretty easy as she lived in Ohio and I lived in Tennessee. I called weekly and made many visits to check on her. Eventually we had to hire a caregiver to help her during the day. After some major health issues, we transferred her from a hospital in Ohio to Vanderbilt Hospital in Nashville. When she was released, we moved her into our home; to cut down on her confusion, my sweet husband moved her belongings including the furniture with us! She had her own bedroom, living room/dining room, and a wonderful deck complete with her old porch swing.

This was an awkward transition period for both mother and I. I am now a caregiver to a woman who has always been so distant and cold to me. Two strangers now forced to coexist in one home together. I wasn't sure that I could do this; then I remembered a saying someone had given me years ago.

> I woke up this morning and realized the problems facing me today. My first reaction was to cry, but then it came to me that the only people without problems are dead. I thanked God that he loved me enough to give me another day and have faith in me to be strong enough, with his help, to handle anything that life throws my way.

It's been four years since we moved Mother to Tennessee; I have watched her progress from a mild form of dementia to being diagnosed with Alzheimer's disease. She spent one year living in our home before having to be placed in a nursing home.

The first year of her living with us was a learning experience for the whole family. One day Mother would be happy, the next day angry at having to live here. I adjusted my work schedule from five to four days a week and had a caregiver stay with her when we were gone. Our thirteen-year-old grandson would come home each day from school and take his shift of caring for her. They would play children's games, eat snacks, and visit till we would come home. Mother can't remember his name anymore but on a good day still talks about how much fun she used to have with him and how much he looks like his deceased mother.

I knew nothing about the nursing homes in our area, but I did trust our doctor. He recommended one highly. He said it was the only one in the area that had a special Alzheimer's unit within the facility. Not really believing that we really *needed* that, I did agree on the facility. After three months, my mom was almost completely bedridden. The director of nursing at the facility called me for a meeting. She felt Mom was depressed and was willing herself to die. Her suggestion was to transfer her from the general population to the special Alzheimer's unit. She took me for a tour of the unit; I was *very* much against it, not feeling that my mom was in as bad of a shape as the people there. We can say denial! The unit was nice, only seventeen patients. They had their own private dining room, their own activities, plus they could also join in all activities with the general population. The nurses and the certified nurse's aide's specialty was working with this type of patient.

The first few days were rough. Mom would not leave her room, and after a few weeks, she began to flourish. At this point she was *a walker*, and this was a lockdown unit, so she could safely walk anywhere she wanted. She began to make friends, play bingo, join a kickball group, and most importantly, smile. She entered two beauty contests and came in first runner-up in both years! My oldest brother, who is a minister, came to visit at Christmas one year and was able to bring the music and message to the nursing home; Mother was so proud.

How has her moving down here changed our lives? We live on Kentucky Lake and have always spent our free time between church and spending time on the lake—boating, fishing, swimming, picnics, etc. Now on all my days off, I visit with her. Does it put a strain on my personal life? Of course, it does! I am very blessed to have a husband who is an understanding Christian man and knows how much Mother looks forward to our visits.

I have had many people tell me it's just too much to handle, or they can't stand seeing their loved ones decline; therefore, they don't visit often. Let me tell you what the Bible says. "Give proper recognition to those widows who are really in need. But if a widow has children or grandchildren, these should learn first of all to put their religion into practice by caring for their own family and so repaying their parents and grandparents, for this is pleasing to God. If anyone does not provide for his relatives, and especially for his immediate family, he has denied the faith and is worse than an unbeliever" (1 Tim. 5:3-4, 8).

When she first went into the nursing home, she hated her room, so I had to figure out a way to make it more like home for her. Mom had always collected beautiful angels, so we bought a tall corner-shelf unit and filled it with her angels (good ones on top, stuffed animals and nonbreakables on the bottom shelves.) I bought two large bulletin boards and filled them with pictures of her mom and dad, brother, sister, aunts and uncles, then our family. I hung a large family portrait of Mom, Dad, and all six of us kids. I had already lost two brothers, a daughter, and my father at this point, so pictures were very special to Mom. I also added a clock so she could keep track of time.

I like to think all of these things have brought her happiness just to look at, but when she is having good days, they bring back a flood of memories of happy times for her. It's times like these when we have found her in her room with a special handmade wooden box that holds a Bible my dad presented to her on Christmas Day 1973 as a gift. It is inscribed, "To my beloved wife, from your loving husband." Seeing my mother trying to read her Bible surrounded by angles is a beautiful sight never to be forgotten.

On a good day, Mother knows I am her daughter; she doesn't know my name unless someone tells her. On a bad day, I am her deceased sister, a friend, whoever she wants me to be! Sometimes she tells me old stories from her childhood; oh, how I treasure these times! We sit and color pictures, she sings to me, I take her for walks; we visit with the beautiful birds in one of the living rooms at her "home." She loves it when my two sisters make a visit or when the grand- and great-grandchildren come spend time with her. On bad days, she cusses at me, threatens me, cries, or fights with her caregivers. She ends the visits by telling me she loves me the most—how sad.

All holidays, special occasions, birthday parties, etc., are especially stressful on my family, as we usually host all such events, which involves preparing our house for the occasion (extra cleaning and decorating.) I also do all the cooking for an average attendance of twenty-five and coordinate picking up Mom from the nursing home so she can join us for the event. Once she is here, she has to be watched and entertained constantly to make sure she behaves herself. Sometimes she forgets that she can't walk and tries to get out of her wheelchair. These events are the highlight of her existence.

She has become so much harder for me to take care of. When she went to the nursing home, she weighed 133 pounds; she now weighs 200 pounds. Just getting her from her wheelchair to the bathroom is a physical struggle for me now. She will be eighty-six years old this August and is in great health, other than she falls a lot due to forgetting that she can't walk.

As her disease progresses, her behavior deteriorates. We try to monitor her sugar intake so she doesn't gain any more weight. While at my home for a birthday party recently, she kept trying to sneak more cake, so my granddaughter moved the cake out of her reach, and Mother took her fork and told my granddaughter that she would stab her if she didn't give her the cake back! People who say "Children say the darndest things" haven't been around an Alzheimer's patient as they progress in their disease!

Do I resent my father for putting this burden on me? Do I resent the fact that it has changed the last four years of my life, and who knows how many more to come? Do I wish my mother would hurry up and go home to be with God?

A resounding NO!

I thank my father for giving me the opportunity to get to know my mom. She is *not* a burden, and I needed to give up my selfish thoughts toward her. We always need to honor our parents. We need to keep in mind that as we honor our parents, we honor God. As we honor our parents, we model how we ourselves will be honored as parents. And depending on our stage of life and theirs, the honor we give our parents will take different forms. It comes through our obedience when we were young. It comes through living righteously when we mature. And it comes through caring for our parents when they are aged.

My Mom
Ruth Lundy Wooten

Laura E. Payne
Owner and Chief Administrator
Queen City College
1594 Ft. Campbell Blvd.
Clarksville, TN
Qcc1594@aol.com

30

LaVon Bracey

(Clarksville, Tennessee)

You prepare a table before me in the presence of my enemies. You anoint my head with oil; my cup overflows.

—Psalms 23:5, NIV

My name is Charnitric LaVon Bracey, and I was born in Brownsville, Tennessee. I am the wife of Horace Bracey, associate pastor of God's Sanctuary Church. I am a mother of two sons, Emmanuel and Gabriel, and one daughter, Magnolia. I have served as worship leader for over ten years and overseer of the children's ministry for over five years. I am currently working on my first CD release, *In Your Presence*. I was blessed with wonderful parents, Charles and Justine Cooper. I am the second born of four daughters. I started singing at the age of two. My mother took a special interest in cultivating each of her daughters. I will never forget one day I was singing "I Remember Mama" by Shirley Caesar when my mother stopped me. She told me I could not sing that song because my mother is still living. "Never sing a lie," she said. "If you sing 'I will trust in the Lord until I die,' then you need to do so." She also told me, "Never make someone beg you to sing or use your talent." To this day, when I am selecting the songs for our worship service, I found myself doing some soul-searching before selecting my songs. Along with worship opportunities, I have had the privileges of cowriting, directing, and acting in the gospel stage plays *Guess What I Heard*, *Guess What I Heard Home for the Holidays*, and *Deception Fooled by a Feeling*. I am a Leading Lady.

I had a wonderful childhood with godly parents who taught me the Word of God. My father was a pastor, and my mother an evangelist. I was an army brat. My father was in Basic Training on the day of my birth. I was born to travel, and this exposure to different people, countries, and cultures has been instrumental in creating the woman I am today. As a military dependent, we moved every three years. As we traveled, my mother always taught me the importance of the company I kept. Looking back, I realize that everyone who has come into my life, whether good or bad, played a role in who I would become. There are some people God placed in our lives to help us reach our destiny, and others to teach us how to pray.

Psalms 23:5 became my favorite scripture when God revealed a spiritual nugget to me. "You prepare a table before me in the presence of my enemies." When reading that scripture, I always thought that it meant everyone who had ever talked bad about me, mistreated me, or hurt me would one day drive by and see my beautiful house, my wonderful job, and my loving family. But God compelled me to look a little closer. At your table called life, there will be people who are there to cheer you on and support you. On the other hand, there are those we call our enemies, haters, or that person who simply cannot be happy for another person's success. So rather than be happy for you, they make a point of exposing your flaws. I am here to tell you that in order to reach your destiny or purpose in life, you must identify the enemies at your table and turn it over to God. Over the years, I have had wonderful relationships and toxic relationships. It is easy to see the blessing in the wonderful relationships, but toxic relationships can be a teachable moment as well. Have you ever been talked down to, betrayed, or controlled in a relationship? You can choose to be bitter or better. Romans 2:28 says, "And we know that all things work together for good to them that love God, to them who are the called according to *his* purpose." A bad relationship or situation can be a powerful tool and even inspirational. So in your last relationship, they tried to control you; by going through this, you can become that friend who will support and suppress those you are in relationships with. We all will have enemies, even Jesus. Jesus was betrayed not by a stranger but by one of his own disciples. At the table of the last supper, Jesus said, "Do what you must do quickly." Jesus could have become bitter, but He knew that this evil act would bring the greatest gift. Which was salvation. There is a saying that goes, "Life is 10 percent what happens to you and 90 percent how you react." What the devil meant for evil, God will turn around for your good.

After reading "You prepare a table before me in the presence of my enemies," God revealed another spiritual nugget. You can be your greatest enemy. Am I my own enemy (in-a-me)? Then, I remember as a child, fear was the enemy at my table. I had a fear of reading out loud. The spirit of fear was so strong. If I knew we would be reading aloud in class, I would have to use the bathroom, get sick, and I even acted like I couldn't see the words. Fear had a hold on me. Every year, on the night before the first day of school, I would cry all night long. I was so afraid that my new teacher would make me read out loud. My mother tried to comfort me by pointing out my new clothes, shoes, and even praying with me. But none of that seemed to help because fear had me imprisoned. I was paralyzed with fear. In the fifth grade, I tried out for my first stage play. Acting has always been my gift, and I loved it. On the day of auditions, I found out the director would select a portion from the part you wanted to read out loud. I knew I could do the leading role, but there were so many lines. Which passage would they pick for me to read? At that moment, I decided to try out for the role as the storeowner. This part only had one line. "My, what a wonderful costume you have left over from Halloween." I got the part, but all during the rehearsals, I regretted that decision. I shared this with my mother, and she asked, "Do you love God? Do you have the love of God? Because God's love is perfect. One John 4:18 states, 'Perfect love cast out all fear.'" The spirit of fear robbed me of many opportunities until that day. Now, I realize that if I would have allowed fear to become my life partner, I would not be able to stand on a stage to act or to usher the people of God into His presence.

As I continue to refer back to my favorite scripture, "You prepare a table . . ." (Ps. 23:5), I heard a sermon entitled "Favor Ain't Fair." I am so glad that when God decides to bless you, He does not hold a board or committee meeting to vote on it. The Word of God states, "If God be for you, who can be against you?" I like to say that if God be for you, who cares who's against you? I do not worry about the enemy at my table. The enemy is not preparing my table, God is. Like the songwriter said, "What God has for me, it is for me." That's why I don't lose sleep or time over what the enemy wants to do because my promote comes from the Lord. Jesus commands, "Pray for them that despitefully use you and persecute you." When you know that your enemies have no power over your destiny, it will change your thoughts toward them. When I go out to eat, my experience at that restaurant is not based on the people at that table but on the ones serving me. If I want more rolls or my drink refilled, I don't ask at my husband but the waiter. The same principle applies at your spiritual table. There were times when I felt saddened. I would ask someone to put in a good word for me or help me with a project, and they did come through. After many disappointments, I learned to put up a wall. I would ask someone to help me with a project, but I always had a backup plan; you know, just in case. However, I enjoy the freedom of knowing God will never leave me or forsake me. If I have a need of anything, I don't call on man; I call on God. The Word clearly stated, "The king's heart is in the hand of the Lord; he directs it like a watercourse wherever he pleases" (Prov. 21:1). All I have to do is ask. Matthew 7:7 says, "Ask and it will be given to you; seek and you will find; knock and the door will be opened to you." When I told God, You prepare my table, I unsteadily noticed the normal obstacles were removed. That meant my past, my education, my finances—nothing could stop what God has for me. There are two biblical examples of this. First, Mary the mother of Jesus. An angel appeared to her and said, "Mary, you have found favor with God. You will be with child and give birth to a son, and you are to give him the name Jesus. He will be great and will be called the Son of the Most High." Surely she was immediately filled with joy. Instead she questioned, "How will this be; since I am a virgin?" God works with the natural to show His supernatural power. Second, I think about Peter the fisherman. Jesus found Peter washing his fishing nets. He asked them if they had caught fish. They answered no. Jesus then told them to cast their net on the right side of the boat. The fishermen replied, "We have been fishing all night," but at Thy Word, they caught so many fish that they were unable to pull in the net. God is not looking for what you have but for your obedience. I've been told it's not what you know but who you know at matters. This being said, if you know Jesus the author and finisher of our faith, you have what it takes.

I read the scripture ("You anoint my head with oil . . .") further. We all have an anointed gift and purpose in life. No one can do what God has called me to do. If it was possible, I would not have been born. I am like a fingerprint. No two fingerprints are ever exactly alike. I know there are a lot of actresses, worship leaders, daughters, mothers, wives, but there is only one Charnitric LaVon Bracey. I am anointed and appointed. James 1:17 declares, "Every good and perfect gift is from above, coming down from the Father." The gift God has placed in me is good and perfect for me. God will not put more on me than I am able to bear. But sometimes I put more on myself than God intended. When I find myself being overwhelmed or frustrated with a project I am working on, I think to myself, *God, did you tell me to walk through this door?* I have come to the conclusion that even in our great struggles, we should have a scent of peace because of the anointment. "For my yoke is easy and my burden is light" (Matt. 11:30).

Finally, the Bible says, "My cup overflows" (Ps. 23:5). Now that I have found my purpose and anointed place at the table, I have overflowed. It is best said in Luke 6:38, "Give, and it will be given to you. A good measure, pressed down, shaken together and running over, will be poured into your lap. For with the measure you use, it will be measured to you." With this overflow, I can be a blessing to my enemies and my friends. Yes, I said, my enemies. I thank God for every bad job, relationship, closed door, or disappoint. It has helped me to appreciate my blessings. I have learned to appreciate a simple thing, simple like breathing after I had a stuffy nose. It is my experience that God can use whomever or whatever He will to help develop your purpose, even your enemies.

I would like to challenge you to enter into a place with God that the gates of hell shall not prevail. You can have what you say. Make a daily declaration over your life. I am fearfully and wonderfully made. I am redeemed. I am the apple of Your eye. I am heaven-bound. I am created in Your image. I am an overcomer. Lord, take me from where I am to where You want me to be. My destiny is attached to God. I will not stagnate. My steps are ordered by the Lord. The Lord has enlarged my coast. I refuse to operate below my divine destiny. Goodness and mercy will follow me all the days of my life. That which will hinder me from greatness will scatter. My destiny will not die. Lord, break the spirit of unfruitfulness in my life. Every weapon and evil design against me will fail. I reject sickness in my spirit, soul, and body. All things that are impossible will become possible in every aspect of my life. Today You will surprise. Today You will give me solution. Today You have marked my destiny, and I have unheard-of favor. The spirit of excellence is upon me. I will see Your wonders this year. AMEN.

I pray this has been a blessing to you. I am devoted to passionate worship, the ministry of the Word of God, and the encouragement of the church. I am available for ministry in worship, for speaking engagements, worship leader training and script for your drama ministry. Scripts vary from funny to serious; however, all of their material is worshipful, evangelistic, and edifying for the church. If you are interested in having me minister at your church, check out the links below to contact me. We would love to hear from you!

Contact Information:
Facebook: LaVon Bracey
E-mail: lavon.bracey@yahoo.com

31

Lisa Lewis-Balboa

Father's Girl

Before I formed you in the womb I knew you, and before you were born I consecrated you; I appointed you a prophet to the nations.

—Jeremiah 1:5

Introduction

My name is Lisa Lewis-Balboa. I am a native and resident of Trenton, Kentucky. I am a pastor in the Christian Methodist Episcopal Church. I have been in ministry for eighteen years. I am an employment and training specialist. I am a graduate of Trevecca Nazarene University. I am the director of my own nonprofit organization, Helping Our Latin Americans. I am the mother of one son, Benjamin Grant Lewis. I am an ecumenist. I enjoy empowering other women through ministry. I am a preacher, pastor, teacher, and prophetess. I am a servant of God. This is my chapter. This is my story. This is my journey. I am a Leading Lady.

Words of Sharing

I am sharing this in loving memory of my father, Bennie "Bubba" Lewis. His death helped me realize that I was born with a purpose!

One of my fondest memories as a little girl was sitting on my father's lap. I would share with him my hopes and dreams. My father would listen to me, and he would share memories of his childhood with me. His parents died when he was in the second grade, and he had to go to work to help take care of his younger brother and sisters. I was the youngest child. I guess you could say I was a latecomer as my older siblings were all at least twenty years older than me. My mother said that my father spoiled me, and I would agree. I was my *father's girl*. My father was an over-the-road truck driver. Before he left for his trips, we would always watch the late-night show. He would tuck me in bed, give me a kiss, and say, "I love you."

On November 11, 1977, while on an over-the-road trip, my father suffered a massive stroke in Lebanon, Tennessee. He stayed in the hospital there until he passed away on December 3, 1977 (my brother's birthday.) This was one of the saddest days of my life. My father and best friend was gone!

When my father died, I was nine years old. It was very hard for me to accept my father's death, and I really did not want to live anymore. I did not feel like I could go on! I was my *father's girl*. How would I make it without him in my life? As I write this chapter, I would like to encourage someone who has suffered the loss of a loved one. Your life is not over; you must go on! God has a plan for your life!

After my father's death, my grandmother encouraged me to pray and talk to God. One night, when I was in my room crying about my father's death, I began to pray. As I prayed and talked to God, God began to talk to me. It is a night of my life that I will never forget. God told me to go on with my life. Yes, that night God told me that He had a plan for my life. He told me that there was work that He wanted me to do. It was that night; I realized that God had a purpose for my life! At nine years old, I had no clue where God was taking me. However, that night, I began to trust God and began to rely on Him to get me through my grieving period.

When we are faced with difficult times in our lives—whether the death of a loved one, a teenage pregnancy, an abusive spouse, or just discovering who we are—it is important to remember in those times that God has a plan for your life! God has created us for a purpose.

Death will cause us to respond in different ways. After my father's death, there were times that I was lonely, bitter, angry, sad, depressed, and happy. When we lose someone dear to us, sometimes it feels as if our entire life has been turned upside down. As my grandmother counseled me, I would like to counsel others who are reading this. Pray and ask God to give you strength. God will give you strength to make it through. "Weeping will endure for a day, but joy will come in the morning" (Ps. 30:5). From the time I was nine years old until I was twenty-seven years old, I was always searching for that joy and waiting for God to show me the work that He had for me to do. Sometimes we look for joy in people, relationships, money, jobs, and clothes. However, true joy can come only from God. When we are empty, it is God who fills us!

When God makes us a promise, we must remember that God will keep His promise. In January 1985, I was a senior in high school. I was a shot-put thrower on my high school track team and had just received a scholarship to attend college and participate in the college track team. I was excited! However, in February 1985, I found out that I was pregnant and would not be able to attend college in August. My dream was to attend college, try out, and make the 1988 Olympic track-and-field team and become a special-education teacher. However, God had another plan. After becoming pregnant, I began to question God and ask Him if He really had work for me to do. In my journey of life, I have found out that God's way is not our way. As I pastor, I minister to many young mothers. I try to instill in them that just because you become a teenage mother does not mean that God will not use you. If we repent our sin, God will forgive us of our sin. After the birth of my son, I began to ask God what my purpose in life was? I asked God, "What is the work that You have for me to do"? That was when He directed me to Jeremiah 1:5. "Before I formed you in the womb I knew you, and before you were born I consecrated you; I appointed you a prophet to the nations." When I read this scripture, I thought, *There is no way that God could use me as a prophet!* However, I knew that God was speaking to me and that one day I would know what His plan for my life was.

In 1993, I heard God calling me into the preaching ministry. It was hard for me to believe that God wanted to use me to preach His Word. So I denied my calling. On December 25, 1993, there was a heavy snow. My mother and I were in a car accident. While I was driving, I hit a piece of black ice, ran off the road, and ran into a tree. Everyone that stopped to help us was amazed that neither of us was injured or killed. After the accident, I knew that God still had a plan for my life and that I could not put my call off any longer. I knew that God would not have spared my life that day if He did not still have a plan for me. I thought, *Suppose I had died without fulfilling God's plan for my life?* I began to pray and ask God for strength to acknowledge my call and to preach His Word. In October 1994, I acknowledged my call. On November 6, 1994, I preached my first sermon at Sebree Chapel Christian Methodist Episcopal Church in Trenton, Kentucky. After I preached my first sermon, I remember breathing a sigh of relief and feeling as if everything in my life would be smooth sailing. I have learned that just because we accept God's plan for our life, it does not mean that life will be easy. However, knowing that God never takes us where He will not carry us is a comfort to make it through the journey! A Leading Lady will face obstacles, but God will be there every step of the way!

In 1995, my mother, Louise F. Lewis, had retired; and she, my son, and I looked forward to doing lots of traveling together. One of her dreams was to go to Orlando, Florida, and to visit Disney World. In May 1995, my mother was diagnosed with liver cancer; and from May until October 10, 1995, I watched my mother battle with this dreadful disease. After her death, there were times I felt like giving up. God was there this time too. He was there to carry me. In the times when I felt like giving up, I heard God speak to me, "You can't give up. You still have work to do." Just hearing God speak those words to me—*You can't give up. You still have work to do*—continues to carry me through today. When God gives us an assignment, we must complete the assignment! I am determined to complete those assignments and work that God has for me do. I am humbled and still amazed that God chose me and uses me to do His work. I am thankful that He has chosen me to be a Leading Lady!

I am a Leading Lady who has been blessed with a wonderful son. God never makes a mistake. My son, Benjamin Grant Lewis, is a pastor, preacher, and church musician. He has been preaching since he was thirteen years old. As I watch him on his journey, I know that God is not through with him yet! I know that God is speaking to him too. "Don't Give up. I still have work for you to do."

In my eighteen years of ministry, God has allowed me to pastor four churches. My first assignment was in Lane Chapel Christian Methodist Episcopal Church in Guthrie, Kentucky. I served as the pastor of that church for six years. During my pastorate there, there were lots of work to be done to the physical structure of the building. There were times that I wanted to give up, but again I would hear God's voice say, "Don't give up. There is still work for you to do." It was through that perseverance that in 1996, I was recognized as rural pastor of the year by the Kentucky Council of Churches. He has blessed me to pastor four wonderful congregations. Lane Tabernacle Christian Methodist Episcopal Church, Phillips Chapel Christian Methodist Episcopal, and the churches that I currently serve: Lane Tabernacle Christian Methodist Episcopal Church and my home church, Sebree Chapel Christian Methodist Episcopal Church. Each place I serve draws me closer to Him.

As God chooses us to do His work, He will always place people in our lives that will be there for us to cheer us on and give encouragement. I am thankful for those people that God has placed in my life and in my ministry to cheer me on and give encouragement: my brother-in-law, the late Stanley Russell, the late Bishop Nathaniel Linsey, Presiding Elder Charles Henry Sr., Bishop E. Lynn Brown, Martha Franklin, Ms. Alice Lucille Martin, my niece Angela McKee, my nephew Greg Russell, and my mentor and dear friend, Father Frank Ruff. The saying is true: "We stand on the shoulders of giants." I am thankful for the giants that God has placed in my life. As a Leading Lady, *I stand on the shoulders of giants*!

When God chooses you to do His work, He will give you gifts for the journey. In high school, one of my favorite subjects was Spanish I and Spanish II. My Spanish teacher, Kathy Harper, was very fluent in Spanish, and she made the class exciting. Speaking Spanish was fun, but I never thought I would use my Spanish after high school. However, God had another plan. In the county where I live, there are many migrant workers.

Most of the workers that come from Mexico do not speak English. In 1991, God stirred up the gift. I began to use the Spanish that I had learned. I became a translator for the county, the Todd County School System, and for the families in the community that needed a translator. As I worked with the families, I realized that the migrant families and workers that come here need assistance with not only translation but also transportation and knowledge of community resources. With the help of a dear friend Paul Witte, we founded a nonprofit organization called Helping Our Latin Americans. I have had the opportunity to attend the National Hispanic Breakfast in Washington, D.C. Our president, President Barack Obama, was the keynote speaker. I remember sitting there in amazement, thinking, *Wow, am I really here?* When we are obedient to God's call in our life, God will take us places that we never imagined!

He has taken me to Jerusalem, where I had the opportunity to preach on the land where Jesus walked. He has taken me to Jamaica, where I had the opportunity to serve as a missionary, and He has taken me to preach in—of all places—KENTUCKY! God has opened doors for me, and I have preached His Word in many places across the United States. I have witnessed God move and work in so many ways! God is truly amazing. What an awesome God we serve! God's plan for us is to *go* and make disciples. It is His desire that we all might be one.

The work that God has called me to do is one of my greatest passions. I work to see the body of Christ become one. He has opened the doors for me to do this in my ecumenical work. I am a Leading Lady. I am an ecumenist. Whether serving as the president of the Todd County Ministerial Association, helping to revitalize the Christian County Ministerial Alliance, serving on the executive board of the Kentucky Council of Churches or on the National Planning Committee of the National Workshop on Christian Unity, I pray that God's people may one day all be one! As I listen to religious leaders discuss issues on Christian unity, it can be frustrating to hear the reasons that we are separated. In my frustration, I hear God speaking, "Don't give up. There is still work to do". A Leading Lady's work is never done. However, we can never give up!

Yes, that is what God was speaking to me when I was nine years old. He was saying, "You must never give up. I have work for you to do." A Leading Lady is called to help people realize that we are family. I thank God for my family, my mother, my father, my sister and her family, my brothers and their families. I am thankful for a praying family. I am thankful for being raised up in a Christian home. I am thankful for my grandmother Lena Parker, who encouraged me to fall down on my knees and pray when my father died. If I had never fallen down on my knees, I would never have heard God speak to me that "I have work for you to do." No, I would never have discovered that I was predestined. I would never have realized that God had consecrated me to do His work and to become a prophet for His people.

Closing

I still miss my earthly father and visit his gravesite often just to reminisce on the old days or to share what God is doing in my life today. However, what I have come to realize is that I really am my Father's girl! I am my Heavenly Father's child. I am called to do my Father's work. In those times that I feel like giving up, that is when my Father speaks and says, "No, you are my child. You can't give up. There is still work for you to do!" I am a Leading Lady called to do the work of my Father!

Contact Information:
Pastor Lisa Lewis Balboa
Hopkinsvillell@aol.com
Facebook: Lisa Lewis-Balboa

32

Mayor Carolyn P. Bowers

(Clarksville, Montgomery County)

Born at home on a farm owned by my grandfather's church on Tylertown Road in rural Montgomery County, I was the third child of five children. My father later purchased a farm located at the corner of Trenton Road and Tiny Town Road. Today there is a housing development on Tylertown Road named Church Place Estates. My first childhood memory is on my third birthday; it was the day we moved from the church farm. I remember looking at the calendar on the wall in our kitchen and asking mother if we were going to take my birthday with us when we moved. The date had been marked on that calendar, and I had really been looking forward to the day, only to discover we would be moving to a new home.

I attended St. Bethlehem Elementary School and St. Bethlehem United Methodist Church. I was an active member of the 4-H Club at school and an active member of the Methodist Youth Fellowship group at church. When I think back to my childhood days and summer on the farm, I remember those lazy days when all I was concerned with was playing outside, riding my stick horse all over those old dirt farm roads, playing house with my dolls, pretending to teach them, or playing office. As I grew older, my personal interests naturally changed, and I began to enjoy reading, sewing, and listening to music. A lot of my time in the summer was occupied with helping out in the vegetable garden, preparing vegetables for canning and freezing.

I developed an interest in 4-H Club beginning in the third grade and participated in 4-H activities and camps throughout my eight years at St. Bethlehem School. During my 4-H years, my hobbies were cooking and sewing. One of my proud 4-H projects was taking part in a room-decorating contest. I made large draw draperies, a coverlet, dust ruffle, pillow covers, and cushion covers out of polished cotton for my bedroom. This also included painting the room a lavender color to match the fabric. My room looked beautiful, even if I didn't win! As a member of the Future Homemakers of America at Clarksville High School, I would sew almost all my clothes, dresses, suits, even coats. Home economics seemed to be my vocational calling. My home economics teachers in high school became mentors to me. Through the Future Homemakers of America Club, I got the opportunity to participate in activities locally, at the district and state levels. When I look back, I realize what an impact those experiences made in my life.

When I was in the eighth grade, I started working at a local florist owned by my aunt and uncle. At first I worked only during holiday seasons, then in high school I began working every Saturday. This gave me my first taste of independence and a little spending money at five dollars per day. It was my way of getting off the farm for a while. My aunt, who was an extremely artistic designer, taught me so much about designing floral arrangements and corsages, working with both live and artificial flowers. I learned customer-service skills through taking orders by telephone and in person. She even taught me how to bill and collect on accounts receivable. Little did I realize at the time that she had quickly become my mentor. We developed a very close bond, and she had a great deal of influence during my adolescent years. My dad was very strict and controlling, so my aunt tried to reason with him on my behalf during my teen years. My employment there continued into my freshman year at Austin Peay.

Entering Austin Peay State University as a freshman on a home economics scholarship after marrying my high school sweetheart the summer after graduation totally changed my life. Entering college as a married student did not sit well with the home economics organization that had granted my scholarship. I remember attending a meeting of the organization with my mother and the group voting to let me keep the scholarship for one year only. I am fairly certain my mother was embarrassed by my actions though she never let on.

College life was not about partying, but it was about working and studying while adjusting to being married. I quickly realized that a college education was an absolute necessity to achieve my career goal of becoming a teacher, at that time, a home economics teacher. This would change after my sophomore year in college into becoming a business and office education teacher while also becoming a mother to our first daughter. I enjoyed my consumer-homemaking classes, but when I enrolled in my first business class, it was like I could just not get enough of it. Business course material seemed like a natural progression of what I was meant to become. I have never looked back.

During my first two years at Austin Peay, I was working part-time and was a full-time student; my husband was working on the evening shift at Trane Co., and my mother had become our babysitter. Evenings were spent bathing and feeding our young daughter and studying. Looking back, I am not really certain how my father accepted all this. Without my mother's help, it would have been virtually impossible for me to continue my college education. She was always there for me, and that is something I will never forget! She was a quiet, soft-spoken woman who never had anything bad to say about anyone. She had her plate full raising five children, gardening, cooking, cleaning, doing laundry, and cooking for farmhands throughout the farming season. She was an accomplished pianist who shared this skill with her family and church. My mother had a profound influence on me growing up, and I miss her every day. Our oldest daughter still tells me to this day that her earliest childhood memories are of my mother, fondly referred to as *Ganky*, and life on the farm with the horses, chickens, and pets.

During the early years of our marriage, there was a fast-paced routine of parenting, studying, and working. It was a very demanding time, but one that would really pay off in the future. I don't mean to imply that it was all work and no play. We did squeeze in some time to play!

I graduated with my bachelor's degree in business from Austin Peay State University in December 1967, the same month my husband became a state trooper with the Tennessee Department of Safety; both of these events propelled both of us forward in our chosen careers. December and January lacked opportunity for business teachers seeking teaching positions, so I took an office job at Jenkins & Wynne Car Dealership. In the next two years, I would learn every job in that business office and become the office manager. However, I still had the longing to teach business at the high school level. So in the fall of 1969, I applied for and was offered a business-teacher position at Clarksville High School. This was the beginning of a twenty-nine year teaching career as a high school business and computer teacher with the Clarksville-Montgomery County School System. In this position, I had many wonderful opportunities to serve students as a classroom teacher, class sponsor, club sponsor, and mentor.

My husband and I became the proud parents of a second daughter in the fall of 1975. Somewhere in between all the teaching and law enforcement, we found time for this wonderful addition to our family. Her ten-year-old sister suddenly realized she was not the only child. She became a minimother to her new sibling and still is to this day. Both our daughters are graduates of Austin Peay State University with majors in accounting and business administration. They are married, and one is the mother of our two grandchildren, with the other daughter expecting her first child in July 2013. We could not be more proud of them both.

Everyone knows the joys of grand parenting are too numerous to mention! Our precious four-year-old granddaughter was diagnosed with leukemia in the spring of 1994. This dramatic event totally changed my priorities and those of my family. The focus shifted to being there to support our granddaughter's treatment and recovery. Friends and neighbors were so kind and giving. Prayers were offered by numerous church congregations. She was in prekindergarten at the Clarksville Academy when she was diagnosed. Her classmates, their parents, teachers, and the entire student body were so supportive. When she was able to return to school the following fall, all her classmates wore hats to make her feel more comfortable, because the chemotherapy caused her to lose all her hair. Trips to Vanderbilt Children's

Hospital in Nashville occurred three times every week. It was like an emotional roller coaster during the three years of intensive treatment. Some of her medications caused her to crave certain foods. Whenever her parents were worn down, we would kick in to provide relief. One particular time she was at our house, she was craving shrimp. I simply looked at my husband and said, "Are you going or am I?" Going through a life-threatening event such as cancer, especially that of a child, can cause profound change, and it affects everyone in the family. I prayed that God would give me the cancer and let her be healthy. After realizing this was not happening, I prayed to God that I would do whatever He wanted me to do with the rest of my life if He would spare her life. I waited a long time before I recognized my true calling, another type of public service. Our family remains very close now, and we never take for granted the precious time that we have on this earth together. In the end, all there is, is love! It is so very important to impart this message to others whose lives we touch. My mission to help others remains to this day and always will.

Professionally as a teacher, I was actively involved in conducting teacher in-service workshops on many subjects to include computer use in the classroom, curriculum coordination, writing state course curriculum for vocational office-education courses, and being actively involved in the Clarksville-Montgomery County Education Association, holding numerous offices and serving on various committees. I served on state committees and held state offices in the Tennessee Vocational Teachers Association, Tennessee Office Education Teachers Association, and the Tennessee Teachers Study Council. These activities offered the opportunity to work with teachers from across Tennessee and leaders in the State Department of Education as well as the governor. I had also earned my master's degree in curriculum and instruction from Austin Peay and sixty hours beyond becoming certified in administration/supervision. I was honored to be voted outstanding classroom teacher by my peers in the spring of 1998.

The years I spent teaching business and computer courses to thousands of students in this community was one of the most gratifying and rewarding experiences of my life. It warms my heart to see those students today and learn how they put to good use the skills learned in those classes. My years as a steno-lab and data-processing-lab teacher gave me the opportunity to really spend time with students over a two-year time period while they developed business and computer skills that would reward them in their future endeavors. For twenty-five years, I sponsored a business club that utilized their business and computer skills and also developed leadership skills. Tutoring students and fund-raising to enable students to travel to skills competition events and leadership conferences instilled a sense of responsibility and dependability in students that did not normally excel in other areas of the school environment. My after-school tutoring sessions included etiquette classes for those attending skills competitions and conferences.

I agonized over the decision to leave teaching and run for the office of county trustee in the spring of 1998. I knew my business skills would serve me well in the trustee's position, but I was not certain about running for elected office. Encouragement from many friends and acquaintances gave me the strength to step out of my comfort zone. People do not get elected to office on their own; it takes lots of people coming together to volunteer and donate campaign funds, give of their time to put up signs and conduct campaign events. It is a very intense process, and it occurs during the hottest months of the year. That summer was spent campaigning from May to August. I was convinced that if elected, I could make a difference for our citizens. As county trustee, I was able to make changes in the computer system used for billing and collecting county property taxes, collecting and auditing hotel/motel taxes, changing office procedures in the flow of work and accountability. During my tenure as county trustee, I was able to revise the way idle county funds were invested to gain a larger return on our tax dollars, earning over $20 million in interest revenue.

Currently, I am serving my second term as Montgomery County mayor after having served two terms as county trustee. Running a campaign for county mayor is much more challenging than county trustee. It requires a complete campaign strategy, a larger campaign team, and more fund-raisers, more speaking engagements, more signs and visibility. My purpose in running for public office is strictly to serve the citizens of our county and be a team leader to a stronger community—a community that is stronger for growing quality jobs for our citizens, a better education for our students, a safer community, and one with more recreational facilities to improve quality of life for everyone.

In early 2006, the county executive announced that he would not be seeking reelection. I was approached and asked to consider becoming a candidate for the seat. A woman had never held either the city or county mayor positions in Clarksville or Montgomery County. After much support, encouragement, thought, and prayer, I decided to step up and declare my candidacy. Fund-raisers and events were scheduled, committees organized, a campaign strategy and theme developed, and a logo designed. Getting permission for campaign-sign locations and purchasing permits occupies a lot of time for candidates and is labor intensive. The months of April through July of 2006 were packed with events while work as county trustee continued by day. Campaign events and activities occupied evenings and weekends. Five candidates were on the ballot, four men and one woman. Election night was electric; I carried every precinct except one small one! It was unbelievable!

The work as county mayor is challenging but rewarding. Serving our citizens as Montgomery County mayor is not something I sought out as a career path. I earnestly feel that God has put me in this place at this time for a purpose. The county mayor serves on fifty-five committees; so meetings occupy a lot of my work schedule. These committees are largely working with department heads, elected officials, county commissioners, and appointed citizens to carry out the work of Montgomery County government. I have wonderful support people working with me to carry out the many duties of county mayor.

The Montgomery County mayor serves as the elected official over seventeen county department heads that are hired to carry out the mission of their specific departments. These department heads also have committees that make recommendations on procedures and improvements in their respective department.

Since being elected Montgomery County mayor, I have had the distinct privilege to work with numerous local, state, and federal government officials. Each year, I have served as part of the Citizens for Fort Campbell coalition, which lobbies for Fort Campbell maintenance and improvements as requested by the current general in command. Currently, I serve on the Tennessee Executive Committee for the Association of County Mayors as secretary. I was appointed by Governors Bredesen and Haslam to the State Energy Efficient Schools Council and currently serve on the executive committee of the Middle Tennessee Mayors Caucus.

My community-service activities include being a member and past officer of the Clarksville Rotary Club, receiving the Outstanding Rotarian Award in 2004-2005; graduate and alumnus of Leadership Clarksville and Leadership Middle Tennessee; recipient of the Clarksville Athena Award for outstanding female business professional in 2006. Also, I currently serve as a member of the Austin Peay State University President's Circle of Advisors and the Clarksville-Montgomery County School System Advisory Committee and am a member of the Immaculate Conception Catholic Church in Clarksville.

I am a life member of the National Association for the Advancement of Colored People (NAACP), Clarksville chapter. This past year, I was inducted into the Phi Kappa Phi Honor Fraternity at APSU for my contributions to education in our community.

I feel honored to have held positions of leadership in the Clarksville-Montgomery County community. Being able to bring people together for a common cause that has created progress in education, jobs, public safety, and recreation for people living and working in the Montgomery County area continues to steer my course.

This community is my home, and I am so proud of the path my life has taken. If someone had asked me when I was young what my aspirations were, I could never have come up with this, but I am blessed to be leading the county that I love. I can only hope that those who fill the county mayor's seat behind me love it and believe in this community as much as I do.

E-mail: mayorbowers@montgomerycountytn.org

33

Mayor Kim McMillan

(Clarksville, Tennessee)

Do unto others as you would have them do unto you.

WHAT ARE YOU COMPELLED TO DO?

If you've ever felt compelled to do something, something that you didn't really plan on or admit that you really wanted to do, you'll understand why I first ran for public office.

First, you have to understand that I am the product of teachers. My mother taught in the public schools and my father was a college professor. Although I was adopted as an infant in the State of Alabama, we moved around for my father's work. We ended up for my "growing up years" in Knoxville where my father was at the University of Tennessee. As the child of teachers, we were always involved in the community where we lived. PTO (or PTA as they were called back in the day) meetings were a way of life, just as parent-teacher conferences, planning days and constant library trips were. I learned to love learning and I learned the importance of making a difference in people's lives.

By the early 1990's, I had my own successful career. I had graduated from the University of Tennessee College of Law, practiced in a large Nashville firm and had moved to my husband's hometown, Clarksville, Tennessee, and begun a law practice with him. Our eventual firm, McMillan and McMillan (mine was the first name on the door!), had a wide-ranging client list. It was a terrific way to meet the people in my new home and to get involved. We had two small children and we were excited to be a part of a growing, family-oriented community.

Something in me wanted to give back. I wanted to make a real difference for the people I had come to know and love. And I felt compelled to run for office. So, anxiously and excitedly, I went to the Election Commission, picked up my nominating petition and was off and running. It was the easiest thing in the world to become a candidate! *Being* a candidate was a different thing altogether.

If you know anything about politics, you know that name recognition is a big deal in any campaign. If you are familiar with Clarksville, Tennessee, you've heard of Austin Peay State University. At the time I'm writing this, it's the fastest growing university in the State of Tennessee system and it's named for a famous Clarksvillian and one of the most beloved governors in Tennessee history. He was also the distant relative of my opponent in my first race.

Yes, in the campaign I felt compelled to run, I faced Austin Peay VI in Clarksville, Tennessee.

Uphill battle anyone?

Two things kept me running that race. First, I couldn't lose that feeling that this was something I was supposed to do. There was never a guarantee that I would win that election—there never is. But I knew I was supposed to try.

The second thing that kept running through my thoughts was one of my favorite quotes:

> If a man is called to be a street sweeper, he should sweep streets even as Michelangelo painted, or Beethoven composed music, or Shakespeare wrote poetry. He should sweep streets so well that all the hosts of heaven and earth will pause to say, here lived a great street sweeper who did his job well. ~ Dr. Martin Luther King, Jr.

I was a candidate for the Tennessee House of Representatives. Following Dr. King's admonition, I would take great pride in how I conducted my campaign. I made it a point to try and meet every single person in the District if possible. I knocked on thousands of doors, visited groups, shook hands, had my picture made and gave so many speeches I lost my voice. If I lost, it wouldn't be because I hadn't given it my all.

I won that first race and the next five. I had the honor of representing the people of Clarksville in the General Assembly for more than a decade. While I was there, I was involved in passing groundbreaking ethics reform legislation in Tennessee. I sponsored bills that would help address domestic violence in Tennessee and I helped to create and pass state budgets that affected every department and every resident in the state.

I'm proud of the work we accomplished while I was a member of the General Assembly. But I was never there to be proud of myself. I was there because I felt compelled to make a difference. I was there because people trusted me to represent them. That's a huge honor and a tremendous responsibility.

Those days weren't always easy and I learned to focus on what we could accomplish together and not how hard it was to do. I earned a reputation for consensus building and reaching across the aisle. That, for me, was the easy part. I'm always interested in new ideas and in improving the way government works. If I could give new legislators one piece of advice, it would be to care more about doing the work than getting credit for having done it. Indira Gandhi once said, "There are two kinds of people, those who do the work and those who take the credit. Try to be in the first group; there is less competition there."

During my time in the legislature, I was elected as the House Majority Leader. It was big news because I was the first woman to ever hold that post in Tennessee history. I spent twelve years in the House of Representatives and then left to be a part of the Governor's cabinet. After I left the Governor's cabinet, I knew I would return to public service but I had no idea where that knowledge would eventually lead.

One of the things I would encourage women to do is listen to that voice that is compelling them to act—even when you don't fully understand why. After fourteen years in state government, I needed to recharge, to take on a new challenge. For me, that's a good thing. I've talked with a lot of women over the years who feel as though they can't change their minds or their lives. Why not? Life is meant to be lived, to explore, to grow. It's hard to get a different perspective if your view never changes.

Fast forward to November 2010. There I was, watching the election results with my family, friends and supporters when the news was officially announced: I was elected as the first woman Mayor for the City of Clarksville. I thought I was stepping back from elected office. It turns out I was simply stepping into a new role.

Why after twelve years in the General Assembly and serving in other roles in state government would I want to run for Mayor? It's simple: I felt compelled to do it.

It didn't take me long to come to the conclusion that I am compelled to live a life of public service. I know the problems are big and the answers aren't easy. I know that I will rarely get complete support on the decisions I make. I also know that people look to me for answers that, quite simply, no human being could really be expected to have. But I also know that I have the opportunity to make a difference every day to the people who live and work in Clarksville, my "adopted" hometown. For me, that's important.

I also know that I am compelled to be a part of the solution. I can't just talk about the problems and wait for someone else to figure it out. When asked why she had taken on so many responsibilities as First Lady, Eleanor Roosevelt replied, "I could not at any age be content to take my place in a corner by the fireside and simply look on." I understand that sentiment completely.

I've been asked countless times how it feels to be the first woman to accomplish something. I've always answered that it's important to recognize that women can (and do) take on any challenge, any job, at all levels. The whole truth, I also explain, is that I have never asked anyone to vote for me because I am a woman. I want people to join me in this work because I am the best person for the job and I happen to be a woman.

On the other hand, being a woman in politics isn't always easy. Let me give you an example. I had just completed my first session in the House of Representatives. One of the last items of business was the appointment of a special committee that would be working over the summer to discuss campaign finance reform. I really wanted to serve on that committee even though I was one of the newest members of the General Assembly.

I was very excited to be appointed by the Speaker of the House to serve on that committee. It was a big opportunity for me and I worked hard to be prepared, especially for my first meeting. These meetings are held in "hearing rooms" and they are recorded. Frequently, the media will show up and video the discussions and the press is always around when the subject is campaign finance. That was the case during this first committee meeting. The room was flooded with media people, other members of the legislature, citizens and lobbyists. I was there early and took my seat where the other committee members, five other members of the House and six Senators, would be sitting.

(One thing I had going for and against me is that I looked really young. I was pretty young but I looked even younger. That's important to this story.)

The other members of the committee started to arrive, including the Chair, who was growing impatient that everyone hadn't arrived yet. In front of everyone, including the press, he harrumphed that the least "that intern" could do was fetch some coffee while he waited for the stragglers to arrive. "That intern" that he was pointing to was me.

Here I was, a proud new member of the General Assembly, ready to work, eager to serve the people of my district, and the Chair was calling me an intern. I was also the only woman assigned to the committee. I had two choices. I could angrily and arrogantly tell him to get his facts straight and invite him to get his own coffee. Or, I could do the last thing anyone expected. I chose option number two. Without a word, I got up and went to the outer chamber, located a pot of coffee, some cups, creamer, sugar, the works, and put them on a big tray. When I brought my impromptu coffee service into the hearing room, you could have heard a pin drop. Apparently while I was out getting coffee, his staffers were explaining that he'd just instructed the new Representative from Clarksville to get some coffee. I came back in the room with a smile on my face. I cheerfully handed out cups and offered coffee to everyone on the committee. The Chair never apologized. No one ever mentioned his gaffe during that meeting. And I never drew his attention to it. He called the meeting, to order and we moved right along.

For the rest of the time I served in the Legislature, I could count on him for support. If I needed a co-sponsor on a bill, he would work with me. If I needed advice from someone who had been there, his door was open. In the end, he was someone I would call a friend despite our rocky introduction.

Being a public servant isn't the only way to make a difference; in fact, some might say it's the hardest way to make a difference.

I'm reminded of a story I heard once about a young woman who was talking to her mother about how things her life was so hard. It seemed, she said, like should could never get ahead in any part of her life.

Her mother listened and then asked her daughter to follow her to the kitchen. Without a word, she filled three pots with water and placed each on the stove so they would boil. Again, without saying anything, she put carrots in the first pan, eggs in the second, and in the last she placed ground coffee beans. She let them sit and boil, all without ever saying a word. The daughter was so caught up in her own misery that she hadn't paid much attention to what her mother was doing.

After twenty minutes or so, she turned off the stove and put the cooked carrots, eggs and coffee in separate bowls.

She asked her daughter, "What do you see?"

The daughter, more frustrated than curious, answered, "I see carrots, eggs and coffee. Strange menu."

Her mother scooped out some carrots and told her daughter to feel them. Of course, they were mushy. The mother handed her daughter and egg and asked her to break it. When she peeled the shell, the egg was hard-boiled. Then the mother asked the daughter to sip the coffee. Finally, the daughter thought, something to enjoy. She took a sip and smiled at the rich flavor and smell.

Her mother, again, had fallen into an annoying silence. The daughter was patient for a few minutes and then asked, "Why did you do all this?"

Her mother explained that these three things, eggs, carrots and coffee, were like people. They all change when they're put in a little hot water. The carrots, for example, went from being hard and strong to mushy and weak. The eggs were initially fragile and runny inside. But the hot water made their insides hard.

"Some people react the same way," her mother explained, "when they find themselves in difficult times. The times change them and turn them into something completely different."

The daughter, now intrigued, asked, "What about the coffee?"

"The coffee, sweet child," responded the mother, "changed the water."

No matter what you do in life, you have a choice to be a carrot, an egg or coffee. You can let the challenges change you or you can change your environment.

I've been very blessed in my life to be able to do the work I feel compelled to do. What if I had not won that first race? What if I had not been elected Mayor? I am confident that I would find a way to be involved in our community. Why? Because I am compelled to be.

What are you compelled to do?

Are you answering that call? Trust me, you won't feel complete until you do, and when you do, the levels of success you reach will astonish you. I had no idea when I picked up that first nomination petition that I would eventually become the Mayor of Tennessee's fifth largest city. I just knew I was compelled to get in the race.

Contact Information:
kim.mcmillan@cityofclarksville.com

34

Minister Suzanna Reese-Wilson

This is the expression of a Leading Lady that can be seen through poetry. Women are strong, resilient, and always adapting to their environment. Life has many ups and downs, and it can take you on a journey that you will never forget. I thank God that He always gives us a word. Though the years go by, His Word always stands. I remember Isaiah 40:31, *"They that wait upon the lord shall renew their strength, they shall mount up on wings like the eagles, they shall run and not be weary, and they shall walk and not faint."* I can attest that God's love supersedes any trial that I have endured. Be encouraged and be blessed. This is my story behind my eyes: It all begins with a trip through time.

A Trip through Time

Time passes so quickly, and sometimes we forget the things that are precious to us. It is only when we are about to lose it, we realize that we never want it to go. The wind keeps blowing, and the silent tears keep falling. But when the tears dry up and the wind stops blowing, does time stand still? The clock ticks seconds, minutes, hours pass, and our love fades like the sand in an hourglass. Can we tip the glass over and start the journey again? Moments change like the ticking of a second hand. Can we take a trip through time? Remembering the love and passion we shared. Can we capture that shooting star that we left behind? Is it that time has gone too far ahead and we can't go back? Won't time stand still for a moment as we gaze at each other and see the pain that we've endured, the stress, the hurt, the anguish, and like a dim lit candle, the love that we share. Twinkling like the fire from a wood-burning fireplace. Let's take a trip through time and see if we can make time stand still as we gaze in each other's eyes and embrace in each other's arms. Warm and comfortable like the light from a bright candle flickering in the wind.

I realized that love can only be found in God, and once you fall in love with God, you can love yourself and others. Now I can truly say He is my all and all. I know that I am a strong woman and a king because He said that I am, and I believe His Word and that I can make it. God taught me how to trust and how to love again. He taught me what it meant to be a true woman.

A Woman

What do you see when you look at me. Look deeper, come closer, gaze into my eyes, and travel through my mind. Do you see fear in my eyes? Do you see pain that creeps into my mind? Can you see my heart bleed each time for a brother of mine that dies? Can you see the tears I fight off with light grins of peace? Can you bathe in my presence? Are you afraid of what my eyes reveal? Is the pain too deep? Is the grief too unbearable? Tell me my eyes tell you a story of my life. What is your story?

My story continues, and it lives on not just through me but also through my children. I am married, and everyone knows things are not always easy. But through it all, I learned that the essence of women is very important. The way she carries herself and the way she presents herself to the world. As I grew, I became more mature in life, and I knew that there was a purpose and a plan for my life. I have discovered that everything we do is not by accident but for a reason, and God is aware of it. Jeremiah 29:11 states, "For I knew the thoughts that I think toward you, saith the Lord, thought of good and not of evil to give you an expected end."

The Essence of a Woman

> Strong, proud, and virtuous a woman whose beauty is beyond rubies, and her inner spirit sparkles like newly shined diamonds. Her words are of wisdom and encouragement. She listens with a willing heart, and she gives beyond measure. She walks with a sense of assurance. Her smile glides across her face like the sun hides behind the clouds. And as the sky cradles the moon, she holds her family dear to her. The essence of a woman, virtuous, strong, and proud. She fears no one and accepts challenges as a new day. She never gives up but perseveres until the end. Her love flows through her like honey seeps from a honeycomb. The essence of a woman.

When I think of the things that God has brought me through, I begin to rejoice. In 2003 I was stricken with a deadly flesh-eating bacteria. I went to the emergency room because I was not feeling well. Then they took my temperature, and it was very high. However, they gave me Tylenol. It brought the fever down, and they thought they solved the problem. I went home, and two days later, I discovered that my skin was decaying. It was all black, and an awful smell was coming out. I called my gynecologist and went to see him. He said he had never seen such a thing. He then referred me to a surgeon and told me to go immediately, and so I did. Upon arriving at the surgeon, he took a look at it. He said to go directly over to the emergency room, which was across the street, sign in, and prepare for surgery. Within two hours of seeing this doctor, I was in surgery, and the end result was I had an open wound two inches deep and two inches wide next to my rectum. The doctor said it was a miracle I am alive today. So when I tell you God has a plan, He has a plan. It takes courage and strength to stand when obstacles are hard and seem unbearable, but that's when we can say, "Glory, hallelujah."

Glory, Hallelujah

Glory, hallelujah! Glory, hallelujah, to our Risen King, to our precious Lord I sing glory, hallelujah. I sing glory, hallelujah, when I am weak; I sing glory, hallelujah, when I am happy and my Savior's with me; I sing glory, hallelujah, because I know He will bring me through.

Now things have begun moving again, dreams unfolding new experiences, and seeing God move in my life. I think back to the time I was on my way to prayer; it was snowing, and the roads were a little icy. I began to go through the green light, and before I knew it, a young lady was unable to stop her vehicle and ran into me. The car spun and landed on the gravel median. Who cannot say that we serve an awesome God? Just two feet more and the car would have landed in oncoming traffic. My life could have been over, but God had a plan. He wanted me to share that though the storms come and go in our lives, we have to know who is the author and finisher of our faith. We have to make a conscious decision to love Him, believe in Him, and accept Him. Just think what can happen in a moment.

A Moment

A thought into eternity; a moment spent in darkness waiting for the enchanting light. One moment that will change life forever. A moment of peace, of resentment, and of happiness. A moment captures years in the making. Can you see it, touch it, and hold it? Will it exist in time; a second, a minute, an hour? A moment when I am trapped in time and embraced with all mankind, Your tender love, affections; and a moment to choose life or death. A moment to know that you cared and that you can fill every moment in my life.

God has been my rock, and even when I fell, He was there to walk with me and teach me. He showed up in times when I thought no one cared. He told me, "I will never leave you nor forsake you, and that's why you are never alone."

Never Alone

Though the way seems dark and the clouds cover your way, there is hope for a new day. The sun will rise, and the morning sheds new light. So don't give up. The night may come and hope is lost, but lean on the one who carried the cross. Strength is yours in moments of despair. Don't give up for you know He cares. Close your eyes and look to the sky, help is on the way. Remember He has not left you. Just open your heart, and He will fill the emptiness. Just give Him your hand, and He will take care of you. God will see you through, so know you are never alone.

I held on to these words, and I can truly say God never left me, and He is still guiding me day by day. He is my counselor, and I go to Him for direction, and I give Him praise because every time I turn around, God keeps on blessing me.

Every Time I Turn Around

Every time I turn around, He keeps on blessing me. God every time I turn around who makes the wind rustle the leaves? Who makes the rain fall to its knees. Every time I turn around I mess up, and who is helping me to clean up. Every time I turn around God allows the sun to rise and the moon to set on me. Murder, death, gunshots, sickness, and disease all pass by me because the Lord keeps on blessing me. Every time I turn around, the Lord has been good to me, and all I can say is thank you for blessing me.

Hallelujah, my testimony is very simply and true. John 15:17 states, "If ye abide in me and my word abides in you, ye shall ask what ye will and it shall be done unto you." What are you asking God for? What are your dreams and visions? God is listening, and he has an answer for you. Go to him boldly. Hebrews 4:16 says, "Let us therefore come boldly unto the throne of grace, that we may obtain mercy and find grace to help in time of need." We must know who we are and that is a king see (Rev. 1:6) and who we belong to (Gen. 1:27). Walk in your authority, and be the king that God made you to be. I thank God that because I have heard the Word, I believe the Word, and I am applying it to my life, and I continue to press for spiritual success.

Spiritual Success

Divine inspiration dedication educating oneself to the highest height in Christ's spiritual success, taking life to new dimensions and increasing visions of ultimate success. Spiritual success is at its greatest depth when observation, interpretation, and application have all come into the arena and they provide knowledge, wisdom, and understanding from the Almighty God. Spiritual success is a step in the right direction when Christ is guiding your path.

The story is never over, and there is always more to say. However, I want to leave you with this that may God forever change your walk to be a confident and a strong Leading Lady. May the words in this book resonate in your spirit, your heart, and your mind because out of the abundance of the heart, the mouth speaks, and you can speak death or life to every situation you encounter; so I close with this. I speak life over you, and God's blessings be multiplied in your life. AMEN.

Majesty Publications
"Featuring poems for all occasions"
Suzanna Reese-Wilson

E-mail: behindmyeyes30@yahoo.com

35

Monica Dunnagan

In your legacy, *you leave* possession, principles, *and* people.

Life is like a book, and you want it to be a good book to read.

Grace and peace be multiplied unto you through the knowledge of God, and of Jesus our Lord. Giving all diligence, add to your faith virtue; and virtue to knowledge; To knowledge temperance; and to temperance patience; and to patience godliness; To godliness brotherly kindness; and to brotherly kindness charity.

—2 Peter 1:2, 5-7, KJV

For These Things Should Begin with You

Hello, my name is Monica Dunnagan. I was born in Charleston, South Carolina, where my father was serving in the United States Navy; but I grew up in the small town of Picayune, Mississippi. I am married to my wonderful and supportive friend Roy, and between us, we have six wonderful children and eleven grandchildren. I say *eleven* because there will be a tiny addition to our family before this story goes to print. I am the author of a children's book entitled *Your Legacy*. *Your Legacy* was written in order to inspire children to learn more about their ancestors and provide them with a simple foundation to begin building their own legacy. The books is also intended to encourage parents, grandparents, teachers, and even siblings to spend quality time together learning about what their legacy means to them. *Your Legacy* is the first of a planned series of children's books that will also be accompanied with instructional workbooks in order to enhance the learning process. I am also a consultant and currently working out of Everett, Washington, on various commercial and military aircraft-engineering projects. My hobbies include anything that allows my creative abilities to shine through, such as painting, writing, crafting, and to also include martial arts and exercising. The biggest journey that I have embarked upon would be completing my PhD.

And This Is My Story

I find that one of the most difficult things that individuals will ever accomplish is to bring into the open something personal and very intimate, such as past life experiences. However, to accomplish such a task can be a healing agent as well as an inspiration to someone else who may be struggling with similar conflicts. Survival in the face of abuse, economic crisis, or even through the process of natural disasters becomes the key to individual success. Survival is a process we learn from many individuals who will impact each of us along our journey in life; the key to survival is how we respond to our lifelong lessons. Charles Darwin coined the theory survival of the fittest, and although some interpret his work to only refer to the animal species, it can also be applied to everyday life, in which, in order to survive we must equip ourselves with knowledge, good health, faith, and support from our family, friends, and our community. In addition, we must also find a way to pay it forward, or as I like to refer to it, giving back. Giving back to me is to encourage growth, strength, and faith to survive any challenge that we may cross on our personal journey through life.

I raised my two sons as a single mother! I am a survivor of spousal abuse! That statement in itself is a hard statement to make, yet it is also a positive one because I chose not to be a victim any longer. I am not a victim of spousal abuse but a survivor! Being a survivor or stating "I am a survivor" gives you a sense of I am taking back control over my life and my life choices. Moving from the status *victim* to the status *survivor* is the toughest part because it requires more than simply stating your choice; you have to act upon the choice that you made. I have often heard others say, "I would never place myself in that situation," or "If so and so tried to do that to me, this is what I would do," or "I would never put up with that." Sounds easy, but I am here to tell you that a person never really knows or understands what will actually happen when they are placed in such a situation. No one chooses to become the victim of abuse of any kind, but once a person is in that situation, you then have to make a choice. Do you remain a victim, or do you become a survivor?

First of all, when a female or male lives in an abusive home life, outsiders and even family are hesitant to become involved, including police officers, because it can become very dangerous, even life threatening. I am speaking strictly from my personal experience, and every situation has the potential to be different, but there are patterns that allow others to see similarities in different situations. This is where victims of abuse become isolated and take on the perception that nobody cares or there is no one to help them. This aspect becomes the control point that the abuser uses to manipulate and isolate their victim from outside interference. For the individual being abused, it becomes the loneliest place in the world to be. It is not enough to ask for help, because you could endanger the helpers' life; you have to be at a point in your life that you are willing to walk away from everything and never turn back. In some more severe cases of spousal abuse, that extreme also carries with it the threat of death, not only for the self but also for the children involved as well. At what point in the relationship can you stop and say, "I will put my life and the lives of my children at stake in order to become a survivor!"? God only knows that you will surely die if you stay, but you and your children could possibly die if you leave. You think these thoughts because this is what the abuser pounds into your head night after night! You are told, "You are worthless," "Nothing, no one comes to help because they do not care for you or those kids," and "I will kill you all if you ever try to leave!" I had come to that point in my life, and I knew that if my boys were to ever have an opportunity to live a life without hatred, I would have to take that chance! So for two days, I remember sitting unmoved in my chair while I stared at nothing, but I told myself over and over that we will die if we do leave now, and I knew in my heart that God had a better plans for us. It was time to go! It would take me the next twenty years to not feel like I was living in a shadow of fear! But now the only person I fear is God because it is His wrath and His wrath only that we are meant to fear.

Life remained full of sacrifices and hard work in order to create a new life while overcoming the fear that lived inside me. One small step at a time, I worked my way through raising my two sons and through accomplishing my associates degree from Poplarville Community College (PRCC) and then onto receiving my bachelor of science degree in psychology from the University of Southern Mississippi. However, being a single mother, I had to make choices that would allow my two sons to grow in a positive manner. I had no support from their father and often times found myself working two jobs in order to make ends meet. Even with a bachelor's degree, higher-paying jobs were hard to find. My degree did lead me to fulfilling opportunities, first working with children in a behavioral hospital, and then I was offered the opportunity to work at the Harrison County Sheriff's Department, where I finally felt my life turning around for the better. At both the hospital and the juvenile county facilities, I received the opportunity to work with children and adults who, for different reasons, found themselves displaced in society. Individuals who were either too young to care for themselves or suffering with mental and physical challenges. I believe the most saddening part of my work was to hear the stories that these individuals had to tell. When you think about a child in jail or a hospital, it is easy for others to assume that there is something wrong with them or that they are nothing but trouble, when all they really sought out of life was to be loved and cared for. There was one child in particular who made juvenile detention and boot camps his second home; he was seen and treated as a bad seed, so to speak. After working with him for some time, I finally asked him, "Why do you keep getting into trouble and returning to us?" This is what he said: "Because here I have a bed, food, clean clothes, and I am not outside in the cold, but most of all, because no one else wants me." As I began to ask the others the same question; most of the time, I received similar answers. That's when I knew more about God's plan for me. That was when I found such a blessing in volunteer work! I conducted volunteer work that allowed me to help others through their toughest times and simply let them know that they are somebody worth loving.

I have worked in outreach programs with children who chose to leave street gangs, children and women who had become victims of sexual abuse and had the desire to become survivors. I have conducted workshops on alcohol and drug prevention, as well as increasing teenagers' self-esteem. Teaching basic remedial classes for kids who have fallen behind in their skill level is one of the volunteer positions that I hold dearest to my heart. Simply watching kids work hard and to see that hard work pays off is indescribable. I even learned to run in the Country Half Music Marathon for the St. Jude's foundation. I have come to a point in my life that I do not feel complete unless I am involved in a nonprofit organization that teaches, encourages, and develops the skills of young children and adults. This is how I give back and how I pay it forward to my community.

I have worked in various organizations, from restaurant management to industrial manufacturing, and I always try to remember one thing: *never forget where you came from, and never lose sight of where it is you dream to be.* I live that philosophy in everything that I do, and I teach it every day. If a person is not able to love their self, if a person is not able to feel complete and whole within their own life, then how can they expect to help others? What is even more important is that as leaders of your own community, you need to be strong enough to understand what you can accomplish and what is beyond your capability. You can be the smartest person in the world, but if you do not know when to ask for help, then you have failed the person who looks to you for guidance. As leaders in our community or work environment, it is important for us to build an environment that others feel safe and secure in. Once this occurs, then they are free to learn, experience, and prosper under the guidance of great leaders. Leaders must always be careful in how to approach others, and always be supportive for it is a true honor to have others follow you! I find it a *blessing* from above to express positive change!

I have never stopped learning, and I have never stopped growing! I have obtained my masters in psychology with an emphasis in public administration, and I am currently working on my PhD in organizational psychology. My dissertation involves studies to further enhance our understanding of what makes a great leader, but most importantly, how great leaders influence and deal with diversity in the new era of contractual employees.

There are a great many influential people in my life: my two sons, my parents, teachers, and my *sifu* (sifu is my martial arts instructor); each and every one of these individuals teaches me that I am worth a lot more than words. God is my spiritual leader, and He will remain above all else; however, there is one person I cannot end this story without giving thanks to. Angella Banks, CEO and founder of Xcellence, Inc., a nonprofit organization that strives to encourage children, teenagers, and college students to become strong future leaders.

Angella has continued to place her faith in me, a faith that comes from a true believer's heart, one that no matter what you do, you could never let down. I received an e-mail from Angella one day, and it said, "Join Xcellence." I had no idea who she was, but when I reviewed her website, I knew that Angella was working toward a higher cause and I needed to work with her. Today, I am Xcellence's national member director; and together with all the regional coordinators and the local chapters, we work within our communities to promote education, growth, spiritual leadership, as well as encouragement for young adults to become the future leaders of our society. The year 2012 has ushered in a great many avenues for Xcellence; one of them includes a scholarship program entitled Book My Future, which provides for young college students the opportunity to obtain assistance with the increasing cost of book tuition. It is not enough to encourage young adults to attend college; with our economic crises, we must find ways to help them pay for their expenses; and through the scholarship, Xcellence is paying it forward for our future leaders.

What I find to be the most important thing to remember is that you are somebody; you have a world of knowledge and experience to offer others. I used to think that I had a community to give back to, but now I see that my community is the world in my backyard. I believe this concept because there is no limit to what each of us can accomplish if we set our minds to it. One of our greatest pop artists made the statement that if you want to change this world, then you have to start with the person that you see in the mirror. Change what you are, and make that change to mirror what it is you wish to see! That statement can confuse anyone, but if you think about it, you can only create a positive atmosphere if and only if you create that positive atmosphere to center around yourself first! Now it is possible to misinterpret that statement! That statement means only to change yourself in a positive way before attempting to lead others.

In summation, I know that I am human and subjected to faults, but those faults turn into life lessons only if we choose them to be. I once had a teacher who told me that if you do not make mistakes, then you are not learning. My life did not begin in a negative manner, yet somewhere on my journey, it did turn into something that no one should ever experience. No matter how long it took to turn that experience around, the most important aspect is that it did turn around. That life experience turned into a creative part of me that is set out to make a positive change on this world. This is your life. As I visited a church, I remember the pastor asking this: "If someone had to make a statement about your life, what would it be?" What is the one sentence that you would want others to say about you? What is your *legacy*? What will you leave for others to say? I want others to say that I never gave up and that I always did my best to make our world a better place to live in! That is my legacy!

I want to thank Angella of Xcellence, State Senator Mrs. Harper, Treva Gordon, as well as the other Leading Ladies who have come together to make this book a great success, for allowing me to be a part of this project! We can only be successful if we share our knowledge and our experiences in life! It is my hopes that the individuals who read this book gain a better perspective on their own life experiences. God bless each and every one of us on our life journey!

Monica Dunnagan

mdunnagan@xcellenceinc.com

36

Nicole R. Scott

(River Rouge, Michigan)

Illegal Fingerprints

What can you give me
that true love
has not already provided?

I've paraded in a world
where I've prostituted
north
south
east
and west.

Messed up
physically
emotionally
and spiritually.

Out of order
I was . . .

Illegally touched by
places
spaces
faces.

Surrounded with laces,
circled in sex tools
of money, materialistic toys, and charms.

Can you draw me near
as a newborn child
nurtured by its mother
unto you and whisper
I love you,
I forgive you,
I am the love
you have been searching for?

Can you offer me,
the way
the truth
and the light?

As I lie down
with this one

and that one,
I wonder . . .

If an x-ray light was placed on my body,
my womb,
I would be guilty of
decades and decades of fingerprints.

Prints of those who
do not know
recognize
or understand
the value of love.

The importance of loving a woman
one woman.
The value of loving a man
one man.

In my dreams,
darkness attempts to
draw and deceive
this temple into
sexual promiscuity.

But I laugh
and I watch
and I look
and I listen
and I fast
and I pray.

See your tricks, Satan
your lies,
the games,
and the charades
are over.

And you
you no longer have power,
but it is he who created the universe

>   who has all dominion
>   all power
>   power over you
>   and you
>   and
>   me.

It was the age of fourteen when I lost my virginity and became pregnant. I can still remember overhearing the conversation my stepfather had with my mother. He was shouting that I could not stay at the house if I was pregnant. This was a very devastating situation for me, not to mention that I had just found out that my biological father was a stone-cold drug addict. The family problems continued to emerge, from disagreements with my parents, to me running away from home. I can still recall the moment during ROTC practice. I remembered the principal wanted to see me in her office. I remembered explaining to the principal about the problems that were going on in our home and how these issues began to affect my progress in high school. Looking for love and a way to escape the problems I had, I began having unprotected sexual relations with those who said they love me. The more I had sex, the lower my grade point average was. I graduated from high school with a 1.9 GPA. My self-esteem was very low, and I devalued, degraded, and deluded myself into believing that every man I had relations with loved me.

Soon, I graduated with an associate's degree in fornication and pursued a bachelor's degree in adultery with a married man. I stayed in that degree program for about seventeen years. Why? Because I wanted man's love and not God's. I knew who God was, but I didn't have a personal, intimate relationship with Him.

One day, I woke up after an episode of being hurt and playing the harlot. I told God that I wanted to give everything that I've been giving to men to Him. All of my time, love, my body, thoughts, and praises unto Him. I wanted to be intimate with God. I felt that the Lord would appreciate me more than any man.

My walk with God was not an easy one. I kept backsliding into adultery with a married man, got pregnant, felt alone, helpless, and kept dating the same types of men that left me brokenhearted and lonelier than I was before. I became depressed and felt that I was not good enough for anyone. I believed that God was punishing me for all my wickedness and sinful nature. After some time had passed, I went to church, and I remembered a preacher was preaching and asked us as a congregation if we all knew what our names meant. Clearly I had no idea what my name meant, and so I called my mom, and she could not remember. So finally, I got on the Internet and looked up what my name, *Nicole*, meant. It means "a victorious people." I immediately began to cry and pray and told myself that I was a king's kid, a royal priesthood, a victorious woman, a Proverbs 31 woman, and I got back on the road to God. It was a path that required faith, honesty about who I was, and trust on my part. So I turned from my wicked ways with a repentant and contrite heart and began seeking after God. I found the Lord in prayer, writing, praises, thoughts, and of course, through His Holy Spirit. He healed all the hurts and pains in my heart as I continued to delight myself in Him and His Word. I would admonish everyone to emerge themselves in God. He knows the very essence of your being, and He will give you the desires of your heart. I PROMISE YOU! I don't care what you've done. God is a forgiving God, a saving God, a merciful God, a just God. He is not a respecter of persons. If he can clean up a wretched life like mine, what more do you think God will do for you? He is the only way. The Word of God says we should cast all our cares upon Him for He cares deeply for us. If you are a drug dealer, prostitute, liar, thief, idolater, adulterer, REPENT! God is waiting for you to come to Him.

As I continued to walk with the Lord, He began showing me the beauty of Him and how the gifts and talents He blessed me with played an important role in His kingdom. So I started confessing scriptures and positive words over my life because I'm in the *now season*! A season in which the Lord, my God, is digging and dunging me; where He's uprooting old things and fertilizing me for new things to grow. As Christ continued to do a new work in this temple, I started confessing scriptures like "No weapon formed against me shall prosper" and, "Greater is he that is in me than he that is in the world," and positive words like "You will become a successful business owner, your name means victory, you are victorious." So "a man **thinketh** so is he" is the Word of God, so why not speak positive and prophetic words over your life?

The message of this testimony is to admonish fathers who have daughters to spend quality time with them. Get to know their likes and dislikes. Learn their dreams, goals, and aspirations and help them to pursue these. Take every opportunity that you have, and tell your daughter how much you love her and how special she is. That way, you prepare her mind, give her confidence, and prepare her path for excellence in God's love. She will know truly if a man loves her by his actions, and she will have you as a father to look to as an example as to how a man is supposed to treat her. Furthermore, I admonish our fathers to teach our sons how to treat our women by being an example as to how you treat your wives. The Word of God says that we should love our wives as Christ loves the church. It is our responsibility as parents to set examples for our children.

For those who don't have children, you can adopt. Join a boys or girls club, be a mentor at your church, or even take on some of your relative's children. We have to do our part and spread God's Word and let every child know that they are loved no matter what the situation or circumstance is. It's our responsibility to spread God's love to all of His children. We will be held accountable for what we do and what we don't do.

I truly know that God loves me. Not just because He sent His Son, Jesus, to die on the cross for my sins, but because he knew that I wanted to be loved desperately and to give that same love to a person who desired to be in a committed relationship as much as I did. God was just waiting for me to give my all unto Him. The loneliness and yearning that I felt was God's way of saying to me that He wanted me closer to Him. I thank God that He saved me and kept me safe from sexually transmitted diseases that unprotected sex can give. It was the Lord, my God, who kept me when I was sexually assaulted in a dating relationship. I repented for my actions on the matter, forgave myself and all parties involved, and began to look at myself and think about who I was in a more positive aspect. When I talk to the Lord, He reminds and assures me that although I had those traumatic experiences, He is still calling me to do a greater work in Him and drawing me closer to Him. I thank God for looking past all my sins, forgiving me, and meeting my need.

My name is Nicole R. Scott. I was born in Highland Park, Michigan. I am a single parent of a twenty-year-old son, a business owner of Victory Given Business Driven, and a self-published author of two poetry books entitled *Poetry from the Heart* and *Can You Handle My Truth?* In my spare time, I enjoy listening to jazz, going to concerts and plays, and traveling. I'm a retired police officer from the Detroit Police Department, and an army veteran from the United States Army and the Army National Guard. I have an associate degree in applied science from Wayne County Community College in Detroit, Michigan, and a bachelor's degree in criminal justice with a minor in communications from the University of Michigan in Dearborn. Currently I'm writing *Making It off of Broken Pieces*, which is a biography about my life, and a book of poetic prayers. In the fall of 2013, I will launch the stage play *Making It off of Broken Pieces*.

I have many scriptures that I love, but I feel that the ones befitting for my life are the following scriptures:

> If My people, who are called by My name, shall humble themselves, pray, seek, crave, *and* require of necessity My face and turn from their wicked ways, then will I hear from heaven, forgive their sin, and heal their land. (2 Chron. 7:14, Amplified Bible)

> But seek (aim at and strive after) first of all His kingdom and His righteousness (His way of doing and being right), and then all these things taken together will be given you besides. (Matt. 6:33, Amplified Bible)

> Keep *and* guard your heart with all vigilance *and* above all that you guard, for out of it flows the springs of life. (Prov. 4:23, Amplified Bible)

> For in Him we live and move and have our being; as even some of your [own] poets have said, For we are also His offspring. (Acts 17:28, Amplified Bible)

A Love Poem to the Father

As you satisfy my very soul
I quench, thirst, and hunger
for you as the goal.

Its veil of truth
stretches and fastens itself
around the globe,
yet your love is not conditional
but unconditional underneath your holy robe.
This spirit shouts unto you as my hero
through a Christian race
leaving behind the worldly zeroes.

Extending the arms of grace and keeping them
stretched out when I turned away,
never did you leave my side or allowed me to stray.

Night after night I cry, lay, and say,
how easy it would be to fall in love

with you day by day.

I can see clearly why I seek
for us to date exclusively,
to lift me up and keep me
committed unto you profusely.

Knowing there are things needed to instill
in me for preparation to marriage,
I wait patiently on you to arrive
with the groom, horse, buggy, and carriage.

The light in times of darkness,
my night and shining armor
in times of saving.

How beautiful is the smile greeting me every day,
when I say, Good morning, Daddy
or Good morning, Jesus.

A God who never throws the past in my face
but in the sea of forgetfulness
and urges me to continue the race.

As I meditate on the goodness to fly like a dove,
the embracement of your soft arms,
sweet words, reminds me of how much I am loved.

And though the storms may come,
I know God that on the contrary
you give me strength enough to say
this is only temporary.

Every struggle
Every storm
Every fear.

Constantly I am reminded that
you are always near.

Long ago I broke your commandments

and therefore I did not know love,
but I love you, Lord.

I love you ...
not just because you died on the cross
not just because you conquered hell
not just because you rose with all power
not just because you are long suffering

But ...
because you are holy
because you are faithful
because you are merciful

My secret place and refuge
you are
you are.

The redeemer and restorer
so far
so far.

The countless hours spent with you, Father
I see change
I see growth
I see trust
I see faith
I see your love
I see ...

You!

In conclusion, it's vital in every human being that we have Christ in our lives and a personal relationship with him. He is the source of our being. Although it took some time to get to where I am today with God, I invite those who don't know the Lord to pray, seek God, and ask Him to come into your life. When you pray unto Him, exercise your faith; it pleases God. There is nothing to stop me now that I have Jehovah-Jireh. I die daily to myself in order that I may hear from God. I'm stronger, wiser, and I grow in Him daily. So today, you choose. Either get busy living for the Lord or get busy dying for the devil. I leave you with this last poem entitled

And the Winner Is

Often times we run a race
yet we have not received
proper instructions and training
to take on obstacles.

As a people, we jump-start
the event and forget to pace
ourselves in water intake.
Esther put her life on the line
for her people
waiting in faith and obedience.
She married King Xerxes
to save a Jewish race,
and the winner is . . .

Martin Luther King had a dream
and the vision came to pass
in freedom
unity
and perseverance
and the winner is . . .

The power of faith, hope, and love
three artists
three spirits
three disciples
and the winner is . . .

Sometimes our feet needs
to take us to different places,
but along the way our vision
becomes cloudy, which allows us
to stumble through mudslides
and sink in quicksand.

Even in suffering
we must continue to move
the king allows us to go through some things,
but like the songstress says,

"I got the victory."

As we continue to press to the mark,
never forget the creator
your children
your family
always strive to win souls with a spark.

Today I stand
educated
retired
poetic
energetic
modeling material
and the winner is . . .

It's you
It's you
and you
and you
and
me!

May God continue to bless all of you!

Father God, in the name of Jesus, I pray, O God, that You will touch and move in the lives of those that read this testimony today, especially the unsaved. Father God, I know that it is Your will for all men to be saved; and so I ask, O God, that you will save all those who seek after You and who desire to know who You are. Lord, You said in Your Word that if we confess with our mouths and believe in our hearts, we would be saved. Father, I lift You up in the name of Jesus. You are holy, awesome, faithful, and a loving God. You said that if You be lifted up, You would draw all men unto thee. I ask, O God, that You draw the single mom, single dad, the backslider, the one who suffers from health afflictions, the bank robber, murderer, O God, I pray that You will touch and change their lives for the good. I pray that you will be glorified, in Jesus's name, amen!

Contact Information:
Nicole R. Scott
E-mail: MsNicole42@gmail.com

37

Omni Mandela Camilla Walker

(Clarksville, Tennessee)

Don't allow people, places, or things sway your reaction because God is looking at your reaction!

My name is Omni Walker. I was born in Cincinnati, Ohio. I graduated from the Great Central State University with a bachelor of arts degree in mass communications. I am currently in graduate school at Academy of Art

University, studying fashion merchandising. I am a business owner; I have an online graphic T-shirt and tutu skirts called Tahirah Style and I am also a personal stylist. I am a Leading Lady.

I am thankful for the testimonies and the trials that I have gone through because without them, I would not have been the person I am today. I am the oldest of four from my mother's side and the fourth child of ten on my father's. I am the only child between my mother and my father. At the young age of sixteen, I graduated valedictorian from PACE High School in Cincinnati, Ohio. I was self-motivated to get out of Mother's house, where I did not feel loved or safe. At the age of eight, my cousin would come into my room and touch me in the middle of the night. I told my mother. She talked to him, but he still remained in the home. This should never be dismissed because it was a relative, but this was something that I dealt with nightly. Sometimes I would try to sleep through it so I could escape it. The abuse did not stop there. I was not always the fashionista I am today; my hair was never done, and my clothes were not the best. Kids are cruel; they pick on me, called me black and ugly. My cousin called me scratch-up dent-up girl. I had no self-esteem; it seemed like I was not beautiful to anybody.

School was not the easiest for me. I could not read or write, which made me even more a target of abuse. I was put in special-education classes, and I had to have an Independent Education Program (IEP). Honestly, this is the greatest thing that could have ever happened to me. It gave me the extra help I needed and gave me confidence and also an outlet. My special education teacher made me start a journal. At first I did not want to; I thought it was pointless. I did not know how to read, and Hooked on Phonics did not work for me. I truly believe that practice makes excellence because I began reading and writing everything it soon came naturally to me. I cannot remember her name, but if she is reading this, I thank you for your patience. After mastering reading and writing, learning became fun for me again. Like when my grandpa taught me to ride a bike and also when he taught me to tie my shoe. I love that man more than he knew; he was my hero. He absolutely do no wrong in my mind. After he whopped me for lying, I still loved on him after. He would take me on long walks, and we would talk about anything. He always said he loved me and cared about me. When he passed away when I was nine, my world crumbled; my hero was gone, and I had no one to talk to who understood my imagination and no one to walk with. Soon after his passing, my grandmother moved in with us. She and I became closer; we talked about Grandpa, which helped me to cope with the pain. At his funeral, I found out that praise dancing was his favorite. Seeing it, I thought it was the most powerful way to get God's attention. I soon began praise dancing, which allowed me to release sadness and feel like I was closer to my grandpa.

I enjoyed church, especially singing. I did not understand shouting; like all children, it scared the mess out of me. Preaching bored me, did not interest me at all. But I could not wait to go to practice to learn different moves. But no matter where I went, I would get bullied; I never understood it. After telling my mom consistently that they were picking on me, we stopped going to that church. Always being picked on made me sad, which soon turned into anger, which also soon became a huge problem with my siblings.

Being the oldest sibling is not easy. Your steps are followed, and it can either cause pain or happiness. In my case it was pain and motivation. Being the oldest child usually means being the test child. My mother would punch me in the chest, call me out of many names, or just plan not talk to me. My sister Gabrielle is exactly the opposite of me and was praised for it. It irritated my soul. I wanted to know why was it that every time I did something wrong, I was punched, but she got a mere talking to and sent on her way. I became angry with my mother and jealous of her relationship with my sister relationship. I was the oldest child; I should have bonded with my mother, right?

My mother had married and had embraced her three stepchildren with open arms, but I felt no love from her or my new father. At the age of thirteen, I had enough of the lack of relationship, and I acted it out. I thought it was okay to hit, yell, and curse at my sisters when they did wrong because it was done to me. That was the worst thing I could have ever done because it caused a strain on our relationship till this very day, and I would get beat up even more by my mother for hitting them. I felt like she protected them more than she protected me. I felt as if I meant nothing to her and she dealt with me simply because my father did not want to be a father.

By this time my grandmother had passed away, and I felt completely alone. I became suicidal; I would take pills and even try to cut myself. I felt that everybody I loved and who loved me back was leaving me. I would purposely rebel and have an "I don't give a —" attitude to match it. My mother and I went head-to-head almost every day. I did not care, and she did not care to figure out why. My mother was a provider, and she also made it possible that I visit Europe, Hawaii, Bahamas, and about seven other states. At the age of thirteen, my mother also taught me and my siblings how valuable being a virgin was by giving us all the Americanized African ceremony called the Rites of Passage.

A year later, I was sexually active. Finally I felt somebody wanted to listen to me, hug me, kiss me, and love me. I had a lot of meaningless relationship that did not last long. I continued this behavior while I was in college at the age of sixteen. I thought I had the right to do what I wanted because I felt alone. My mother had moved to Clarksville, Tennessee, on my second week at Central State University. I believed it was time to take care of myself and figure things out on my own and just use my mother for money, because talking to her about how I was doing was pointless; she did not care. I carried on with this behavior until I woke up one night out of nowhere and began to count my sexual partners. I became instantly embarrassed. The things I had been taught about my value all began to smack me in the face. I decided then to get my life right. I joined Daughters of Nia Anaya, a sisterhood, on my sophomore year; and I meet my sister, who during our process of becoming a part of the organization, had done a complete transformation from being a lesbian to being on fire for God. I needed to get back to that, so I went to church with her. The message was on point, and coming down my street, I joined Church of Judah Family Worship Center in Xenia, Ohio, that day. I began to reading God's Word and understanding. I wanted to be pure again and keep my body holy for my husband like I was taught by my mother. I began my journey of begin a Christian. I struggled to follow the rules; I had got into such a routine opposite of what authority said that it was natural for me. I would become convicted for messing up, knowing all God wanted to do was love me. I had stopped having sex, but I began partying, drinking alcohol, and smoking weed. I praised God every Sunday and acted like a heathen Monday through Saturday. I thought I was sneaking, but the fact is at every party, I would take pictures or put things on Facebook. My pastor, Tina, came to me and asked me to take them down because I am a king's kid, and I should act as such. I did what she asked, continued to go to parties but dodged the pictures. I was off and on with having sex because God could not fill this hole of abandonment like I wanted Him to, so I went back to what I knew. I would talk to people at my church about my problem, but it seemed to me that they had passed me and was on another level with God, so I struggled with this in my own mind and began to separate myself from them.

I began dating this guy, and he was a sweetheart, but he had just as much or more baggage than me. I just wanted him to love me, and he did just that. I was sinking in sin with him because I could not relate to church people, and my friends said it was okay. I never really liked me still; even though men wanted me, I did not like me. I made sure when I got my hair done that I kept a swoop over my right eye because I did not like that side of my face. I did not love myself or value myself. I could not see that I was fearfully, wonderfully made, and marvelous are the works, and my soul did not know it at all. The enemy knew how to attack me, and he did it very well. One day while I was looking through my pictures, the young man I was dating with told me that I needed hair to be cute. He cut me deeper than he ever would have known, but that was what I needed for God to move. I had gotten a quick weave that I kept in for months. I went to Tennessee for Christmas break 2009 and had my cousin, the hairstylist, take my hair down.

When she got the weave out, my hair was so damaged that she had to cut my hair into a fade. I had to start from scratch. I begged my cousin to make a wig. I went to Ohio to spend New Year's with my godmom. I was comfortable around her, so I walked around the house with the wig off; but when people were around, I would quickly put it on. She watched me do that a couple of times, and one day when it was just me and her in the house, she told me I looked better without the wig because it really showed my face it reminded her of when I was a baby. Those words planted a seed in that deep womb that he had cut. I began to look at myself in the mirror and see my beautiful face for the first time. She even talked me into getting color because it would make my face pop. Her influence helped me see me for the first time. I thank God for the seed she planted because without that seed, I would have never made it through this trying time or the worst storm of my life. I went back to school with "I am beautiful" attitude, and the India Arie song "I Am Not My Hair" was my theme song. I went back to church, and my pastors had to take a double take because they did not recognize me.

At church that night, we had a back-to-school revival. Pastor Tina's husband, Pastor Jones, is a prophet of God and spoke into my life that night. He told me that he could hardly recognize me and that God was starting something new and that I would be a fashion designer who would make clothes for girls with low self-esteem because I knew how to reach them. I felt like I was being downloaded into and something on the inside of me was being awaken. I was on fire for God like never before. I began sketching, and I named my company Tahirah Style. *Tahirah* means "pure," and I wanted everything that I created for my company to be pure and pleasing to God. I cut off that young man and began to seek God again and praise dancing. I even did the Miss Virtuous Pageant that Pastor Tina had held the year before. I won second place, but it was still a great experience, and I did feel I was God's wife.

But still I had blemishes that I could not hide. During the pageant, I began dating a guy. I soon became pregnant with twins at nineteen. He and my mother told me to get an abortion. He didn't speak to me for the first four months, and my mother stressed me out. My pastors loved me through it all; they covered me. He came back to me and apologized for leaving; I instantly took him back. A week later, I had a miscarriage. This was the worst thing that could have ever happened to me. I fought so hard to keep them, and then God allowed them to die. I could not take it; the doctors said they were healthy, but twins are a high risk. I could not understand why God allowed it. I hated God for it. The guy soon showed his true colors again and left. My godmother gave me words of encouragement, but it still did not stop the pain even though she also had a miscarriage and could relate to me. I felt that she could not relate because she had three children of her own and God had stripped me of both of my children. I tried to I handle it on my own, but I could not. I tried to kill myself again, but it did not work. When I finally allowed God to love me and heal me through the storm, I became stronger. God gave me the motivation to get up and go to class. With God I was able to graduate a year later from Central State University. I still have my moments when I would think about my children and cry, but I think about all my accomplishments. I graduated on time from college, I started my company, I am able to provide for myself and not have the struggles of being a single parent with two children. I am also able to focus on goals of being a high-end fashion designer and go to graduate school without the worries of not being a great parent. Now I see the miscarriage as a blessing because I have absolutely have no ties to that man, and I am free. I recently have moved back with my mother, and it was rough for the first three months, but we finally got to the root of the problem, and we are closer than ever. I apologized to my sisters, and we are closer than before.

This is why I believe you should never allow people, places, or things affect your reaction because I could have handled each of my situation different, but I allowed anger to control everything. I'm not saying that everything would have been perfect and I would have never made mistakes, but I do believe that a lot of things that I went through could have been prevented. But I give God praises for a praying grandmother; her prayers covered me when I could not cover myself. I am thankful now that I can speak to you and say you're beautiful because God said, "You're fearfully and wonderfully made," and God is not a man that He should lie. It's okay to be different; know that you are the best you there is because God did not create no one else in the world like you. You are perfect in God's image and likeness. If you don't believe anyone loves you, know that God loves you and I love you. Never be afraid to be you.

Contact Information:
Facebook: http://www.facebook.com/AllFreedomQueen
Twitter: https://twitter.com/tahirahstyle
Website: tahirahstyle.webs.com
E-mail: omnimcwalker89@gmail.com

38

Pastor Diana S. Washington

But Jesus beheld them, and said unto them, With men this is impossible; but with God all things are possible.

—Matthew 19:26, KJV

Behold, I am the LORD, the God of all flesh: is there any thing too hard for me?

—Jeremiah 32:27, KJV

My name is Pastor Diana Washington, and I was born in Blytheville, Arkansas. I was raised in Dillon, South Carolina. I graduated from high school there. Growing up in the church, we were taught to fear and honor God. As a child, we attended New Jerusalem Holiness Church. My mother was a praying woman. She always made sure that we understood that God was our source. God always provided for us.

I left home after graduation at the age of eighteen years old. I stayed in Trenton, New Jersey, for one year and later lived with my sister in Newark, New Jersey, for two years. I joined the military, where I served for eight years. I had several jobs (referred to as MOS, military occupation specialty), from supply clerk, clerical work, and later food service as my secondary MOS. I loved and enjoyed working in the army. I took great pride in serving my country. I was blessed to travel throughout the world by way of military and preaching. I held the highest Physical Training (PT) Award until I ETS (Expiration Term Service) from the army.

I met my husband, Robert Washington, while on my first permanent-duty station. After a long three-year courtship, we married in September 1980 while on orders in Korea. I had to leave for six months to go to Seoul, Korea, and he later joined me. This is where my journey began, where the Lord saved me while waiting on my husband to arrive. I am so blessed and thankful that today we have five children and ten grandchildren.

While in Korea, several girlfriends and I were preparing for a night out to go clubbing and dancing. When we split to get dressed, I was left with the left-handed cigarette (known as marijuana or reefer) to roll up; and while rolling it up, I decided to set aside one for myself. When I got ready to light it, I could feel a very strong breath blow the match out. I attempted three times. It would not light. I checked out all the windows, and there was no draft. I didn't understand where this was coming from. On the third attempt, again it was blown out and a voice spoke to me, "Why die when you can live?" At that moment, I found myself on the floor calling on Jesus, and the most wonderful feeling came over me. I was cleansed. As I continued to praise God, the young ladies came back for me. When I opened the door, I began to tell them that Jesus was real and how he had visited me. They called me crazy and thought I was high off the left-handed cigarette. I gave them everything back, including the one that was set aside for me. I told them I was high off Jesus.

As I continued to minister, His joy kept flowing in my life. I let my friends know that God is real. It was the most beautiful thing that ever happened to me in my life. God led me to attend Christian Man Service Center, a church where Roy and Ann Humphries were the pastors. I was baptized and filled with the Holy Ghost. My friends were also led to the Lord at this church after they observed my life, and asked questions of me, they were eventually saved. They witnessed God moving in my life and how He delivered me from smoking a pack and a half of cigarettes per day. Because God saved and delivered me so quickly, it was hard for even Christian people to accept that God immediately took all the smoking, cursing, drinking, and everything away from me. Just like that, God took it all away from me. I no longer had the desires. I was instantly a new creature, now delivered and set free. After my transformation, my friends Anita and Barbara were saved. They knew that God's hand was upon me.

It was in Korea that God also began dealing with me about ministry. As a woman, I faced many issues about my calling into the ministry. I would ask God, "Why me, and what about my husband?" I was struggling with women preachers and being called to preach. I asked God, "Don't you understand that I am a woman?" I could not understand. I was always told little girls do not preach. One night while my husband was lying there sleeping in bed, I wondered, *Why didn't God call him?* Because I was told that women were not called to preach, I struggled with that. Like me, many women called by God have struggled with the same issue. However, God gave me a ministry, a Midnight Witnessing Team. I told my husband about this ministry. My husband replied, "No wife of mine will be out witnessing to anyone in the night." Wanting to be in order with God and my husband, I prayed about it. God spoke and said, "Trust Me and obey Me." As I was preparing to go out to witness, my husband locked the door. At this time, the power of God took over my husband so strong. My husband began to jump up and down as the power of God literally shook him up and down that he cried out, "Yes, Lord!" After God released him, my husband told me I could go and do whatever God wanted me to do and had his blessings. At this moment, it was Elder Washington's spiritual awakening. It later led him to seek God more, and he was later filled with the Holy Ghost in Germany. He was on fire for the Lord.

One day, after I left my apartment and went to open the elevator, there stood the same two ladies I planned to party with in Korea. They were now saved and running for the Lord. They told me that God had led them as well to the Midnight Witnessing Team. We were all praising God. Although neither of us had spoken to one another, coincidently I noticed that we were all wearing the same color of clothing as we were led to go out to witness that night. The anointing of God was upon us all very strong. We would go out in threes, and many miracles followed us as we obeyed the Lord.

God used us to show His glory to many people. One night as we went out to witness, God led us up to a big flight of stairs; and when we got to where we were going, God instructed us there what to do. I knew God was leading us because it was in a place where no one would have thought to look. When I looked around, there was a young man who was about to commit suicide. I opened my mouth as God ministered through me. The man said that he knew God sent us. We led him to the Lord. The next day he went to church. Another time, there was a boy born with no fingers; and he came to us and asked if God can heal him. God led me to pray for him, and his fingers formed right before our very eyes. He came back the next night looking for us, and we were not there. He later brought his mother to church.

The Midnight Witnessing Team served for three years in Korea until I departed. The church was overflowing. I returned to the states and was stationed at Fort Carson, Colorado. When I arrived, I needed to make housing arrangements. The anointing was still very strong upon me. While in the process of establishing my living arrangements, God was still moving, and people began telling others about the Good News. People whom I had witnessed to along the way soon began gathering at my apartment. God was moving. I was led to a church there called House of Prayer under the leadership of Bishop and Mother Emma Harp, where I worshipped and continued to evangelize and minister until my departure back to Germany.

My ministry continued in Germany. I was led to Christian Outreach Fellowship Church under the leadership of Pastor Charles and First Lady Debra Moss. While there, I went through many trials. I later realized that this was all in preparation of a new level in ministry. God says, "I will not give you more than you can bear." I eventually became the pastor of this church. For five years, I served as pastor in Germany, where miracles and the power of God continued to operate highly. You know, God has a sense of humor, because most of my members were men. God continued to move.

I was finally brought to Clarksville, Tennessee, and was stationed at Fort Campbell, Kentucky. I had hoped not to pastor anymore. I also begged God not to send me to Clarksville. I heard how cruel it was to be a woman preacher in this town. God let me know that He had not released me from the calling of a pastor. I had several run-ins with certain men of faith in this community. One male pastor in particular approached me and my husband concerning me being a pastor. I believe that I addressed the situation as God led me to do so. I since have had no more problems from this pastor. Today there is a great deal of respect between the two of us.

I met other women pastors in the community; one in particular personally came to my hotel room to meet me because of a good pastor friend in Germany who had informed her of my arrival. I thank God for that pastor. Another female pastor I met opened fellowship to me, and being a new pastor, I appreciated that. To this day I still fellowship with both pastors. I began to minister, and after accepting the fact that I was going to live in the city, God began to open doors for me. There was a local male pastor who helped me a great deal. He blessed me with the furniture for my church and helped me in other ways too. We moved into his old building. This pastor gave me a Word from God, saying God had not released me from my position of being a pastor. I was pregnant at this time. I said to God, "If I am to pastor, I will need a building, and it will have to be furnished." God moved. I am thankful for that pastor who obeyed God and blessed me. Now all I had to do was to move in and preach.

Being a street preacher, I had a burn in me to preach. I was set on fire. I was high off Jesus. "Be not drunk with strong wine, but with the spirit" (Eph. 5:18). The name of my church is called Remnant of God Outreach Ministries in Clarksville, Tennessee. As I continued with the ministry, God added to the church. We started a tent ministry years later. Since then, healing and deliverance have taken place. Cancer patients healed. The power of God moves greatly in our church. I am thankful for my faithful members, church mother, and armor bearer. I am thankful for each and every one of them and their support.

I have preached in many women's conferences. I also have met people along the way who I thought were my friends. I have had my share of life's ups and downs. I have had people to turn on me, but I continued to show love. I will continue to love others just as God loves me. God gave me a message in Germany, years before I preached it in Clarksville; it is entitled "Birthing Forth the Word." This message came to me when I was discouraged about my calling as a woman pastor and how men were speaking against me. God began to minister to me about how he used Mary to bring forth His living Word, which was His Son, Jesus Christ. John 1 reads, "In the beginning was the Word." God did not have to use Mary, but He entrusted her with His Holy Son.

As God began to minister to me, he asked me, "How can you carry the Holy Son of God and not preach My Word?" Not only did He use a woman, but He also used her to bring forth the Holy Son of God and raised Him into His manhood. I would like to say to all women everywhere, you are worth something. According to Luke 1:28, you are blessed among women. So stop trying to prove that God called you and start walking in it. You're walking in your calling. John 4:11 says, "Believe Me that I am in the Father, and the Father in me: or else believe Me for the very works sake." According to Galatians 3:28, God says that there is neither male nor female in Christ. God does not discriminate. Our worst enemy is sometimes other women. At times, we can be very cruel to other women who are called into the ministry. Sometimes women tear you down because they don't think very highly of themselves. I pray for these women and that they will know their worth as they look closer at the birth of Jesus. You are somebody in Christ Jesus.

I would like to say to all women, love yourselves, your husband, and your family. Keep God first because God is love. In the past few years, I had to trust God. There were times when I felt alone. I never had a lot of female friends, and those whom I entrusted to be my friends had proven false. So during these times, I had to trust God. I found out that I cannot have a better friend than God. Some people have only come around just to see how bad things are, but God says in His Word, Psalms 110:1, that He will make your enemies your footstool.

No matter how bad the situation seems or what trials or tribulations you will endure, God says that He will give you no more than you can bear, and I have found Him to be faithful to His Word. We must trust God (Prov. 3:5).

Whatever you pray, believe God, and don't doubt in your heart. With God, all things are possible (Mark 9:23).

We must remember to show forth love in spite of. Jesus tells us to love one another (John 13:34). For he that loveth not his brother whom he hath seen, how can he love God whom he hath not seen? (1 John 4:20).

Pray for your enemies, love those who despitefully use you and pray for them (Matt. 5:44).

For those reading my and have a calling from God upon your life in the office of a pastor, minister, evangelist, teacher, missionary, etc., you are not exempt from being a wife or a mother. Women should be submissive, and husbands, love your wives as God loves the church (Eph 5:21-25).

Just remember that God didn't have to use Mary to bring forth our Lord and Savior Jesus Christ; But He did! Remember, God did use a woman, and ladies, you are worth something. Allow God to use you.

Contact Information:
Pastor Diana S. Washington
Remnant of God Outreach Ministries
1208 ½ Paradise Hill Rd.
Clarksville, TN 37040
E-mail: DianaWashington@bellsouth.net

39

Pastor Dr. Jane W. Garland

Trust in the Lord with all thine heart; and lean not unto thine own understanding. In all thy ways acknowledge Him, and He shall direct thy paths.

—Proverbs 3:5-6

The Journey to and Beyond Becoming a Pastor in Clarksville, Tennessee

Upon our (the Garland family) arrival in Clarksville, I wanted to work with a ministry. Since the Baptist church was our roots in religion, we decided to go to one of the local sanctuaries.

Let me make myself clear on why I said that I wanted to work with a ministry and not we. I know and I honor the Word of God that states, "Man is the head of the household." I am saying I because my husband was off to school in the military and the children were not decision makers in the family at that time. Therefore, I was left with the decision making for the family. We went to one of the local Baptist churches. But to my surprise, I found that I could not work in the office of a minister being a female.

As a teenager growing up in the Baptist church, I had an encounter with my grandfather. I had gone into the pulpit to collect an offering. My grandfather angrily forbade me not to ever go back into the pulpit again. As a matter of fact, his exact words were, "Don't you ever let me catch you in that pulpit again." Well, the Lord called my grandfather home before I was called into the ministry. I had no problem accepting my call because we were active-duty army. In the Gospel Hour Service, we were all denominations. We had traveled extensively with the military with very little contact with the civilian community. And Clarksville was at least 50 percent prior—or active-duty military, but it's also about 75 percent, if not more, hardcore Baptist (not modern).

I met with the pastor of that sanctuary and told him that I had been called into the ministry as a minister. The Lord had called me first to teach, then to preach. How do I know I was called? Moreover, what is the difference in the calls? Well, for my call to minister as an evangelist, Mark 16:15 resounded in my spirit, in my reading over and over again. And He said unto them, "Go ye into all the world, and preach the gospel to every creature. He that believeth and is baptized shall be saved; but he that believeth not shall be damned." It would not go away until I said yes to the Lord.

My call to teach was assured by Matthews 28:19-20: "Go ye therefore, and teach all nations, baptizing them in the name of the Father, and of the Son, and of the Holy Ghost: Teaching them to observe all things whatsoever I have commanded you: and, lo, I am with you always, even unto the end of the world," and the song by the Reverend Shirley Caesar that says, "Go ye therefore and teach all nations. Go! Go! Go!" Even though the call to teach and the call to preach were not heard until 1980 and 1981, I realized after looking back at my life that I was anointed to teach at the age of nine years old. I found that I didn't have to study my Sunday school lesson but came up with the same interpretation of the scripture as the author of the book. I didn't know about the callings and anointing at that time. It was not until 1978 that the Lord began to teach me about anointing, accepting the call of God, and being led by the Spirit of God. I must also say that prayer played a key role in me accepting the call of God. First of all is hearing the call. Because you first have to hear the call to answer.

It was our second tour in Germany when God started putting images or faces of people in my spiritual vision. I asked Him, "Why do I keep seeing these people? All I know to do is to pray for them." Once that was spoken, a floodgate was opened in the Spirit, and the Lord began to pour people into my spirit to pray for. Many times, I had not a clue, but I prayed what clues I felt or sensed in the Spirit, and God would reveal to me later why I was praying for a particular individual or situation. I remember distinctly the first petition that I offered up to the Lord when I realized what He was saying to me. I remember seeing the face of one distant cousin, and as I began to pray, another face appeared. They were the younger sons of an older distant cousin that had always believed in me. I prayed as the Spirit gave me utterance, not in the tongues but with my understanding. I kept praying until the Lord revealed to me that my elderly cousin was on her deathbed in the hospital, and my prayer was to bring comfort to those sons.

Another incident occurring after my call to intercession occurred in the afternoon before my children came home from school. The Lord spoke to me and told me to pray. I knelt down briefly to pray. As soon as I got up, the Lord told me to pray some more. I prayed some more, a little longer, and got up. No sooner than I was up off my knees, the Lord said, "Pray some more. What if something would happen to your children on the bus?" I immediately plunged into groaning in my spirit, weeping and crying out for my children on the bus. You know Romans 8:26 tells us, "Likewise the Spirit also helpeth our infirmities: for we know not what we should pray for as we ought: but the Spirit itself maketh intercession for us with groaning which cannot be uttered." This is what was transpiring. I did not know what to pray, but the Spirit did. I cried out until I felt a break in the Spirit; then I waited to hear what had happened. The children came home but didn't say a word. Then I waited to see if it was something with my husband. He said nothing! Was I mistaken? Why was I praying so hard?

Well, we had a fellowship with another service that night. As we started on our way, one of the children said, "Mama, the bus bumped a car." I knew in an instant that this was what my prayer was about. We continued to the service, and there in testimony service, God revealed another intercession. I had been praying for this young soldier that I didn't even know. I had seen her once or twice in fellowship, but that was all. There was no former communication between us. Well, she stood up to share her victory over a problem she had encountered in the army. That really gave me a boost of faith that I did and do hear from God.

I worked diligently in interceding for all of those that the Lord would put in my Spirit or send my way, until one day a friend of mine, much younger than I had just been saved, was called to preach. I was so happy for her, yet I felt like the prodigal son's brother. I was so jealous because I had been with the Lord since I was a child and had not received a calling. All I did was pray.

It was time for me to go to the Father on my behalf. I began to pray, "Lord, I love what You are doing for my sister, but I'm so jealous." The Lord spoke to my spirit and said, "You don't have anything to be jealous about. You have the ministry of intercessory prayer and testimonial witnessing." He said to me, "Prayer can go where no man can go." I felt so ashamed yet so honored that He had trusted me with such a gift. Who was I that God would trust to bring the burdens and problems of His people before His throne and get answers for them? I wept before the Lord with great humility and admiration. No one was more blessed than I. After humbling myself under the mighty hand of God, then I was called to teach, then to preach. I was very active in my ministry from duty station to duty station, always remembering to acknowledge God in all my ways, thus allowing Him to direct my paths.

In my ministering in different congregations and with different denominations, the Lord taught me to always respect and obey leadership unless He tells me differently. He said, "It is better to obey God rather than man".

Upon my meeting with the pastor, I shared some of these things with him, hoping that the Spirit would bear witness. But unfortunately, denomination overruled the voice of the Spirit. He laughed at me and asked if I had eaten some fatback and collard greens, went to sleep, and had a dream. He said that he could make me a missionary but couldn't let me in "his" pulpit because they would run him out of Clarksville. I told him that I had to obey God, that I was called to be a minister and not a missionary. And by the way, the pulpit does not belong to man because Christ is the Head of the church. There's neither male nor female in Christ Jesus. It is written!

Although I was not allowed to preach the Word or teach, I continued to intercede as the Spirit unctioned me. I shed many tears during the services but remained humble. For it is written that weeping may endure for a night, but joy comes in the morning. And if you will humble yourself under the mighty hand of God, He will lift you up. We stayed there until the Lord released me, which was about three and a half months.

Yet determined to work with another ministry, we went to another church; this time under a female pastor. It was there that we discovered that God was calling us to a different ministry. We were sitting in Sunday school when the Lord began to speak to me. I heard the voice of the Lord say, "Build my church." I began visualizing a building. The voice came to me again. Yet visualizing, the voice came a third time. Now! I needed some revelation. I asked the Lord for understanding. What did He really mean? In my quest, He began to lead me in a plain path. He told me that the church is His people, and building it meant to meet the needs of His people. I began to think, "Oh, my Lord, we've gotten it so wrong!"

Again, we remained faithful until the Lord gave us further instructions. He said, "Start Bible study in the home." Of course, we obeyed. God poured His anointing upon us in a mighty way. He blessed us beyond measure. Many were blessed by our ministry from both large and small congregations. People didn't want their pastors to know they were hurting (losing their cars, homes, going through with their marriages, having no food, among other things.) Therefore, they came to us. We didn't turn anyone away if we could help. Why? Because the Lord said build His church and not my church. Some people came to us not knowing anything about church. They learned to speak and pray before a congregation. They learned to operate under the anointing (the power of God) then went to larger congregations. Because we obeyed the voice of God, many began to call us a cult. Because our ministry was different, "we were not of God," they said. However, the Lord reminded me what He had told His disciples that He had other sheep that was of a different fold. Just because sheep are under another shepherd in another field does not change the fact that they are sheep. We are all many members of one body. Search the Word!

We were enjoying the works of the Lord, seeing Him bless so many and answer our prayers. Then the Lord began to speak to me about pastoring.

He wanted me to be the pastor. Our organization is designed to be copastors with the man as senior pastor. I told the Lord that He would have to tell the bishop because I wasn't going to tell him. The Lord said, "No, you will tell him." Of course, the tears started again. I prayed for the Lord to reveal to them what He said to me, to no avail. I cried for months.

The Lord sent my husband overseas to force me into position. He was copastor and radio host in Honduras. I was acting pastor here. We had a convocation at that time. The bishop praised him for his works, never mentioned the works here. I was so broken, continually weeping and seeking God for directions. Finally, the Lord told me to write a letter to the bishop. I waited for the timing. A few months later, the bishop's wife called saying she had had a dream about me. We were on our way to Salt Lake City, Utah, our headquarters, to collect my inheritance. I knew then that the time was right for me to write the letter. I told her what the Lord had told me and that I was waiting for the right timing. She had just confirmed to me that the time was right. I wrote the letter in obedience to the Lord as unctioned by His Spirit. The bishop received it. After reading its contents, he called me and said that the Spirit concurred with every word. At last, the burden was lifted. He came and did an emergency ordination. Thus, making me the pastor of True Vine Worldwide Gospel Church Ministries.

We have continued to provide for the needs of God's people. Many have counted us out. People have taken advantage of us (so they thought). But God has given us a watchful eye and a spirit of observation. He said in His Word that He would not have us ignorant of Satan's devices. He has given us much wisdom in our struggles. There is a song that says, "If it had not been for the Lord on my side, where would I be?" I can truly say that He's been on my side. I have had both internal and external struggles in my leadership. But through much prayer and fasting, giving much, receiving little, I have remained faithful to the call. The Lord promised me that if I be faithful over a few things, He will make me ruler over many.

The doors are beginning to open. The storms are ceasing. The promises of God are being made manifest as I speak. I have begun to see the fruit of my labor as I've endured hardness as a good soldier. He revealed to me a few days ago that the woman completes the man, but she also completes His creation. There was nothing else created after woman. Hallelujah! Women, don't be afraid to accept the call of God. Trust in Him with all your heart; lean not to your own understanding because our thoughts are not His thoughts, and our ways are not His ways. He promised us He will always be there. Since we have been faithful in building His church by helping His people, He is allowing us, at this time, to start building the building. To God be the glory! Remember one day is as a thousand years to God, and a thousand years is as one day. Amen.

Pastor Dr. Jane W. Garland

E-mail: jawg4jays@yahoo.com

40

Pastor Judy D. Quarles

Love All The Time—From Food Stamps to Faith

That I may know him, and the power of his resurrection, and the fellowship of his sufferings, being made conformable unto his death.

—Philippians 3:10

My name is Pastor Judy D. Quarles; I was born in Nashville, Tennessee. I am married to a retired veteran, Pastor Marvin Quarles; and together we have four children, George (34), Lavar (26), Shaquita (25), and MaKayla (3). I am CEO and founder of Abigail Ministry Incorporated, Resurrected Life Christian Center, and Bethesda House of Recovery.

I'd like to dedicate this to a woman of faith, courage, strength; a woman who, in a world of uncertainties and the in the midst of trials, trusted God. My friend, example, and my mother, Minnie Marie Sherron.

On July 1971, my sister Evelyn had a dream. She said, "Hey, y'all, guess what I dreamed?" "What?" we said. "I dreamed Daddy shot Mama." We all said, "Sure, that'll never come true." So we all went back to playing the eraser game.

Living in a two-bedroom house, one of only three houses in our immediate area, no running water, outdoor toilet, cooking and heat with coal. We had only two neighbors: the Bell family lived directly behind us, and Mr. Glen lived about fifty feet up on a hill. Six girls and two boys. The oldest four were referred to as the older ones, and the youngest four were referred to as the four babies. I was the youngest of eight children. Everybody referred to me as the baby of the family.

Most people knew my mom as the lady with all those "chillums" (children); some referred to her as that church lady or that lady with the no-good husband; others referred to her as that lady that can sing, and others called her Ms. Minnie. To her children, all those names described her; but most importantly, she was our mom, a lady who worked all the time, prayed, and acted as our sole breadwinner. It seemed as though she never had a day off. She cleaned Mr. Butler's house on Monday and Wednesday, Ms. Todd's house on Tuesday and Thursday, and another house on Friday. I remember going to one of their houses with her one time, and they left her check on the counter; it was $20. But because of her work schedule, she had to depend on my older sisters to cook, bathe the smaller kids, and get us ready for bed. My mom always sang in church and sang with a gospel group called the Echos of Zion. She could really sing. I remember that every time she would stand up to sing, everybody would start clapping; and before she started singing, they would holler, "Sing, Minnie!" And boy, she sang. Everybody loved to hear her sing.

Christmas was good; most of the time, we were grateful to get used toys from the fire department. Most of the time, we didn't get Easter baskets for Easter; we always got colored chickens. We would identify our chickens by their colors; some were yellow, purple, blue, pink, and really cute. As they grew up, the colors would fade, and they were all the same colors, and they became dinner. Sometimes my mom would leave instructions for my brothers to get a chicken ready for dinner, which meant to go in the yard, ring the chicken's neck, pluck the chicken, clean and cook the chicken for dinner. Everybody had their parts to play. My brothers killed and cleaned the chicken, my sisters cooked the chicken, and everybody ate. We finally understood why we never got Easter baskets.

Everybody referred to my dad as Billy. My dad came by occasionally, especially when he was drinking; so when he came by, they were always fussing and fighting. My mom always said, "I know you've been drinking." So I later learned that he was an alcoholic. He sang in quartets and lived with other women. Every time he would come home, my brothers would listen to make sure he wasn't trying to hurt Mama. It was like he always wanted her to be handicapped because I remember seeing cut scars on her legs and arms where he tried to cut her arms and legs off.

It's July 3; we heard a truck drive up, and we peeked out the door. Mama went outside. It's my dad; he had his friend nicknamed Shorty bring him to our house. We were all in the house, playing the eraser game. They sat on the long porch. He, on one end; she on the other. We couldn't hear their conversation, but suddenly we heard *bang, bang, bang*! Since it was almost the Fourth of July, we thought it was fireworks; so we kept playing, but my brother stopped and said, "Those were not firecrackers." He then ran outside, hollered, "Daddy just shot Mama!" We all ran to the porch, seeing her covered in blood, beginning to weep. My brothers carried Mama and put her in Mr. Bell's car to be taken to the hospital. My dad got back in the truck with Shorty and left.

My mom would often say, "If something happened to me, I don't want my kids separated." They arrived at the hospital; Mama had to have immediate surgery. We were left at home, crying, scared, until my uncle Zeak came to get us. Worried, scared, and in fear of Mama dying, we knew we would be split up to go to different homes because nobody had enough room to house eight children. My aunt Rosie took some of us; some stayed with my other aunt, Marybell, and some stayed with our cousin Elizabeth. So as my mama feared, we were separated.

I remember one night staring and thinking and picturing her in church, singing, "Trouble in my way, I have to cry sometimes. So much trouble I had to cry sometime. I lay awake at night, but that's all right, 'cause I know Jesus will fix it." The background kept playing over and over in my mind as though I was singing the background. "Jesus, He will fix it, Jesus, He will fix it, Jesus, He will fix it." I didn't want to say "after a while." I wanted him to fix it right now.

Thinking about her being shot three times. Once in the back, left arm, and chest. I was reminded of another song she sang, "He Touched Me and Made Me Whole." And I wanted her made whole again.

For about two months, she was in the intensive care unit; and at that time, children were not allowed to visit in intensive care. Later she was moved to a room, and only ages twelve and up could visit. So the four babies were unable to visit.

Too young to visit her in the hospital, we would ask day after day, "What is the doctor saying about Mama, is she gonna live?" The replies were always with reluctance. "Just keep praying." My aunts always said, "Your mama's gonna be all right." But because we could not see her and only remember all the blood on the porch and the blood that filled Mr. Bell's car, we just knew she was not going to make it. Confused, scared, and crying myself to sleep for days, weeks, and months, I could not understand how my dad could do this to my mom. Time would pass, and it seemed like we would never see Mama again. Our breadwinner, our instructor, our encourager, our mama, daddy, and friend. When we talked to each other, we would ask, "Have you heard about Mama?" hoping that another aunt or cousin was saying something more positive and different.

As the sole breadwinner in our family, my mom could not afford to give us allowance; but every month when she got food stamps, she would give each of us a fifty-cent food stamp. One day my aunt Rosie went to the hospital, came home, and gathered us together and said, "Your Mama will be getting out real soon, she's doing better now, and she told me to give you this. She handed each one of us a fifty-cent food stamp. It was amazing; we were overjoyed! It was like the food stamp could talk. It gave us hope, assurance, joy, and confirmed that Jesus has fixed it. It confirmed the fact that Mama was in her right mind and was not going to die. As we were all so closely knit together, the food stamp comforted our hearts and increased our faith.

Thinking back, the food stamp was not just a food stamp; it was assurance. She sent the food stamp to comfort our hearts and tell us that though we were physically separated, we can stay together in love. "That their hearts might be comforted, being knit together in love, and unto all riches of the full assurance of understanding, to the acknowledgement of the mystery of God, and of the Father, and of Christ" (Col. 2:2).

October 1972, two weeks after my mom was released from the hospital, she took us to see our new home. The city was building new housing projects called Cumberland View. What a blessing; we were so excited to move in a five-bedroom brand-new apartment. It was like heaven. We had our mom back, we were no longer separated, we had a bigger place—*five* bedrooms, *two* full inside baths, only two people to a room, running water, no more wood and coal stoves—we even had *electric* heat. WOW!

Sometimes we never know what God has in store or what He will use to show us His glory or to increase our faith. Who would have thought a food stamp could bring so much assurance, hope, love, and faith. Who's to say that public housing is not a blessing?

Of course, my dad went to jail, and she divorced him while he was incarcerated. During his incarceration, she took us to see him. I resented and hated him so much, was always afraid he was going to try and kill her again. I never wanted to see him again and gave her every reason why she shouldn't take us to see him. She replied, "What happened between me and your dad is not your business, he's still your dad." She never talked about him; she always said, "That's your dad." She always made sure we got him a Father's Day card, Christmas gifts, and went to see him. As he was aging and getting ill, she helped take care of him, took him back and forth to the doctor to get his medication, always made us go see him and take care of him as well.

My sister's dream came true, but fire will not destroy gold; fire purifies gold. When God gets ready to polish His gold, He uses fiery trials. Unfortunately, nothing brings luster to your character and commitment to your heart like opposition. The finish product is a result of the fiery process. I saw my mom in the fire, and I saw her shine with the kind of brilliancy that enables God to look down and see Himself. God places His prized possessions in the fire.

The bad news is, even those who live godly lives will suffer persecution. The good news is, you might be in the fire, but God controls the thermostat.

Never satisfied with my aunts' answers, always worrying, going from aunt to aunt to get different answers about her condition, God sent proof, assurance, joy, and love through a simple food stamp. Like Noah sending out the dove and the raven to make sure the land was dry after the flood.

> After forty days Noah opened a window he had made in the ark and sent out a raven, and it kept flying back and forth until the water had dried up from the earth. Then he sent out a dove to see if the water had receded from the surface of the ground. But the dove could find nowhere to perch because there was water over all the surface of the earth; so it returned to Noah in the ark. He reached out his hand and took the dove and brought it back to himself in the ark. He waited seven more days and again sent out the dove from the ark. When the dove returned to him in the evening, there in its beak was a freshly plucked olive leaf! (Gen. 8:6-11)

When my aunt Rosie came home that day, there were eight fifty-cent food stamps that brought hope, assurance, and confirmation that Mama was going to make it.

I thank God for a strong role model, that lady with all the chillums (childrens), that church lady, that lady that taught us to trust God in the midst of trials, taught us commitment, forgiveness, sacrifice, prayer. That lady with courage, endurance, courage and strength. That lady that still reminds us that regardless of what it is, "Jesus will fix it." In 1975 the oldest ones married and moved into their own places. Mama, a single parent, was able to purchase a very nice home in a very nice neighborhood to raise the four babies. *"Now unto him that is able to do exceeding abundantly above all that we ask or think, according to the power that worketh in us"* (Eph. 3:20).

LOVE FROM THE START
Judy D. Quarles

On August 10, the day I was born; I didn't know the price of milk or corn

You raised us up well, sent us to school, always
taught us to pray and the golden rules

You took us to church, worked hard and prayed,
and asked the Lord for better days

The days sometimes got harder, and very very tough,
that sometimes the money just wasn't enough

Enough for eight kids, buy food and pay bills; I know it
wasn't easy, and you said, "It's the Lord's will"

Going to work cleaning beds, floors, and rooms;
oftentimes missed lunch at noon

Working so hard trying to make ends meet, to put
clothes on our backs and a decent meal to eat

Always talked about and never praised; you knew the Lord would make a way

Somehow you managed to keep us in line, scrubbing
at work with prayer all the time

Now that I have responsibilities, I can relate, to how
hard it can be without help from your mate

I can remember one Christmas, without toys under the tree;
you paced the floor and asked, "Where could he be?"

He, we thought, was Santa and just running behind;
but wasn't Santa at all, but Daddy at the time

Now through all this, you kept a smile; you knew
Santa wasn't coming in just a little while

Still you continued smiling, praying for a better way; you
showed us your faith and love, each and every day

Now that I'm grown and out of my own, the love
I have for you has never left home

One thing I can say and mean it from my heart,
you showed us love, right from the start

From Ms. Minnie to you

Don't stop trusting and believing God—Exercise your Faith.

Endure. The race is not given to the swift, nor the battle to the strong, but to the one that endures until the end.

Though thy beginning was small, yet thy latter end should greatly increase. (Job 8:7)

Minnie Marie Sherron

April 18, 1932-January 10, 2001

Booking information—Judy D. Quarles
e-mail: resurrectedlifechristianctr@gmail.com

41

Pastor Yolanda Morgan

But blessed is the one who trusts in the Lord, whose confidence is in him.

—Jeremiah 17:7

I asked the question, *Why me God?* I had been raised in a Christian home, had served God all my life, and did not understand why this was happening to me.

In 2002, we were making preparations for our annual The Glory's in the House Women's Conference. In the process of preparing for it, I became very ill and began to experience vertigo and nausea. Realizing I had so much to do, I decided to go to the doctor. He diagnosed me with a severe sinus and inner-ear infection and sent me home with an antibiotic to rest.

Forcing myself out of bed the next day, I attempted to get ready to go to the church to pull things together for the conference. As I got in the shower, I experienced another episode of vertigo and nausea. Holding onto the wall, I made my way back to the bed. I could not do it. The thought of going out overwhelmed me.

I called the church and let our conference team know that I could not participate in the planning meeting. Even though I did not go into detail about how sick I really was, I felt like I was letting them down. I was taught at an early age to put a smile on my face and persevere regardless of what was going on in my life. I was to be more concerned about the people who surrounded me than my own situations or problems. I thanked God that He surrounded me with wonderful women who understood and cared for my well-being.

As I was getting dressed for the opening night of the conference, I noticed everything seemed a blur. Trying to focus and get my thoughts together, I said to myself, "How am I going to do this tonight?" Determined to be at the event, I prayed, "God, touch my body so that I can be at my post of duty."

At the conference, I stood on the platform, thinking to myself, *How am I going to do this?* Walking to the podium to welcome all the guests, I thought, *What is happening to me? Is this really a sinus infection or is something else going on with me?* Looking back now, I can't recall driving to the church or returning home—it's all a blur.

The second night of the conference—I remember this so vividly in my mind—we had a reception for all our guests after the service. Slipping away from the crowd to the back of the reception hall, I prayed, *God, I have got to get home and get in my bed.* Then I turned back to the room with a brave face so no one would know how truly sick I was.

The conference ended that Sunday morning. After service, our special guests came to our home for lunch. At this point, not only did I have vertigo and nausea, but also I had developed a tremendous headache. Trying to keep my sickness to myself, I discreetly left the room and went upstairs to lie down.

Following the conference, my husband and I had plans to get away to relax for a few days. With trepidation, I began packing, although I remained aware of my sickness. Realizing I wasn't getting any better, I decided to call my doctor. He responded by increasing my antibiotics, which I desperately hoped would make a difference.

On Thursday of that same week, we drove to Daytona Beach, Florida, towing our motorcycles to meet with friends for the weekend. We arrived that morning at around 3:00 a.m. and were very excited about cruising our bikes along the beach. After a few hours of sleep, my husband woke me up and said, "Are you ready to go?"

I was anything but ready. Entering the bathroom to take my shower, I realized that I had double vision. I became very fearful and went back to lie down, saying to my husband, "You have to go without me—I cannot go."

Concerned, he asked, "Are you sure?"

I replied, "Yes, I'll be okay. I think I'll feel fine after I rest."

After sleeping for a couple of hours, I actually woke up feeling worse. At the hospital in Florida, I was diagnosed again with a serious sinus and inner-ear infection. All they did was send me away with another antibiotic. Still puzzled about my lingering illness, I began to realize something more serious was going on.

We returned home Sunday night. The next morning, our daughter-in-law walked in my bedroom to see how I was doing. When I looked up at her, she saw that my right eye had shifted abnormally to one side. Trying not to alarm me, she said calmly, "I think we need to go to the hospital." My family rushed me to the ER.

After being admitted to the hospital, the doctor started a long series of tests. I was oblivious to what was happening around me because I was so ill. The first diagnosis was a severe migraine headache; later doctors changed that diagnosis to a stroke. The doctor prescribed blood thinners and ordered a spinal tap for the next day.

As the procedure for the spinal tap began, the radiologist noticed that I was being given heparin (a blood thinner) through my IV. He stopped the procedure and came in the waiting area to tell my husband that if he had continued with the spinal tap, I could have been paralyzed. He explained that a spinal tap while on blood thinners can be deadly! It was only by the grace of my amazing God that the error was caught before the test was performed.

After that incident, my husband made the decision to transfer me to another hospital. I stayed there for an unimaginable twenty-seven days. During this time, I endured a battery of tests and procedures including 11 IVs, five MRIs, and five spinal taps. I vaguely remember the last spinal tap because my sister was there, holding my hand and praying for me during the procedure. I thought, *God, when will this ever end?*

Nothing the doctors did made any difference: all the tests were inconclusive. Because I was relentlessly vomiting, I lost sixteen pounds. My body was so worn and so weak that I had no clue what was going on around me.

My precious husband stayed by my side every minute, sleeping on a cot in my room every night. One night in particular, while lying on the hospital cot around midnight, he remembers hearing me whisper and thought I was calling his name. He got up, walked over to me, and put his ear close to my mouth so he could hear me clearly. I was so weak and frail that my speech was difficult to understand. What he heard me whisper was, "My faith is healing me, my faith is healing me." Over and over again, I repeated it. "My faith is healing me." I was not consciously aware of what I was saying, but my inner spirit knew exactly what to say.

Eventually, I was sent home. My weakness was still such that my son had to carry me upstairs and put me into bed. Things did not go well at home, and three days later, I was readmitted to the hospital. The doctor admitted that he had sent me home too early and that I needed to remain in the hospital awhile longer to regain my strength.

A week later, I left the hospital again. Still battling double vision but believing in faith for my total healing, I thanked God every night for my vision to be corrected.

On Thanksgiving Day, my husband and I were sitting at the table talking, waiting for our children to arrive to have Thanksgiving dinner. While looking at him, I suddenly realized my vision had been restored. I shouted out, "Oh, dear God! Baby, I have single vision!"

We were both so excited; we leapt to our feet and danced with joy! As our children walked in, we all began to weep tears of joy because we knew that God had started touching me with His miraculous healing power.

In the early part of December, my children thought it would be a great idea for me to get out of the house for a change of scenery. When I went into the bathroom to get ready, I flicked on the light and noticed everything was gray. Once again, I was gripped by fear because I had no idea what was happening to my eyesight. Fortunately, my doctor at the hospital had given us his private cell phone number in case we needed him. We called, and he instructed me to get a regular eye exam. The ophthalmologist who administered the eye exam told us that I had optic neuritis, a condition in which the main nerve in my right eye was damaged. After my exam, I called my doctor again and told him the diagnosis. He instructed me to return to the hospital right away and even arranged for someone to meet me so I would not have to sit in the waiting room. Again, I witnessed evidence of the favor, grace, and mercy of my awesome God.

I was admitted to the hospital immediately and started a four-day course of steroids for the optic neuritis. The next morning, the doctor came in with several interns. As they surrounded my bed, my doctor looked at me and said, "Mrs. Morgan, I hate to give you this news, but we are diagnosing you with multiple sclerosis because of the lesions we found on your cerebellum."

For a moment, I was speechless, breathless, and shocked. Fear gripped me, but in that moment of fear, I still had faith to look my doctor in the eye with boldness and say, "I do not receive this report. You have no idea the God I serve."

The doctor seemed a little stunned by my response, so his reply was very short. He said, "Okay, Mrs. Morgan."

I left the hospital with a prescription for four more days of steroids. At night, I was overwhelmed with torment and fear. My precious husband would get out of the bed to walk with me and help me pray. During those times, I thought God was so far away. I would say aloud, "Where is God?"

Early one morning, I slipped out of bed as quietly as I could, trying not to wake my husband. I carefully made my way to the kitchen table to pray alone. As I prayed, I said, *God, give me peace in my mind, and help me with this tormenting fear.* At that moment, God gave me this scripture, Psalms 91:5, which says, "Thou shall not be afraid of the terror by night, nor of the arrow that flies by day." His promise to me was that He would be with me when the terror came at night. I definitely felt the hand of God lift the fear from me that day.

I had been so sick that I had to have someone stay with me when my husband went to church to minister. That Sunday, I told him I would be okay to be alone. As he left, he asked me to please stay in bed and not go downstairs.

While I was watching a service on television in my room, the minister spoke as if directly to me and said, "I see you lying in that bed. You are tormented. Go get your Bible; I have a Word for you."

Knowing that minister was speaking to me and that I had to get my Bible, I slowly made my way down the stairs, praying, *God, please protect me.* I could hear my husband's voice in my mind, saying not to leave the bedroom, but I knew I had to get this Word. I made it safely back to my room just as the minister instructed his viewers to turn to Jeremiah 17:7, which says, "Blessed is the man who trusts in the Lord and whose hope the Lord is." I was hoping for a healing scripture, but I realized this scripture was meant for me.

The next thing I did was pray for God to give me a plan. I said, *God, what is your strategy for my healing?* I had been to the specialist recommended by my doctor, and he wanted me to take daily injections that promised only a 30 percent success rate toward slowing the progression of the disease. The overall prognosis he offered was terrible; he predicted I would eventually be in a wheelchair permanently. That's when I decided to contact a doctor specializing in alternative medicine.

Upon meeting the doctor specializing in alternative treatment, I told him I was desperate and needed help. When I shared with him my medical condition, I looked at him and said, "Doctor, I believe God orders the steps of the righteous, and I also believe He ordered me to see you. With your knowledge and God's power, I will be totally healed."

He was a bit stunned by my bold statement, but he looked at me and said, "Okay." I started a healing journey with this doctor and did everything he told me to do along with declaring and prophesying over my body daily. The first week, I ate a diet of only broccoli and cauliflower, changing my eating habits completely. It wasn't always easy, but I remained committed. Within three months, the lesions on my brain were completely gone. (Normally, they take at least one year to go away.)

I remained faithful to my healthy diet and my commitment to getting well. Three years later, far from being confined to a wheelchair, I was released by the doctor who gave me my initial diagnosis of multiple sclerosis. At our last visit, he looked at me and said, "You do not need me anymore. I release you."

Did you notice that the lesions were gone in three months and my release came in three years? In terms of numerology as it relates to Biblical matters, the number three equates divine manifestation. My healing had divinely manifested the day of my release, and no one has been able to squelch my praise since!

As I told you in the beginning of this story, the question I asked God while walking through this process was, *Why God? Why me? After I have served you for years, why me?*

The answer was given to me one day during my desperation. I cried out to God and asked, *Why?* It was then that I heard the audible voice of my faithful God as He said, "Because I knew I could trust you."

Just as He did with Job, God allows us to go through a process so He can test and prove us to be his servants. Satan came to God; God asked Satan, "Have you considered my servant Job?"

Satan responded, "I cannot get to him. You have a hedge around him!" I believe God instilled a hedge around me as well, even during my suffering. Just like Job, I made it through my test; God delivered me, and now I am a walking testimony that He will bring you through it all.

If you are walking through a process, know that God is with you. He will *never* forsake you.

Contact Information:
Celebration of Life Church
Website: www.celebrationoflife.com
E-mail: office@celebrationoflife.com
Twitter: @YolandaChozen1
Facebook: https://www.facebook.com/pastoryolandamorgan

42

Servella Lee Terry

The Lord is my light and my salvation; whom shall I fear?
The Lord is the strength of my life; of whom shall I be afraid?
When the wicked, even mine enemies and my foes, came upon me to eat up my flesh,
they stumbled and fell. Though an host should encamp against me,
my heart shall not fear: though war should rise against me, in this will I be confident.

Psalms 27:1-3

I, Servella Lee Terry was born to the late Tyree Sims and Emma Lee Broomfield in the city of Dayton, Ohio. My father was an AME pastor and the founder of Ramson Memorial Church, located in a small community named Crown Point. My family comprised of four brothers and me.

God has always been the center of the Broomfield's family. My dad was killed in an auto accident at an early age of thirty-one, which left my mom a young widow to care for five children. With her faith in the Almighty God and her family's support, she managed to raise all of us. Even though life for us on a day-to-day basis was a struggle, my mom managed to keep food on the table and a roof over our heads. She worked as a housekeeper for many years for a wealthy Jewish family before finding work at the local hospital in the dietary department. She chose not to remarry for fear of someone being unfair to her five children.

I firmly believe that it is very important to know where a person comes from in order to get a glimpse of their values and character. My humble up bringing has allowed me to work and understand the least and the loss of our society. There is an old adage that says, "If you have never experienced not having, you really can't understand the emptiness." I believe this.

I would be remiss not to introduce a great man of God, Jimmy Terry Sr., my husband. He has been very supportive of all my dreams, desires, and work down through the years. I spent fourteen years working for the Tennessee Black Caucus as the chairperson of the women's issues task force. This committee was comprised of ten women in an executive leadership positions. We were tasked by the Speaker of the House and the Honorable Lois DeBerry to bring programs to the legislative training conference for women. Many wonderful things came out of this experience. Our overall goal was to empower women and to address issues ranging from domestic violence, health, education, career changes, child protection, and many more. Terry, my husband supported me as I traveled across the state to conduct these various workshops and group gatherings.

My passion for helping people began when I was very young. I organized a cleaning effort whereby we cleaned two elderly homes two streets over from where I lived. Because of our thoroughness and willingness to clean for the elderly, we were requested on a regular basis for small house cleaning jobs in our community. Those dollars earned assisted my mom in purchasing groceries and kerosene for our house heaters. I was twelve years old at the time. It has always been clear to me that there was a special purpose and/

or calling on my life to help others. Perhaps, it was the calling to become a missionary. My husband, Terry, for over forty years has shared with me a poem by Ellen Gates called "Your Mission," which states:

> If you cannot own the ocean, sail among the swiftest fleet,
> rocking on the highest billows, laughing at the storms you meet,
>
> You can stand among the sailors, anchored yet within the bay,
> you can lend a hand to help them as they launch their boats away.
>
> If you are too weak to journey up the mountain steep and high,
> you can stand within the valley while the *multitudes* go by.
>
> You can chant in happy measure as they slowly pass along;
> though they may forget the singer, they will not forget the song.
>
> If you have not gold and silver ever ready to command,
> if you cannot toward the needy reach an ever open hand,
>
> You can visit the afflicted, o'er the erring you and weep;
> you can be a true disciple sitting at the Savior's feet.
>
> If you cannot in a conflict prove yourself a soldier true,
> if where the fire and smoke are thickest, there's no work for you to do,
> when the battlefield is silent, you can go with careful tread;
> you can bear away the wounded, you can cover up the dead.
>
> Do not stand then idly waiting for some greater work to do;
> fortune is a lazy goddess, she will never come to you.
> Go and toil in any vineyard, do not fear or dare;
> if you want a field of labor,
> **YOU CAN FIND IT ANYWHERE!**

This poem reinforces my efforts for mission work the more; if you want a field of labor, you can find it anywhere.

Our community was extremely poor and mostly rural; as a matter of fact, everyone was at the same status, i.e., no running water, outdoor toilets and coal-heating stoves. Yes, those were the times in which I grew up. Through it all, Psalms 37:25 says, "I have been young, and now am old; yet have I not seen the righteous forsaken, nor his seed begging bread." It is a quote my mom would always say growing up. In many ways, I have grown to love this Biblical quote.

I accepted Christ at the tender age of five years old. My pastor recognized my singing abilities and immediately asked my mom if I could join the choir at Ebenezer Baptist Church. My faith grew strong as I sang "Amazing Grace," as well as many other hymns and gospels. I was requested by the choir director and identified as the main leader for the adult choir. I was now about seven years old. Wow! Wasn't that amazing? My favorite song as I remember during that time was "To Me He Is So Wonderful."

When I am lonely, or I should feel sad, I am so contented and my heart is glad. Joy bells are ringing and my heart I am singing, it is wonderful to know that He is mine. When I am discouraged or filled with gloom, God sent His angels to sing in my gloom, I joined the singing, for I can't decline, it's wonderful to know He is mine.

My community work started in 1968, working with the Model Cities Program in Dayton, Ohio. This was an opportunity to aid local struggling communities to become better informed about community resources. I had to identify leaders within the communities who were able to articulate various needs of their neighborhoods. This position allowed me to share positive and healing messages to families who lived within a targeted area of high crime and poverty. Several folks during this process were recognized and became great leaders in local government. This could not have been done by myself only; God was working through me for His good. As I said earlier, there has always been a calling on my life to assist in promoting the least and the lost. I am convinced that God desires strong and positive soldiers in His army. A favorite song as I grew up was "No Coward Soldiers," and I say praise God, because I have never been coward to speak the truth.

In the seventies, I was recruited to become the director of a halfway house for the Federal Bureau of Prisons. As director, my responsibilities were to provide oversight to staff in an effort to allow offenders opportunities to start a new beginning and to make a positive transition into the local community. Additionally, I have been blessed to work in many executive roles within many organizations. I share this testimony to those who will be reading my life's journey by encouraging them that God uses ordinary people for extraordinary work. Within these roles, I have continued to allow God to use me to make a difference and to let my light shine so that men and women see good works and glorify my Heavenly Father, who is in heaven. In 1976, I was recruited to become the executive director of a local program funded by the National Council of Negro Women. This program provided resources to divert females from the juvenile justice system. We offered tutoring, family crisis intervention, health assistance, and career planning. That program was a blessing to many at-risk young females and their families. I was blessed to serve in that capacity and had the pleasure to meet Dr. Dorothy Heights, executive director of the National Council of Negro Women.

In 1979, my husband and I relocated to Clarksville, Tennessee, where he was called to pastor the Mount Olive Missionary Baptist Church. All my life I have been a true servant and follower of His. Initially my life felt useless, due to the fact that I was in a place much different from where I grew up. This relocation brought about much anxiety within me, not knowing anyone in the city or state. However, God knew that He needed me here to continue His work as I was doing in my hometown.

In August of 1979, I started my career with state government as the coordinator of volunteer services for Middle Tennessee. This position allowed me to meet many wonderful people across the state. I soon realized that God was still on my side and that I still had much more work to do. I was blessed with His favor because He allowed me to connect, motivate, and to encourage people regarding volunteerism within the faith-based communities. *Southern Baptist Church Administration Journal* recruited me to write an article entitled "The Church and Volunteerism." That article addressed how local parishioners can be a blessing in the following areas: mentoring, mother's day out, after-school programs, prison ministry, and more.

I have been blessed to share my faith and walk with Christ throughout my state-government career. What I have learned is people want to see a sermon, not hear one. If you live each day what you believe, your living will not be in vain. The last years of my career was spent being a voice for the most vulnerable of all, grandparents raising grandchildren and foster children. Much prayer, as well as community involvement, is needed for this population. I submit to you that we must be more proactive rather than reactive.

Local faith communities should play a major role in this area and request information and/or training from local regions. The faith-based guide for the Department of Children's Services was developed by my division several years ago. Several faith-based round tables were rolled out in two regions, Davidson and Southwest. They were very successful, with large numbers attending. I worried that there may not be anyone in place after my departure from the Department of Children's Services to champion this cause. Tennessee's kinship programs were under my watch in the mid to late nineties. A colleague and I were responsible for the promulgation of kinship and statewide training.

My faith and trust in God has taken me many places, and I would like to share a few. Several years were spent traveling across the country sharing with pastors and minister's wives on "How to be an effective and supportive wife to your husband in ministry." In many ways, this was helping me to work through my own fears as a pastor's wife. On June 30, 2011, I retired from state government after thirty-three years. It has always been my desire, hope, and dream to leave footprints of my work across the state.

I knew upon retirement that I had much more work to do for God. A commitment was made to my husband and the Tabernacle Christian School Board that I would give much more attention to the further development as well as oversight to our school after retirement. I assumed full time status as the executive director July 5, 2011. As executive director, I believe that Jesus Christ should be at the center of all learning. Our goal is to provide students with a curriculum from a biblical perspective that prepares and inspires students for success in life. Our educational program provides students with the skills and abilities necessary to sustain and defend a Christian worldview. "And all thy children shall be taught of the LORD; and great shall be the peace of thy children" (Isa. 54:13). To God be the glory; great things He has done.

September 7, 1999, Tabernacle Christian School opened its doors with sixteen students. This is our fourteenth year of teaching and training champions for Christ. I am proud to announce that for fourteen years, we have been serving our community with high quality and godly standards for pre-K through the sixth grade.

Our school provides a safe and nurturing environment that enables a child to obtain academic excellence, spiritual, emotional, and physical development through the teaching of Christian principles and values. We provide each student with an opportunity to grow in the nurture and admonition of the Lord.

And thou shalt love the Lord thy God with all thine heart, and with all thy soul, and with all thy might. And these words, which I command thee this day, shall be in thine heart: And thou shalt teach them diligently unto thy children, and shalt talk of them when thou sittest in thine house, and when thou walkest by the way, and when thou liest down, and when thou risest up. (Deut. 6:5-7, KJV)

In 2011, I was honored to meet Treva Gordon, who in many ways has made a very impressionable impact on my life. I believe what she is doing is what God has ordained her to do. My husband and I are on board with supporting this ministry. We have always felt that anyone who feels led to step out and exercise the faith that Treva has done should be rewarded with local means. It is an honor to participate in this Leading Ladies project, and my prayer is that much will come out of each of the stories that are being published. I was blessed to attend Michigan Leading Ladies Conference in October 2012. That conference was a true blessing to more than five hundred people, mostly women. I witnessed the anointing on the lives of many women as they sang, prayed, preached, and presented. This is probably the best-hidden secret of this time.

As we prepared to fly out of Nashville en route to Michigan, my sisters demonstrated great love and joy for one another; much conversation, laughter, sharing, praying, crying, fellowship, as well as anticipation of arriving in Detroit. It was a blessing to have my godson Pastor Wess Morgan join me and his mother, Pastor Yolanda Morgan. He was, as always, phenomenal, as he let God use him in song.

In summary, my prayer is that you have been blessed by reading my humble beginnings and life story. This is an opportune time to encourage you to find out more about this great women's movement. My experience with all of Treva's events has been very positive and encouraging. I have partnered with her in the planning of the next upcoming Leading Ladies Conference coming October 2013. There is much excitement in the anticipation of it being a great success. Come and join; you will be blessed, and you will learn from other leading women.

This book of the law shall not depart out of thy mouth; but thou shalt meditate therein day and night, that thou mayest observe to do according to all that is written therein: for then thou shalt make thy way prosperous, and then thou shalt have good success.

Have not I commanded thee? Be strong and of a good courage; be not afraid, neither be thou dismayed: for the LORD thy God is with thee whithersoever thou goest. (Josh. 1:8-9, KJV)

Contact Information:
Servella Lee Terry
E-mail: *servella.terry@aol.com*
Web: TabernacleChristianSchoolTN.org

43

Sha Jackson

(Hopkinsville, Kentucky)

So if the Son liberates you [makes you free men], then you are really and *unquestionably free.*

—JOHN 8:36, AB

My name is Sha Jackson. I was born in Los Angeles, California. My husband, Johnny, and I have been married for thirty-six years. We have two adult children and seven grandchildren. I am the assistant manager of Taylor Motors, Inc. I am the founder and president of Daughters of Destiny Women's Ministry, a member of Rhema Word Jail Ministry, and owner of Sha Chic Accessories. Also, I am the author of *Booty Call: It's the Truth*. I have been a faithful member of Holiness Church of Deliverance for over twenty years, where I serve on the praise team and other boards. I am a Leading Lady!

I was born to the most wonderful parents a child could ever have. I am the second child of four girls. My childhood was bittersweet. I had to overcome many obstacles as a child: molestation, constantly being talked about because of the color of my skin, and being overweight. Because I was raised in the church and accepted the Lord at an early age, I believe that is what helped me to make it through.

I thought I was in love, so I gave up my virginity at sixteen, at which time I became pregnant. Against better judgment, I aborted (murdered) my baby. This horrible act haunted me for many years. I became pregnant again at the age of seventeen, at which time my boyfriend and I decided to get married seven months before our son was born. We separated just a few years later, and that was when my life began to spiral out of control. The ditch I dug for him, I fell into myself. I tried to make him jealous by turning my back on God, going to the clubs drinking and using drugs; it backfired on me, and I became a drug addict on the streets of Los Angeles for ten years.

During all those years of using drugs, I tried to live a normal life, but it wasn't possible. My life just kept getting worse and worse. Often times I would cry out to God to save me and deliver me or just let me die and put me out of my misery. I have been pistol-whipped, raped three times, and almost died from malnutrition and dehydration. I have almost been killed, and I have even wanted to kill. That was when I knew I couldn't go on living that way. I knew what I was doing was not right, but wanting to kill people for the wrong they were doing to me was too much for me to handle. I would cry out to God to please do something. People would tell me all the time that I needed to stop doing what I was doing, but what they didn't understand was I could not stop! The forces of darkness bound me, and I was out of control. The good I desired in my heart to do and spoke out of my mouth, I could not do. The wrong that I did not want to do was exactly what I kept on doing (Rom. 7:14-20).

My mother was praying for me, and my husband whom I was still married to. It hurt my heart to the core to see the pain that I was causing her. She arranged for my children and me to come to Kentucky to visit my husband for a vacation (I conceived my daughter during a one-night stand with a total stranger). After a few days, my husband asked me to stay. Immediately I told him no! Then I heard a voice ask me, "Isn't this what you've been praying for?" I hadn't actually been praying for my husband and me to get back together, but I had been praying for the Lord to deliver me from drugs or let me die. He did the exceedingly, abundantly, above all I could ask or think (Eph. 3:20)!

A short while later, I realized that I had been totally delivered from drugs. I had no desire whatsoever to use any more. I was consuming a little alcohol and smoking cigarettes, but no other drugs at all. A flight from California to Kentucky, and that cocaine demon was gone! I was totally delivered!

Immediately I rededicated my life to the Lord. When I couldn't go to church, I would have church in the apartment with my children. God had delivered me and set me free by the blood of the Lamb, and I was glad about it. I had struggled for so many days, until it was a beautiful thing not to have to chase those drugs day in and day out. But it wasn't long until I knew God had not set me free just for me. It was time for me to pray my husband through, as well as continue to work on myself. I still was a mess spiritually. There were many things in my life that I needed to get delivered from, and I needed to forgive myself as well as others. I was truly a work in progress.

I wanted to work, but the Lord told me to stay at home and take care of my family. In the process of doing so, I had plenty of time for prayer and Bible study. The Holy Spirit taught me so much during that time. I had to grow, and I had to grow fast. In the beginning I didn't have any friends, and I knew I didn't need any at this time. After a little while, I did begin to pray for one good Christian friend, and the Lord blessed me to meet a lady who ultimately discipled me. Together, we attended Assembly of God Church in Clarksville, Tennessee until she left the area.

As the years went by, the Lord moved me to a new church home, Holiness Church of Deliverance in Hopkinsville, Kentucky, where the pastor is Gloria Leavell. It isn't a coincidence that the Lord moved me to a deliverance church. Only God knew that I would have a ministry dealing with deliverance. Soon after, I founded the Daughters of Destiny, a ministry that ministers to the mental, physical, and spiritual needs of women. Then I was asked to be a part of the jail ministry. Because I, too, had done twenty days in Sybil Brand, the jail in California for women, I knew I was in the right place.

On my first visit, I was told I was to do nothing but pray and observe; but after the praise and worship, I was informed that the Spirit of the Lord wanted me to share my testimony. I spoke just what the Lord wanted me to speak. That was also how I came up with the name Rhema Word. When you're ministering to people, you must know what needs to be said. We can speak many things to people, but the Holy Spirit knows exactly what is in the midst and what needs to be delivered to the people at that time.

We went back two weeks later, and the room was packed with women who said they had to come out and see the woman that the girls were talking about. I am not sure what they all told those ladies, but it drew a large crowd. They told me that I didn't look like I did anything I was claiming to have done. I let them know, that is just how good God is at cleaning us up. When He cleanses us, He leaves no residue.

Even though I go in with a team to minister to a group of women, I spend sometimes as much as four hours ministering one-on-one. Because I have overcome many obstacles, I can relate to much of what the women are going through. Truly what the devil meant for my harm, God has turned it around for my good and the good of others. It has become my quest in life. I (we) not only lead them to the Lord but also help them through their struggles and help to bring understanding to their misunderstanding. I tell them the truth in love, and that, sometimes, is hard to accept. I have to have an ear to hear what the Lord is saying to me to tell them to bring about deliverance. Because they tell me so much, I have to have discernment. My ministry is a ministry of deliverance!

Many are bound up and don't even realize it, and once that person is set free by the blood of the Lamb, the struggle is gone. You become free indeed. It is as if you have never had that problem before. I can truly say that in over twenty-five years, I have never struggled with the temptation of cocaine, alcohol, or cigarettes, which I was delivered from in November of 1987. The cocaine was in June of 1987.

Many times these women come in and out of jail like a revolving door. It can be discouraging, but because I know that as long as they are alive, they stand another chance at getting it right, I don't give up on them. Because I struggled so much, I know what it means to struggle. I know all about the spiritual warfare. I know that the Lord can take a terrible person and make them great. It is not the man but it is the spirit behind the man. Jesus overcame the world, and thus I am an overcomer too.

I know that no matter what challenges I face here on earth, God can and will see me through them all. There is nothing in this life that God cannot take care of or give me the strength, wisdom, or knowledge to take care of myself. Nothing is too hard for God, and because the greater one is living on the inside of me, I know that there is noting that I can't accomplish. It does not matter how hard or difficult it may seem or look. God is a miracle worker!

God is just, faithful, trustworthy, loving, kind, wonderful, praiseworthy, etc.! He is my all and all, and I don't say this because I have read about Him; I say all this because I have experienced it for myself. Many of the scriptures have been fulfilled in my life. I know firsthand that the forces of darkness are real. The enemy really is trying to do his job, which is to kill, steal, and destroy. I also know that he is a liar, and the truth is not in him. I know the Lord God is powerful, mighty, and He is a miracle worker because my daughter is a miracle. I know that the Word of God is living and powerful because I use it on a daily basis.

I have to stay connected to my Lord through prayer and the reading of His Word. I am not only a hearer of the Word; I am but also a doer of the Word of God. I stay close to the church and the members of the household of faith, realizing that we all come together in the unity of faith. I let nothing run me out of the house of the Lord. Jesus is the rock of my Salvation. He is the rock that is higher than I, and because of Him, I no longer have to chase the cocaine rock!

The enemy wants you to give up and throw in the towel, but I encourage every woman that may be going through issues, struggles, disappointments, situations, frustrations, and fears to hold on just a little while longer. God has a plan for your life (Jer. 29:11)! God will work it out if you let Him. You don't have to fall by the waist side; you don't have to give up or give in. The amazing thing to me when I think about my deliverance is, once I gave my life back to Christ, many evil desires left immediately. They were gone! The things that I loved to do on a daily basis, I no longer desired to do them. I used to party at the club sometimes four nights a week. I can truly say I have not desired to go to a club and party in over twenty-five years. It's as if I became a totally different person in June of 1987, and I have continued to both add and subtract from myself to become a better person as the days go by.

"And I am convinced *and* sure of this very thing, that He Who began a good work in you will continue until the day of Jesus Christ [right up to the time of His return], developing [that good work] *and* perfecting *and* bringing it to full completion in you" (Phil. 1:6, AB). I know God is not through with me yet. I have not arrived. I am still a work in progress. What He continues to do in my life, he can do for you also. I am no better than you are. No matter what you have done or are doing in your life right now, God will forgive you if you ask Him to!

Forgiveness is powerful and key to living a successful life. I walk in it everyday. I forgive myself, which is really hard to do sometimes, and I have learned to forgive others. I ask God's forgiveness on a daily basis. We must forgive in order to be forgiven. God really does give us the power to forgive. If you don't know the Lord as your personal savior, I encourage you to do so according to Romans 10:9-10.

I was raised in the church, participated in Bible quizzes, and sang in the choir. When I was a teenager I began to experience life. I didn't turn to what I had been taught all my life. I decided to try another way, darkness. I knew what the Bible said, but I did not abide by it. It is only by the grace of God that I am here today, able to share my story with truth and confidence. I know now for sure that Jesus really is real, and it does make a difference who we choose to live for. I had to make a choice! I guess because I believed the devil and his lies and got nothing from him but heartache, pain, and almost death in return, I now have no problem walking with the Lord and sharing my story of deliverance. I thank

God I am a Leading Lady and no longer a follower of darkness.

Since my testimony has been so profound among the women at the jail, the Lord told me I would put it in a book. It was prophesied to me; that it was going to go to the nation. I get calls from women I don't know, telling me how blessed they were after reading my book. There are women in the jail that have asked me to minister one-on-one with them after they read my book.

Sometimes it is like a dream, experiencing the goodness of the Lord. Not to say I don't have times in my life when everything is not going just right, but it's because I have my joy back. Joy like a river flowing enables me to keep pressing on! I don't lose heart, but I live to share this with all of God's children.

Again, the title of my book is *Booty Call: It's the Truth*. *Booty* is in the Bible (Numbers 31:32KJV), and it means "spoils of war." There is a call for man to come and get their goods, but the enemy has a booty call too. Let us take heed to the right call. I hope and pray I have encouraged you today! You, too, can be a Leading Lady!

You can purchase a copy of my book from Amazon.com, barnesandnoble.com. If you would like a personalized signed copy, you may contact me on Facebook. My e-mail address is *sjdodministries@gmail.com*

I am blessed to be a blessing!
I Will Always Love You!
I am a Leading Lady!

Sha Jackson
Servant of the Lord

44

Tameshia Mayfield

Be the change you want to see in the world.

—Ghandi

My name is Tameshia Mayfield, and I was born in Pageland, South Carolina, and raised an Army brat I am happily married to my best friend, lover, and partner Rapfeal; and together we have one son Isaiah, whom we love very much. Currently, I am an U.S. Army Recruiter in Clarksville, Tennessee.

The best part about my job is being able to help create a positive change in someone else's life.

The first thing that I want you to understand is that you are holy and you were created to be holy and set apart. Yes, the person reading this book, you are holy. This is the verse that helped take me out of captivity of low self-esteem. I first read this verse and thought, Really? My body is really God's temple? And He wants to dwell within me? It is overwhelming when you really sit down to think about it. Well, how do I know that God thinks of me as holy? You are holy because God says you are holy. You can see for yourself in the verse above. It is very important that you understand that God created you to be sacred and set apart. If you do not understand how important this is, it will be very hard for you to walk in it. You cannot just simply claim that you are holy, you must own it. This does not mean that you use this as a right of passage to judge someone else's life or make someone feel like they are less of a person. On the contrary, it means that you accept them the same as Christ accepts you because of God's grace. You have to own it, in your God-given right. It is something that you live out loud. Even though you were created to be holy, you still have to make a conscious choice to live differently, because it is what God has called you to do.

The second part of the verse talks about our body being a temple; well, friend, I am here to echo that divine truth. Your body is God's temple. It is a place where God can dwell, but it can't be true if you allow yourself to be defiled. You see, God carries us back to the same basic principle as before we are holy. When we begin our relationship with God, in order for us to understand that our body is God's temple, we must understand that we are called to be holy. You see, God cannot dwell where sin dwells, so we must not defile our bodies with drugs, alcohol, and sex or anything else that does not reflect God's beauty. We should treat our bodies as something sacred because they are. The important message that I want you to understand is that just because you have already traveled down a path where you did not exactly respect your body as God's temple, it does not mean that it is too late to start. I know what it's like to have a guy you really care about who uses you for sex. I've been in the back seat of a car in wooded areas, wondering how I let it get that far and thinking that this guy really loves me and that we would be together if I just gave in. I just wanted to feel loved, and I thought this was how you showed someone you loved them. Sometimes in life when we don't feel loved, we go looking for it in all the wrong places; sometimes it's deception fooling us with our feeling. We become wrapped up in what we think is love or what feels like love, and this is how we get caught up. It is during this time that we should cling to God's claim over our life and remember that we are called to be holy. If the person you are dating cannot respect your decision not to have sex, or if you have friends who do not respect your right not to get high or drunk, it is not that your standards are too high. It's that theirs may be too low. It is okay to rise to the standard that God has set for you. God wants what is best for us, not sloppy seconds, so why should we settle for less than what God has for us?

> I praise you because I am fearfully and wonderfully made. (Ps. 139:14).

The second thing that I want you to understand is that you are fearfully and wonderfully made by God. I want you to just sit there for a minute, close your eyes, and try to grasp this concept as much as you can. This is a very simple truth that we need to embrace. God designed you in such a way that you cannot be duplicated. God knitted you in your mother's womb. Every hair on your head, the color of your eyes, the shape of your nose, your hips, your eyes, your hands, everything about you is God-designed. You were created in God's image. It is time that we accept that fact. It's time for you to celebrate who you are, flaws and all. We all need to understand that our flaws come with part of the package. They are a part of who we are.

Please recognize that we all have imperfections that we do not like; but if we do not learn to accept our flaws it will be easy for the enemy to use this against us in an emotional and spiritual battle. Now when it comes to speaking to our human nature and character, we will also be flawed in those areas as well. But your relationship with the Lord will allow those areas to be improved. The more you spend time with the Lord, the more you want to change, not because God simply demands it but because you are compelled to. If you do not have a relationship with God, now is a great time to start one; the rest of your life depends on it. Becoming a Christian is not based on how perfect we are; it is about realizing how perfect God's love is for us because it allows us to be accepted, flaws and all.

God is already aware of our flaws. The Bible tells us that for He created our inmost being, He knows us well. So God is not surprised by any of our mistakes or inconsistencies. God loves us, in spite of them. Once you have accepted this fact, take time out to celebrate and delight in yourself. When you learn to celebrate yourself, learn to celebrate other people as well. It is okay for you to compliment another female; it's okay to befriend someone who may feel is prettier than you or has better clothes than you. Now would be a good time to stop sizing them and comparing them to you or vice versa and get to know them as a person. Many of us have struggled with the same insecurities and self-esteem issues, and maybe all we needed was a positive word from someone; we just needed someone to come and encourage us.

True beauty really does come from the inside out, and the more you focus on becoming a beautiful person on the inside, the more it is liable to manifest itself in physical form and be seen on the outside. Your aura will change, your entire countenance will change, and people will be attracted to the Jesus that lives inside of you. God created you in His own image, and God is love, and so you are created out of love and for love. This includes loving other people for who they really are.

> "For I know the plans I have for you declares the Lord, plans to prosper you and not harm you, plans to give you a hope and a future." (Jer. 29:11).

The third thing I want you to understand is that God created you with a purpose. You were designed to carry out God's purpose. The Lord wants to give you hope and a future that is prosperous; that is His heart's desire. Who you are or who you will grow to be cannot be found apart from God because it can only be found in God. Because you were created by God and for God's glory, isn't it kind of silly that we keep trying to find our purpose without Him. Let's take it one step further because many of us never even asked our Creator what He wanted for our lives. Your identity and the understanding of who you are cannot begin without God, and when you understand this, it will set you free and free indeed. I say this because all too often, you see situations where people are trying to be someone they are not. For example, there are many parents who try to live vicariously through their children, through broken dreams they had for themselves, When we try to live a life that was not created for us, you can be sure that disaster will follow, because we are not doing what God has designed us to do. To find out what one should be doing in this life, one should ask God; but here is the key: the only way for you to hear Him would be for you to have a relationship with God. God could have been speaking to you all this time, but you were unable to decipher which direction to go because you didn't recognize the voice of the Lord. Once you have established a relationship with the Lord and not a rapport, it becomes easier to recognize when God is speaking to you. Too often we treat God like a vending machine, picking and choosing what we do not like and when our relationship with God is much more crucial than that. Many times we want to continue to treat God like an acquaintance, but we want Him to be serious about what we have going and what we should be doing in life. Well, friend, I am here to tell you that God will not get serious about you until you get serious about Him, and I am not telling what I heard; I am telling you what I know. There are many times, that we want the blessings that God has for us without giving him any type of commitment. But the truth of the matter is why should God pay child support for a child that does not belong to him? What I mean by this is why should God hand out blessings and we can't learn to even make him a priority and take the time to create a relationship with Him?

When we treat God like an acquaintance, that is when we find ourselves in situations that make us unhappy, and we end up not being fulfilled. This can sometimes stem from doing something we are good at but we are not necessarily passionate about. God does not want you to be doing something that you just like doing, but He wants you to love what you are doing and moved by what you are doing. God will give you a strong heart's desire to be doing whatever it is that He has called you to do, and whatever resources that you need to accomplish that goal will be made available. Since when does God call people to do things that HE has designed them to do without being prepared and without the proper resources? Oh yeah, that's right, He doesn't; that is not even in God's character. Do not be afraid of where God is taking you if it leads you down a path of unfamiliarity. This is done so God can place you in your seat of purpose.

God has to take us out of our comfort zone sometimes to place us in a zone of faith where we depend totally on Him and not with things that we see going in a positive direction. God wants you depend on Him for everything. Think about when Peter walked on water with Jesus. God was showing us a picture. If you stay in the boat of religion, you will only meet disciples; but if you want a relationship with me and find your purpose for your life, you have to meet with me out here on the water. Your main job in finding out your purpose is to maintain your relationship with God so that you will be able to hear Him. If you cannot hear God, how will you know which way to move? I want you to understand me clearly; you have to be able to hear from God, so put yourself in position where you are able to hear the voice of the Father.

The simplest way to establish a relationship with God is to admit to God that you are sinner and believe that Jesus is God sons and that you need him in your life. Also begin to spend time talking with him and reading his word and finally commit your life to Lord and ask him to be Savior. As long as you continue to follow Jesus you will not get lost and remember you have already got the victory in Jesus' name.

Contact Information
Email: mayfieldswifey@gmail.com

45

Tamika Christian

You Have Value

Are not five sparrows sold for two pennies? And not one of them is forgotten before God. Why, even the hairs of your head are all numbered. Fear not; you are of more value than many sparrows.

—Luke 12:6-7

Recently, I went to a women's conference that was hosted by Pastor Angela Jones at Greenhill Baptist Church, and it was totally awesome! The name of the conference was Extreme Makeover! The Holy Spirit was all over the building. There were many different speakers, such as First Lady Dominique Miller, Pastor Kirby, and many more. The special guest speaker was Pastor Yolanda Morgan of Celebration of Life Church in Hendersonville, Tennessee. The conference included lunch, a fashion show, and giveaways.

At one moment I found my hands shaking with excitement, tears cascading down my face. I kept thinking to myself, *My God, You have blessed me with the ability to witness all of this!* Women, for once, were all on one accord seeking a Word from God, seeking a touch of His Spirit. The lessons that were taught dealt with the *whole* person, attitudes, personal image, etc. I began to ponder, *What do I see when I look in the mirror? What is my very own personal image?*

As I closed my eyes, I saw a shelf in the grocery store; and on that shelf is a row of canned goods. On this row, all the cans are perfect except for one dented can. I saw myself as a *dented* can. A tear slowly rolled down my face. I thought to myself, *My God, I take pleasure in uplifting and encouraging people all day, how can this be?* Do you know that you have value? I mean, do you truly know you have value? I have to say that God had to remind me that I did. Most of us keep ourselves so busy during the day to keep from having to go home and deal with ourselves. We will do anything to not have to get personal with ourselves because we have past hurts that are buried and have not healed. God wants you to know today that you are not bound to your past. No matter your past faults in God's eyes, you have value! Saints, it's not so much the *fall*; I believe God is more concerned with how you *recover*. God wants you to know you are stronger and wiser than your past! Remember, in the Bible, God took all the dented cans (Paul, Moses, Peter) and made a difference for the whole world.

In the story of Moses, he was a baby that was saved instead of slain. He was also was raised by the very people that wanted to kill him. He took a stand and murdered a man in the process, and all the while, when he went into hiding, God still called him for his purpose. Moses had a speech impediment, and in his self-image, he thought to himself, *Why would God use me? I can't even speak.* God had already known of his fault and shortcoming; however, He still used him to bring His people out of Egypt. And although he never made it to the promise land, he played a very valuable part in ensuring that God's people made it there.

Paul was a Pharisee who was extremely intelligent; however, he attacked and killed Christians. However, on that road to Damascus, it became very evident that it was no longer about what he knew himself to be; it was about what God had seen him to become—one of His chosen. After his conversion, he had a different battle; he knew he had to teach, preach, and gain the trust of the people he used to kill. Can you just imagine his self-image once his eyes were open? Imagine the pain that he must have felt after he knew the truth about himself and the mere fact that God still saw him as the apple of His eye, a soldier for the Lord's army, someone of value. The Bible says in Psalms 73:26, "My heart and my flesh may fail, but God is the strength of my heart and my portion forever." Please take a second and think about this scripture and what it means to you personally. As I meditated over this scripture, I began to feel peace. I began to look at myself through another set of eyes. I began to see me.

People of God, life has its ups and downs. You will go through challenges, you will struggle, you will be hurt, your heart will hurt so bad some days that it will be hard to breathe. Remember, God is the strength of your heart and your portion forever. And you have to know that beyond the shadow of a doubt, God will never leave you nor forsake you. That means that on your loneliest days, God is right there beside you, comforting you, reminding you that you are beautiful, you are worthy, and He is going to take care of all your needs. God is going to do all these things, not because of something you've done but because the love that He has for you is more than what you will ever have for yourself.

God wants you all to know that you all are worth so much more than you think; He loves all of you so much! Pray about those past hurts, and ask God to heal you and set you free from them; He will do it for you.

> But you, O Lord, are a God merciful and gracious, slow to anger and abounding in steadfast love and faithfulness. (Psalms 86:15)

May you all look past your dents and know that God loves you.

My Father Said

Tamika D. Christian

A whirlwind of confusion surrounds me as I stand still and pray
Heavenly Father, which art in heaven, what thou art of me to do in this whirlwind of confusion?

Shall I lay prostrate in the eye of the storm?
Shall I throw my hands up in defeat?
What does thou art of me, O Lord, God of all gods?

In my life there is no physical companion,
There is only the spirit that I have to comfort me—
Is this the way that it is supposed to be?

Father, what do I do for financial relief?
Do I continue to stand firm on my belief?

How do I tell my physical body to go on when I am so tired?
How do I bear the heat from the fire?

So many days I just want to give up
I just want to give in—

But your strength in me, Lord, won't let me give up
It won't let me give in—

Your presence surrounds me and makes me smile and gives
Me comfort on my most low days—why?

Why do you love me so much, when I am so unworthy of thy love
and affection?

Why do you grant me grace and mercy day after day?

"Because I am within you and you are within me. If I have suffered, so shall you. You are of my heart, created by me. You are my child, and I will always be there for you. Ask and you shall receive."

I will provide you all that you need, if you just ask, be patient and have faith—

Why? I ask.

And my father said, "Because I love you."

Contact Information:
Tamika D. Christian
E-mail: Tchristian40@gmail.com
Facebook: Tamika Christian

46

Tangie Conecha Smith-Singleton

Proverbs 31:10-31

> *Many daughters have done virtuously, but thou excellest them all.*
>
> —Proverbs 31:29

My name is Tangi Conecha Smith-Singleton, and I was born in Eastern North Carolina. I grew up in a small town called Fountain. I am a sergeant first class in the United States Army (active duty,) and I am also the owner and lead jewelry designer for Kute, Katchy, Klassy, a couture boutique in Miami, Florida. I am also a Certified Law of Attraction life coach. I enjoy traveling, meeting, and talking to new people. I love the army. I love designing and creating jewelry. Everything that I do, I do with my family's best interest in mind. I am a lover of people, and I am a lover of God. I am a Leading Lady.

I grew up in Fountain, North Carolina, a small town on the coast less than one hundred miles from Virginia's border. Growing up in Fountain, there was never really much to do. There were only two other girls my age to play with in the entire town, so to say I was a tomboy would be an understatement. From those little boys, I learned to be tough, to take stand for myself, and to not take anything off anyone, skills that served me well later in my life.

From the beginning, I've always known that the towns that I grew up in where much too small for me. I've always known that I was destined for more, that there was a greater purpose in my life. I just had no idea how to achieve it. Even as a small child, I was *different*, something I know now as being very creative. Which, let me tell you, was not widely accepted in the Church of our Lord Jesus Christ (COOLJC) Apostolic Pentecostal. Growing up, we girls were not allowed to wear pants, so with my mother's help, I created and designed outfits that were suitable and respectable in the church but also showed our creativity, although I often pushed the envelope on that one.

Other than being bored out of my mind, I actually had a very loving and stable childhood until I was twelve years old. That was when my parents split, and I fell into a great depression. Until this time I never really knew what it meant to struggle, as I had more than the average child could ever want. But seemingly, in a blink of an eye, it all changed, and life as I knew it turned upside down. My mother, little sister, and I went from having everything to absolutely nothing. We moved from our newly renovated house to a small mobile home in a trailer park (my, how my life has changed.) The father that doted on me so much in my earlier life acted as if he didn't know who we were. I often cried myself to sleep praying to God that my parents reconciled. I thought, *Why doesn't Daddy love me anymore, even if he's mad with Mommy, why won't he come get me?* For years, I blamed my mother for my father being no longer in our lives. Now, I know it was not her doing; there was no way she could have ever stayed and continue to endure what she endured. I have long since asked my mother's forgiveness, and I have recently forgiven my father. It was during this difficult time in my life that I started to crave the attention of the opposite sex, although I was still very skinny by anyone's standard. I was no longer a tomboy. In my freshman year of high school, I gave birth to a baby boy less than two months after learning I was pregnant. He only weighed 2.8 pounds at birth and stayed in the hospital's neonatal intensive care unit (NICU) until his original delivery date, which was a total of seven months. Kenzar Danielle came into this world, facing a ton of obstacles. At only two days old, he had to undergo an open heart surgery. Neither his lungs nor liver were fully developed, and he could not breathe on his own. The head doctor encouraged me to pull the plug on this little boy. He said that I'd rack up hundreds of thousands of dollars on medical bills that would plague me my entire life, and there was still less than a 50 percent chance that my son would survive. Being the teenager I was, I saw no other way and decided to go along with what the doctor suggested I do. However, my mother intervened. She saw things differently. She began to pray over that little baby, declaring and decreeing that nothing was too big for her God to handle! Well, that little boy survived and to this day is a healthy and vibrant young man. Throughout my whole ordeal, my mother, my church family, and my son's father's family were with me. My father, however, was nowhere to be found. I often wonder, *Did his neglect cause me to do some of the things that I did, looking for that father figure in all the wrong places?* To this day, I never miss an opportunity to tell every man I meet who has a daughter how important it is for him to be a part of her life. It really does make a difference, and it really does matter!

After high school, I was all set to attend North Carolina Central University in Durham, North Carolina. After touring the school and adding up the total cost, even with tuition assistance and grants, the price would be overwhelming for my mother alone as a single parent with three younger children, including my son, at home. I knew that I would have to work while attending school, and I have always been one to have to study and focus. Besides, I wasn't sure that I would actually succeed in college. I really wasn't enthused about spending a bunch of money on something that I was sure I would fail, so I decided to join the military strictly for college money and to possibly learn a trade and, most importantly, get away from Eastern North Carolina. In the army, I excelled. Everything about it came naturally easy for me. I thoroughly enjoyed my newfound freedom, meeting new people, and traveling to new and distant cities and countries. In the army, I met my first husband, someone who to this day is still one of my very best friends. However, after ten painful years of a struggling marriage and numerous sessions in marriage counseling, we realized that we were much better friends than mates. During all my years and my various duty stations (Germany;

Korea; Washington, DC; San Antonio, Texas). Fort Campbell, Kentucky, and Clarksville, Tennessee, always stood out as two of my best. It was a place where I felt at home and could truly rest, so in 2009, I made my way back to Fort Campbell. I was a newly divorced single parent, but that didn't matter because I had a cache of friends and helpers living in the area, and I knew we could be okay. There I purchased my first home and went about making my mark in the community as well as in my military career. I had always been very aggressive in my military career—the tomboy in me—and I held positions that were higher than my pay grade. At this point, everything in my life seemed perfect. I'd often go to work singing, "I love my job, I love my life, God is so good to me!" Now, how many people know that when things are going too well, the devil always try to throw a little salt and lemons in your life? Less than a year of being at my beloved duty station (Blanchfield Army Community Hospital), I was given orders to report to the 101st Combat Aviation Brigade (CAB) to be deployed to Afghanistan with them as their Fifth Battalion's noncommissioned officer in charge (NCOIC) of their battalion's aid station and Forward Operating Base (FOB) Wolverine's senior combat medic. Initially, I was less than enthused, but at the same time, I was excited about my new adventure; and for the very first time in a long time, I was extremely nervous. As the time got closer for me to leave, I was super excited and just ready to go! Arriving in Kandahar, I decided that aside from the horrible smell that often woke me up at night, Afghanistan wasn't so bad. Later after arriving at FOB Wolverine, I thought, *This isn't going to be so bad.* After all, aside from the fact that I was extremely lonely and a bit misplaced, I was a MEDDAC (hospital) soldier; and I honestly knew very little about being a medic and the rouged living of a typical soldier. I was officially the *new girl*, but with my outgoing and bubbly personally, it didn't take long for me to fit right in and become one of the guys. I loved my job in Afghanistan, and I loved the position that I held. God had done it once again, and here I was, excelling in a way that only He could permit. One of the unofficial duties I served in was counselor. Soon after I arrived, the social worker that served as the behavioral health provider left, and no one new was sent to us. Because I was a female, easy to talk to, nonjudgmental, an Equal Opportunity representative, and the NCOIC of the battalion's aid station, it was only natural for soldiers to confide in me. They'd often come to the aid station under the guise of going to morning *sick call* to talk and ask my opinion on several aspects of their lives. It was during this time that I met a male that I noticed was scorned by other soldiers. It's as if he had a scarlet letter on his chest, and he always looked so sad and walked around so lost. I inquired about his status and was told to stay away from him because he was this and that, yet no one had any proof; everything was hearsay. Tangi, being the person I am, an advocate for human rights and equality for everyone, thought that it was horrible for someone to be ostracized there on such a small stand-alone FOB. That it wasn't fair and couldn't be well for his mental psyche not to have friends or an outlet. So I started speaking to him, and initially he looked shocked that I had said anything to him, which made me feel worse about the way that others were treating him. Up until that point, I always ate my dinner alone at 6:00 p.m. in the dining facility, reading my Kindle. One day he asked if he could sit with me, and I said yes; from that day forward, we always met and ate dinner together. I found that he was very funny, actually hilarious, and we would sit there for hours after the staff had cleaned up and closed down everything, laughing, joking on each other, and just giggling like high school students. He certainly made my time in Afghanistan go by faster than I'm sure it would have gone without him there. But as always, there was a price to pay.

He was redeployed home a month before I did, and since he and his entire immediate family lived together, there was nothing much for him to do upon returning except unpack. When I returned, I had to prepare my house back to its original living condition. Although, my custodial was very good at keeping my house up to par, there was something about an unlived house. My flight landed at Campbell Army Airfield a little after 9:00 p.m., and he expected to see me that night. For the next few days, he didn't want to let me out of his sight and would get angry and yell whenever I would state that I was with friends or even working. Something that he, being a soldier who had recently been redeployed, should have very well understood better than most. On my sixth night home, I decided that I had had enough; he was not my husband, not my boyfriend, and I wouldn't tolerate it. However, when he called asking me if I wanted to go riding on his motorcycle, knowing my fascinations with them, I couldn't resist. The ride went smooth, and afterward I invited him into my house. Something I would later regret. I showered, and he relaxed. He later said that he drank some alcohol that I had stored on my German bar before I was deployed, yet I never saw anything missing. After I put on my pajamas and invited him upstairs to watch a movie, he started looking at me really funny. I still remember my hair standing up on my arms at the anticipation that something horrible was about to happen. That's when he started yelling at me, saying that I thought I was better than everyone else and how he started to make me have an accident on the motorcycle when we were riding earlier. That night, aside from being beaten from within an inch of my life, he sexually assaulted me and held me hostage at gunpoint for over six hours. I remember thinking, *Oh my God, who is this person? Everything that everyone said in Afghanistan was true, and now I am going to die in my home, in my bedroom, only six days after returning from Afghanistan.* I thought of my children and how I wouldn't get to say goodbye to them. I thought of my mother and siblings whom I had insisted not to come to my homecoming because I wouldn't get to spend time with them; I would just come see them after reintegration, when we were released to go home on vacation. How I may have deprived them of ever seeing me alive again. I thought of all this, and I cried, I cried, and I prayed. I thought, *If I am going to die, Lord, if this is Your will, then I would die praying. I would die asking You to cuddle my soul and welcome me home.* Needless to say, I didn't die that night. God answered my prayers. I often wish that someone else were in that room that night to see the transformation that took place, because as I began to pray, he began to stop hitting me. It was as if my prayers hurt his ears, and he had to stop to cover his head and face. He went from yelling at me to stop praying to pleading and begging me to pray for him, and as quick as it started, it stopped. Telling you how I got out of that house that night is another altogether.

His trial in Clarksville went on for over a year because it happened in my Montgomery County home, so they had jurisdiction. I can't describe the anguish and failure I felt when they said that the case was being released with prejudice, meaning while he wasn't technically found not guilty, he wasn't guilty either and would have no record. I then had to move from Fort Campbell, and that was how I came to live in Miami. I remember thinking what a failure I was and how the *system* had let me down. I still remember Bishop Kenneth Smith telling me, "Tangi, your delay is not your denial." Something I really didn't want to hear at the time. All I knew was I was the victim and I was being treated like the criminal. My beloved army had failed me. For months, I was very bitter.

A few months before I was scheduled to leave Clarksville, things started to turn around for me. Once again God was proving that if I let Him be in control and release everything to Him, he would take care of me. Within one week, I started ministry school, and my boyfriend of three years proposed. He had been with me throughout the entire ordeal and was very patient in all aspects of our relationship. I made the sergeant-first-class promotion list, and I found out that not only would I merely be an army recruiter but I'd also be stationed in Miami as a health-care recruiter, recruiting only health-care professionals such as doctors, dentist, nurses, etc. It was then that I realized I had forgiven him. When I forgave, that was when God opened His floodgates and bestowed all the blessing and favor that were truly mine.

Had events in my life not played out the way they did, I probably would not have been able to successfully have the custom-jewelry business that I have today. In Miami, things just flowed openly to me. Everything just worked out in my favor. I remember that when I first arrived, I'd go to my prayer closet and ask God, *Okay, now what? Why did You bring me here away from my church, away from ministry school that I so enjoyed, away from my support group, away from my comfort zone?* I realize now that sometimes God has to do drastic things in your life to grab your attention, so you can focus on Him and the things that truly matter in life. My advice to all who read this would be to always put God first and never give up. Even when it seems there is no way out, never give up. I only pray that I will be able to reach others with my story and that my beacon of light will shine bright for them to follow.

Accessory Boutique: www.KuteKatchyKlassy.com
Life Coach: www.RedCarpetReady.vpweb.com
Facebook: tangi.c.smith@facebook.com
Twitter: @kutekatchyklass
Instagram: @tangising @kutekatchyklassy
E-mail: tangicsingleton@gmail.com or tangi.c.smith.mail@mail.mil

47

Tiffinea Reid-Breaux, LCSW

Psychotherapist

(Nashville, Tennessee)

1 Thessalonians 5:24 (NLV) [24] *The One Who called you is faithful and will do what He promised.*

I am a native of the cotton littered fields of Brownsville, Tennessee. I am blessed to have a blended family. My biological parents married young, divorced and both remarried. I was raised by my mother and stepfather Justine and Charles Cooper, who together, with Christ as their guide, laid the foundation for the Woman of God I have become. I am the oldest of four daughters on my mother's, side of the family. My biological father and stepmother, Stanley and Sharon Reid were an essential part of my life. I am the oldest of three and only daughter on my biological father's side of the family. I am a keeper of my blended family. I am honored to be the wife of my wonderfully support loving husband, a proud Louisiana native, Melvin Breaux. I am the mother two beautiful daughters, Taylor Jones and Justice Breaux. I am a graduate of University of Kentucky, where I earned both my Bachelor and Master of Social Work degrees. I am an Arizona State University, DBH Doctoral Candidate. I am a Psychotherapist, Licensed Clinical Social Worker, Board Certified Diplomat and co-owner with my husband of the private practice, Reid, Breaux, and Associates. I am a case manager for Homeless Veterans with the United States Department of Veterans Affairs. I am a community advocate for persons living with HIV/AIDS. I am a Children's Ministry Coordinator at Clark Memorial United Methodist Church. I am a United Methodist Woman, serving my local congregation in the role of Mission Coordinator of Social Action. I am a Leading Lady.

My Plan

Theoretically speaking, I would be best characterized as a Type A individual. It is true that I am motivated, structured, and a practical high achiever, however these characteristics have been a blessing and a challenge for me my entire life. Women like me tend to create a plan and then take meticulous steps to ensure that it is followed precisely. We leave very little room for chance and even less for faith.

According to the plan I set for myself years ago, I would complete college, get married, have children, and live happily ever after. Sounds good right . . . Wrong! In reflection, I have to admit that the God I serve is a gentleman; he extended his permissive will and allowed me to "work my plan." And so it began. Soon after I finished college, I hurriedly married without my parents' blessings. At the time, it did not matter, because it was the next box on my list to be checked. There was no stopping me, I was on a roll, and then came the baby in the baby carriage. Time passed slowly. I had checked all of my boxes on my list, but still was left with this dark empty feeling of despair as "my plan" failed. I was experiencing a true lack of direction and my world began to crumble. It was during this time, my biological father passed, suddenly of a myocardial infarction. Not long afterwards, my marriage ended despondently in a divorce.

Those who know me best can attest that this was a transformational time for me. Up until this point, I had known God though the example set forth by my parents. I believed, because they said to believe. I relied on their faith, their words, and their guidance. This was my Achilles heel because I did not know God for myself. I found myself at fork in the road. I did not know which path to take. To be honest, I had become paralyzed by the fear of making the wrong choices and poor decisions. I was overcome with depression. Time passed slowly. Thinking back I had settled in to a weekly routine that left me stagnant for months: counseling, work, and church. I went to counseling to cry and as an endeavor to process the emotional and physical traumas that I had experienced. I went go to work simply to earn money so I would able to provide for my child. I went to church to pray for insight with the hope that a positive change would occur in my life. In looking back I recognize that this each place, counseling, work, and church, had its purpose in God's divine plan for my life.

Trust the Lord

I first embraced the importance of learning to trust God on this part of my journey. Several months had passed when my mother, who had been unusually quiet, not offering advice or suggestion, reached out to me and asked, "Are you ready for things to change in your life?" I remember thinking to myself, "Where have you been? Of course I am ready for change!" However, I responded with "I am so tired of the way things are going. I thought I was doing everything right. It feels like I am stuck. I can't move forward. I am frustrated. I am angry. Why did God let these things happen to me?" Time passed slowly. She offered her listening ear then responded by reminding me of the scripture in Luke 22:32 (NLT) where Jesus admonishes Peter, by saying "[32]But I have pleaded in prayer for you, Simon, that your faith should not fail. So when you have repented and turned to me again, strengthen your brothers." She went on to say "You have to go through tests in order to have a testimony. Sometimes you go through things so you will be able to help others." This concept resonated with me because I am a social worker and we are often considered the helping profession.

Now that she had garnered my attention, she assumed her role as Evangelist Justine Cooper, and began to speak life into my spirit. She explained that she had been in prayer and could not offer support or advise until it was the right time. She took every one of my concerns and provided insight as follow:

On the comment, "I thought I was doing everything right." She offered a reminder of first of the Ten Commandments as outlined in Exodus 20: 1-3 (NLT)20 Then God gave the people all these instructions[2] "I am the LORD your God, who rescued you from the land of Egypt, the place of your slavery.[3] "You must not have any other god but me." She lovingly reprimanded me for what she deemed as the root of the problem, I had allowed my plan and my will to become a god in my life. On feeling stuck, like I can't move forward, she highlighted Proverbs 3:5-6 (NLT) Trust in the Lord with all your heart; do not depend on your own understanding. Seek his will in all you do, and he will show you which path to take." I was there. I had reached the point where it was time to stop trying to do it my way. I would have to go to God for direction. On feeling frustrated and angry, she then suggestion these words from the scripture, Jeremiah 29:11 (NLT) [11] "For I know the plans I have for you," says the LORD. "They are plans for good and not for disaster, to give you a future and a hope." On the question of why did God let these things happen to me? She reminded me that not only does he allow things to happen, but he will restore back to you what was lost. Joel 2:25(NLT)[25] The LORD says, "I will give you back what you lost to the swarming locusts, the hopping locusts, the stripping locusts, and the cutting locusts. It was I who sent this great destroying army against you." Finally she ended with these words of encouragement 1 Thessalonians 5:24 (NLV)[24] "The One Who called you is faithful and will do what He promised."

These insights were further confirmed by other women of faith whom God had strategically placed in my life such as my First Lady Prophetess Abigail Orusa who, during those seven years, partnered in prayer with me at God's Sanctuary Church. Pastor Roselyn Oduyemi, who declared that I should in faith ask God for the impossible, because as stated in 1 Thessalonians 5:24 (NLV)[24] "The One Who called you is faithful and will do what He promised." Mrs. Cynthia Pitts, my spiritual mentoring mother, reassured me that God will heal my broken heart. I am so blessed to have such wise woman in my life. I encourage all women who are in transition to surround yourself with persons of like faith and like belief. I am forever grateful to all those women, whom names I have not named that partnered with me in prayer. May the peace of Christ be with you.

Lessons Learned

In the spirit of being truly authentic it took me seven years to work through all of what had been poured into me during that season of my life. I continued to remain committed to my routine of counseling, work, and church. It seems that over the years the order of importance will shift intermittently. Currently, it aligns more closely to church, work, and counseling in sequencing as I am experiencing clarity.

Contemplate the Necessity of being God-Centered

The greater part of my journey focused on me actively ccontemplating the necessity of being God-Centered. I needed to be able to visual this concept for my life. Time passed slowly. I knew what spirituality looked like for my parents, family members and friends; however, I felt strongly that for my journey it needed to be clearly defined. Being God-centered has been a process for me. Foundationally is the reading of God's word through devotion and prayer daily. I read devotional books and I utilize apps on my phone and tablet. In this hurried world, there are days when it is more challenging to stay committed, often I have to stop and prioritize my actions. I pray and meditate daily because I made a declaration, to trust the Lord. This means I have to be patient and wait on God for guidance and confirmation when making choices and decisions. I also incorporated repentance and forgiveness. Romans 3:23 (NLT) reminds me "For everyone has sinned; we all fall short of God's glorious standard." When I find myself in a situation in which I have fallen short of God's standard, I repent, forgive myself, and move on with the intention of not making that same mistake. If you feel unbalanced, make the shift. Make spirituality a priority in your life.

Invest in the Cultivation of Your Family

My husband and I are making an effort to lead by example. We shared similar levels of commitment to faith in our families of origin. We would like to pass that tradition on to our children. This concept was echoed in Joshua 24:15 (NLT)[15] But if you refuse to serve the LORD, then choose today whom you will serve. Would you prefer the gods your ancestors served beyond the Euphrates? Or will it be the gods of the Amorites in whose land you now live? But as for me and my family, we will serve the LORD." We have taken the practical step of attending a faith based parenting workshop and incorporating some of the suggestions into our family lifestyle. An example would be clearly defining for our children our values, moral, and beliefs. We value service and fellowship, which is why we are active participants within various ministries at our local church and attend church service regularly.

Not everyone is married, so it is important to consider this concept outside of the marital relationship. Many of us are daughters, sisters, aunts, cousins, and so on. We must also remain connected in ways that will enrich the lives of our extended family members. I am reminded of the movie Soul Food and the tradition of having Sunday dinner together. Each one of us is responsible for being our family's keeper. As aging family members' transition from this earth to Glory, we are left with the memories of what they valued and held dear. We are responsible for passing the torch to the next generation. If not you, then who will step up and invest in the cultivation of your family?

Serve Altruistically in Your Community

I am reminded of the scriptures that focus on the importance of giving. So often the word giving evokes fear into our purses and wallets. For some, the resources to give financially may not be an option at this time. Do consider serving in your community. Christ reminds us in Luke 6:38(NLT)[38] Give, and you will receive. Your gift will return to you in full—pressed down, shaken together to make room for more, running over, and poured into your lap. The amount you give will determine the amount you get back. Consider the shoulders on which you have stood. The helping hand or kind words you were given at a time when you needed it most. We ar e further reminded in Luke 12:48 (NLT) [48] But someone who does not know, and then does something wrong, will be punished only lightly. When someone has been given much, much will be required in return; and when someone has been entrusted with much, even more will be required. Find your passion and serve. I am a community advocate for persons living with HIV/AIDS. I attend community meetings and serve on committees to ensure that resources are allocated to provide needed services. You may not be able to serve at this level, but you can serve in some capacity. It starts with one step, you having a desire to help your community. I encourage you to do the research, find a cause that evokes passion within you and begin to volunteer.

Be Open Both Give and Receive Love

Many of us are hurting. We are holding on to hurts of the past, present, and in fear of future hurts. That is not God's will for our lives. We are reminded of what love is in the 1 Corinthians 13 (NLT) 4 Love is patient and kind. Love is not jealous or boastful or proud [5] or rude. It does not demand its own way. It is not irritable, and it keeps no record of being wronged. [6] It does not rejoice about injustice but rejoices whenever the truth wins out. [7] Love never gives up, never loses faith, is always hopeful, and endures through every circumstance. Five years after I had begun this healing journey, I met my husband. When he came into my life, I was open enough to both give and receive love again. I had done the healing work. I had gone to counseling to process old hurts and unresolved issue. God had restored my broken heart. I was ready. Two years later, after premarital counseling and blessings from both of our families, we were united in Holy Matrimony. When it comes to matters of the heart, one must seek to find truth and comfort in God's word.

I am convinced that each of us will come to a fork in the road. It was only after my plan crumbled before me, did I even take the time to acknowledge God in my life. For me, time moved slowly, but that was a part of God's plan so that I could learn these essential lessons. As you begin your healing journey, contemplate the necessity of being God-centered, invest in the cultivation your family, serve altruistically in your community, and sanction yourself to be open enough to both give and receive love again. Peace on the Journey.

Reidbreaux@gmail.com

48

Treva R. Gordon

Leading Ladies, Inc., Founder

I can do all things through Christ who strengthens me. (NKJV)

—Phil 4:13

My Personal Story

I am a 70's child. I was born in Detroit, Michigan, and at the age of two, my family relocated to River Rouge, Michigan. I was raised by my mother and father. I have three sisters. In our home there was love, but also lots of arguing and fights. However, I recall some of my best days were going to our church with my mother, and also to grandmother's house. I grew up in the River Rouge Public School System and graduated from River Rouge High School in 1988. I later attended a junior college for one year.

In my early years, I faced many learning challenges. I was a poor reader, and had difficulty with reading and comprehension. I was not learning at the rate of my peers. As a result of this, I was placed in special education from the first through the sixth grade. I often felt like I didn't belong and was frustrated for being placed in this class. I never felt smart or good enough and could not envision myself ever going to college. I daily battled low self-esteem. Have you ever felt this way in your life?

Other issues also affected me while growing up. I was unhappy with my appearance; I thought I was too tall, too skinny, or too black. I didn't like any of my features. I hated looking in the mirror. I actually thought I looked worst than Frankenstein. I did not like my appearance. Even as a teen, I wondered when I would develop as most other girls in my class. Many times I was ridiculed and teased as a teenager for having a flat chest. Although I often tried to make light of the situation I was unhappy on the inside. Why was I taller than all the girls in my class? Why did mother shop at the goodwill? I never liked my clothes and sometimes was teased at school because of them. Plus, I was dealing with issues at home, and peer pressure, all while developing as a teen and trying to figure out the woman into whom I was becoming.

In February 1992, at the age of twenty-two, I entered the army. My basic training camp was held at Fort Leonard Wood Missouri. My schooling was also held here at this base. The army later stationed me at Fort Campbell Kentucky. My military occupation was a motor transportation specialist (truck driver—88M). After only a few months of being in the military, I met the love of my life, Robert Gordon. We met July 1992, and were married on March 13, 1993 at the Memorial Chapel. I am proud to say that we have been married for twenty years.

Together, my husband and I have three children. We are proud of them all. They are each unique and well loved. Our oldest son's name is Robert, our middle son's name is Tevin, and our baby girl's name is Robyn. In our home, there's always something to do. Throughout the year, our children are involved in school and various activities. They keep us very busy but we are blessed.

Today as I reflect back over my life, I am thankful for neighbors, school teachers, pastors, friends, employees, and family members whom God has placed and is still placing in my path. I truly believe that if it had not been for the Lord who was on my side where I would be. I will admit there are times in my life where I have quit at certain things, or have wanted to quit by throwing in the towel. One thing that I love most about God is that He never gives up on His people. I also know that my Father loves me. God is always there.

In 1993, my mother died of cancer. This was a very hard blow to our family. I thought at one time she would pull through. I wanted her to live. However, it really hurt me to see her suffer in this way. She was only forty-five years old when she passed away. After my mother's passing, it seemed as if the sun would never shine again in my life. I now felt alone and didn't know how I or my family would go on without her. There were times where things seemed impossible, but God made the way for our family. Today, all I can say is God. I am so thankful for my mother's love. Yes, she loved her children. Our family may have had issues growing up, but one thing I can say for sure is that mother loved her girls. She was a woman who was full of strength.

As I think about what mother had to go through—years of chemotherapy treatments and radiation, losing her hair, losing weight, the suffering and pain, all while trying to keep a smile on her face, and trying to stay strong for her children; I don't how she did it. She was the most courageous person I have ever known in my life. I will not complain about the brief years spent with my mother, but instead I will give thanks to God for what she instilled in me and my sisters. I would not be the woman I am today if it had not been for my mother. She was very tough on me. Sometimes I felt it was too tough. But that's another story. I believe my mother is in a better place and she would be proud of her girls. I believe she is cheering us on in heaven.

I would also like to thank my father for being a great dad and grandfather to my children. Growing up he instilled within me a great work ethic. He taught his daughters practical things in life. To this day, I am most thankful for the relationship we all have with our father. I am a daddy's girl. He lives in Michigan, so therefore we spend a great deal of time on the phone catching up.

As far as my sisters, I am thankful for Alesia, Melissa, and Melanie. They have humbled me and are my rock. I am the second to the oldest child. They each keep me grounded, and I am so thankful for them. I am again blessed to have a great husband in my life who is a hard worker and a great father too.

I am a miracle. I am thankful to God for my healing testimony. In 2004, after giving birth to my daughter Robyn, I suffered toxemia. Preeclampsia or toxemia is a condition that occurs only during pregnancy. Diagnosis is made by the combination of high blood pressure and protein in the urine, occurring after week twenty of pregnancy. Toxemia is often precluded by gestational hypertension. While in my third trimester of pregnancy, I went from feeling healthy and fine, to the next day literally fighting for my life after giving birth of my daughter.

I was rushed to the emergency room. While in the hospital and in the intensive care unit, I recall many conversations I had with God. He was right there by my side. He never left my alone. People from all over were praying for me to live. I was fighting for my life. The toxemia caused my internal organs to fail. My liver and kidneys stopped functioning. I suffered high blood pressure, severe edema, blood clots, cardiac arrest, excruciating pain, unconsciousness, and multiple episodes of hemorrhaging. As a result of this, I had to receive several blood transfusions, and was immediately placed on a dialysis machine. After two days of being in the critical care unit, I was airlifted to a nearby hospital in Nashville, Tennessee. The hospital had then notified family members about the severity of my condition. They soon arrived to Tennessee. They could not believe what was going on with me. They stayed by my bedside in love and in prayer.

During this time, my husband was serving in Iraq in the military. Red Cross contacted his unit with a message for him to come home immediately. Upon his arrival, he met a very ill wife. I thank God for his prayers. I cannot even imagine what he must have been going through. I mean just the thought of losing his wife and having to care for our three children alone must have been a whole lot to bear. Many people came from everywhere to be with me and my family at this time. I am thankful for those who came to visit me in the hospital and for their overwhelming expression of love and support. My dad and my sisters were also there. I am especially thankful that my pastor, church members, classmates, prayer warriors, friends, hospital staff, and even strangers remained strong for me.

I love this scripture found in James 5.16:

> Confess your faults one to another, and pray one for another, that ye may be healed. The effectual fervent prayer of a righteous man availeth much.

While in the hospital, God gave me space and time to pray and to repent. I am so thankful for a second chance to live. After my release from the hospital, I still had a great deal of recovery to go. My kidneys were still not functioning at 100 percent; I was now living with high blood pressure, heart palpitations, swelling, pain, loss of appetite, pain in my extremities, and depression. My daughter on the other hand was strong and healthy; she is a miracle.

I was assigned a home health nurse for three weeks and a physical therapist for two weeks. While at home, I was still not physically strong. I was not allowed to hold my baby. I was taking twenty-three pills per day. My blood pressure was high and often times I was rushed to the emergency room for difficulty breathing and pain. My husband became my around the clock caregiver. He was very loving and nurturing. He was very protective of me.

People often ask me today, are you healed? The answer is YES. I am so thankful that God allowed me and my daughter to live. My recovery took several months, but God made the way. I am thankful for life. God gave me a second chance. Praise God.

Isaiah 53:5

> But he was wounded for our transgressions, he was bruised for our iniquities: the chastisement of our peace was upon him; and with his stripes we are healed.

Whatever your situation is, you must speak life. Speak life to your situation. Don't be quick to settle and take out time to pray. Maybe you have received some very bad news, but don't let that be the end of your story or allow your hope to fade. Faith is very valuable in our lives as well as prayer. I believe that God IS a healer. I believe that He can make a difference in each and every one of us. In Christ, there is hope for tomorrow. Each day I stood on the word of God for my healing and claimed it. I spoke the word by faith. I read scriptures only pertaining to healing over and over again. I spent many days alone in commune time with the Lord. I would tell myself daily that I was healed. The key is that you must believe.

So just what are you asking or believing God to right now? Whatever it is, keep the faith my sister or brother because God isn't finished with you yet. In 2013, I was blessed to have my testimony air on the *The 700 Club* (Christian Broadcasting Network—CBN), and also on the Trinity Broadcasting Network (TBN) with host Pastors Joseph and Yolanda Morgan. It has also aired for television on the *Lois Banks Show* (Impact Network), as well as heard on the Boston Praise Radio, and more. To God be the glory for allowing me the opportunity to share my story with millions of viewers around the world.

Remember, in the beginning of my chapter, I shared with you about growing up in special education? In 2000, the Lord blessed me to enter back into college. I was age thirty at the time. My first day back in school brought about many old feelings. I felt uncertain again, but God gave me the strength to stay to the course. In 2005, I graduated at the age of thirty-five with honors from Austin Peay State University. To God be the glory. I obtained a bachelor's degree in corporate communications and marketing. I am thankful for the victory.

Immediately after my graduation in 2005, my husband and I started a business. Together we publish *Convenient Shopper Magazine*. The first issue was published on my birthday July 8th. What seemed impossible, God made possible. We started out with no money for this business but we had faith. Yet God provided. As the years went by, I began getting more involved with community events and also assisting several non-profit organizations. In 2011, God called me as an evangelist. I said *yes* to the call.

In 2012, I was honored as the Business Woman of the Year by the Gospel Music City Awards, and also in 2011 as Citizen of the Year by Omega Psi Phi Fraternity. I will always say that God is good. No matter how high or low, good or bad, things can be at times; God is still good. Keep looking to Jesus, and let nothing stop you from achieving your dreams in life. Discover your passion. There is purpose for your life. Ask God to help you. Matthew 6:33

I am blessed to have worked in television and radio throughout the years. I have shared platforms with Ambassador Dr. Bobby Jones, Pastor Wess Morgan, Dr. Dorinda Clark-Cole, attended the Stellar Awards from backstage, and more. I have had opportunities to interview Artist such as

Vickie Winans, David and Tamela Mann from Tyler Perry, Kirk Franklin, Comedienne Lavell Crawford, and many more. I am thankful for everything God has given to me. He is amazing.

I am looking forward to many things to come through Leading Ladies. In October 2012, Leading Ladies connected with the Women of Transition in Michigan and we were blessed to have had our first women's conference. This event was a great success. I wanted God to do something special in my hometown. A placed where I had grown up. Special thanks to Leading Ladies Janine Folks and Yvonne Hill for their loving support. Together with God's help we were able to make this happen. I would also like to thank Union Second Baptist Church and River Rouge High School.

Don't Quit

When things go wrong, as they sometimes will,
When the road you're trudging seems all uphill,
When the funds are low and the debts are high,
And you want to smile, but you have to sigh,
When care is pressing you down a bit,
Rest, if you must, but don't you quit.

Life is queer with its twists and turns,
As every one of us sometimes learns,
And many a failure turns about,
When he might have won had he stuck it out;
Don't give up though the pace seems slow,
You may succeed with another blow.

Often the goal is nearer than,
It seems to a faint and faltering man,
Often the struggler has given up,
When he might have captured the victor's cup,
And he learned too late when the night slipped down,
How close he was to the golden crown.

Success is failure turned inside out,
The silver tint of the clouds of doubt,
And you never can tell how close you are,
It may be near when it seems so far,
So stick to the fight when you're hardest hit,

It's when things seem worst that you must not quit.

Unknown Author

I would like to dedicate my entire chapter to my mother, the late great Mrs. Joan Sanders. My mother is the reason I have kept going strong. Also to Leading Lady Bernadette Fox. She was one of our first Leading Ladies starting out with us in 2011. She passed away in 2012. She will be forever missed. To Leading Lady Helene Waters, my former elementary school teacher, I would like to thank you for always believing in me and encouraging me. Special thanks to Ms. Lucille Cook.

I would also like to thank everyone who has supported our magazine. To every reader and advertiser, thank you. Special thanks to my assistants and supporters Denise Bell, Ashley Sisco, and DaShaunda Turner. Thanks to Jameka Horton for assiting me too.

Yes, throughout my life, I have been blessed to live, work, and serve in my community. I am the creator of an event I founded in 2010 called Unity Day. A yearly event that honors local heroes in our community. In March 2013, I was honored by Ambassador Dr. Bobby Jones and presented with a community service award. It meant so much to me. Special thanks to Ms. Rosetta Perry and entire staff at the Tennessee Tribune for your recommendation.

I am also a singer and a songwriter. I released my first CD in 2011. My first single "Devil U's A Lie" is about my testimony. Since then, I have been writing plays and directing them. In 2012, I wrote *Deception "Fooled By A Feeling."* I am the executive producer, director, and writer. In February 2013, the play made it's first debut and has had sold out performances. The play features Dove and Stellar Nominated Artist Pastor Wess Morgan. It is also co-written and directed by LaVon Bracey, who is also featured in the play. We are currently on tour. I am grateful to have such a dynamic cast of dedicated actors along with a great production crew as well.

Now I would like to say a prayer for you:

> Father, in the name of Jesus, I thank you for this believer. I ask that You will help him or her to advance Your kingdom even more. Thank You for being a healer, a deliverer, a friend. Help us to go further in You. Now Lord, bless our families. Please keep Your

hand of protection all around us daily. Help us to look unto You, from which all of our blessings flow. Amen.

Contact Information:

Stay in contact with me. If you would like to book me to come and minister, sing, or emcee at your next event or function, here is my contact information:

Websites: TrevaGordon.com
Cshoppermagazine.com
Facebook: Treva Gordon
Twitter: Treva Gordon
E-mail: ccshopper@bellsouth.net
Or Booking@TrevaGordon.com

49

Deaconess Winsome W. Brown-Blackford

(Clarksville, Tennessee)

Perseverance

I was walking down life's highway a long time ago. I saw a sign that read Heaven's Grocery Store. As I got a little closer, the door opened wide; and when I came to myself, I was standing inside. I saw a host of angels, and they were standing everywhere. One handed me a basket and said, "My child, shop with care." Everything a saint needed was in that grocery store, and what you couldn't carry, you could come back the next day for more. First, I got some patience; love was in the same row. Further down, understanding; you need that everywhere you go. I got a bag of two of wisdom, a box of two of faith. You couldn't miss the Holy Ghost for it was all over the place. Next I got some strength and courage to help me run this race. By then my basket was getting full, but I remembered I needed some grace. I didn't forget salvation, for salvation was free, so I had to get enough of it to save both you and me. Then I started up the counter to pay my grocer's bill, for I thought I had enough to do my master's will. Then I saw prayer, I just had to put that in, for I knew that when I stepped outside, I would run right into sin. Peace and joy were plentiful; they were on the last shelf. Songs and praises were hanging near, so I just had to help myself. Then I said to the angel, "How much do I owe?" He smiled at me and said, "Just take them everywhere you go." Then I looked at him again and said, "How much do I really owe?" He looked at me again and smiled and said, "My child, Jesus paid your bill a long time ago."

I am a deaconess residing in Clarksville, Tennessee, USA. Apostolic by faith, originally from Jamaica, West Indies. I was born in Saint Andrew and grew up as a city girl with my father, stepmother, and brothers and sisters from both parents. I am a mother of two lovely and successful children, Lecepth and Skeeter, and five grandchildren: Abigail, Amir, Jaheem, JaMarcus, and Andre. I had the pleasure of vacationing in the rural area while school was out. This gave me the opportunity to bond with the other side of my family. As a child, my life's ambition was to become a nurse; my mother thought different due to religious belief, and so I was placed in the classroom as a teacher, which I wasn't comfortable with. She also was a teacher along with two of my younger siblings. This did not go well with me due to the stumbling blocks in my path from those who thought my opportunity to succeed came too early. This was a great setback for me, and then the critics followed. I was told constantly that I would never make it in life; I wouldn't reach my ultimate goal. They did everything in their power to hinder and stop me. I did odd jobs here and there below my qualifications without lowering my integrity.

They scuffed at the jobs I held and remarked that they would not take such a remedial job. I did not look at it that way. I had financial needs to meet, and I had no intention of remaining in the position permanently. When you fall in life, it is not a disgrace; it is a disgrace when you stay where you fall. You have to start somewhere, most likely from the bottom of the ladder. I made several attempts to enter the nursing field. I was successful on the interviews and entrance examinations and awaited to be called for training. However, I never received the call. Only to discover years later that I was selected to be trained and called on more than one occasions. However, someone very close to me, who should have had my best interest at heart for my success and theirs, intercepted and deleted my opportunities. On one occasion, one person came to me and said, "I received your acceptance letter as a trainee nurse, but I withheld it one year after the course started because I could not allow you to go and train and leave me behind." Despite this, I continued to pursue my dream. I forgo the nursing career for a while but did not give it up, just focused my attention on other areas. Another medical opportunity arose; I succeeded in the normal procedures, only to be cheated once more. I finally relocated to another part of Jamaica, West Indies, called Saint Mary. One day there was a community gathering among some youths, and I went along to observe. They were organizing a youth group and selecting officers. They didn't have a president because there was none qualified among them to perform this duty. I was asked to become their president because of my background in teaching. I hesitated then accepted because I needed to be productive in the community. This was the beginning of my ascension toward my goal. I placed myself aside and concentrated on helping others. I organized and trained the youths and made history by being the first person to bring a representative from the Parliament of Jamaica. This representative was for the constituency of this particular area. He came unlike many others who never visited this area for over thirty years. The political group that was present in this area at the time protested and declared that this representative should have come through their organization. I told them that they were right; however, they did nothing, and I saw the need, took the opportunity, and it benefitted the community. As a result of his visit, the youths received much-needed assistance from this member of Parliament; I became the youth organizer, secretary, and area leader of the member of Parliament's office until voluntary retirement. I also worked closely with the Saint Mary Parish Council in various offices for many years.

Although the obstacles and numerous stumbling blocks continued, they were not successful. It only motivated me more to push forward. You have to understand that I am a child of the universe, no less than the trees and the stars. I have a right to succeed like anyone else. As time went by, I met a senior officer of the island's special constabulary force. He has been my mentor and encourager through all my ups and downs. He used to always tell me that "I was the mother in Joseph and the mother of Job." When others say there is no way out, he says there is hope for me. I didn't understand it then, although I knew the story of Job and Joseph very well. Those who were trying to crush me down have made it, so why not concentrate on themselves and in furthering their lives? Not until I met Jesus for myself, the scriptures could not unfold it, and the pastors and others could not explain it. Until you get your own Damascus experience and your eyes are spiritually opened to see the adversaries around you and how they work to destroy your dreams, life, goals, and purpose in life. For example, your mother's sister, the closest ones to you, your own blood, your husband, wife, son, or daughter, and others you completely trust, knowing the distance you went for them, will take the merit for individuals in your life that they have little or no input, rendering you helpless when nothing is farther from the truth. One day I said to my mentor, "I wish I could be as spiritually high as you are." He said, "One day you will be." I understand today as I am there, regardless of those who try to keep you down, you still have to love them. If you keep revenge and bitterness in your heart, you will not succeed in your goal. The Lord prepared a table before you in the presence of your enemies. He will anoint your head with oil and let your cup run over. I knew a nurse during her final examination who failed; her own church sister, a nurse of a lower degree, was pleased that she failed, and I was in disbelief. She was given another chance to retake the exam; unknown to her, I prayed and fasted for her success, and she was successful. I told her after what I had done; she was thankful and grateful that she sought out avenues for me to enter the nursing field at another level. Despite the fact that my age for entering the field had passed, there was an opening in the field under a different specialty that gave me the opportunity to climb to the top. My zeal for nursing lifted higher than before, and I said that if it's the hem of a nurse's garment, I will touch it. So I pressed on like the woman with the issue of blood that touched the hem of Jesus's garment and got healed regardless of the obstacles and detours she faced. I enrolled and graduated with distinction and was first in my class. It did not come easy nor was it expected by my batch mates. I was absent from class very often due to circumstances beyond my control; I could not afford books and equipment to work and study with. I went to class extra early and borrowed from my batch mates and accessed nurses and doctors in the field to guide me along the way. I also assisted my batch mates with their exams and classes, which resulted in them graduating. I was blessed to be given a job I did not apply or inquired about. The nursing instructor hired me to train the junior nurses and first aiders. This proves you can succeed regardless of the obstacles and circumstances around you. I thank God that one of my students became a teacher at the same nursing school. I started to pursue my career at the tender age of eighteen and did not achieve it until I was forty-five. I used the training I received in the nursing field to help those in my community. I not only knew the medical side of the house, but I also was blessed to have learned about natural cures. The people that resided in my community could not afford medical attention, so I volunteered my services for free. I remember a very touching experience. There was an old man from another country who came to live in Jamaica. He had no family and never married. He was old and suffering as his mouth got infected, and he could not eat, so he was starving. I went to visit him every day and used the natural herbs along with medicines that I acquired with my own money to care for him. He recovered and was able to eat and fend for himself. This person, like so many others, depended on me for assistance, whether it was writing a recommendation from them to receive housing assistance, being accepted into nursing school, or just stopping by to get something to eat. Despite the fact that I, too, did not have much, God blessed me, and I was able to share and give back to others with the little I had. I thank God that through it all, He gave me the mind and heart to help others.

Just like me, others will have setbacks in their lives too. Don't give up, and don't give in. If you have to detour to sidetrack the enemy, do so to keep your eyes on the prize and touch the finish line. Now God has challenged me in another area. He told me to concentrate on the spiritual walk, although I just wanted to be a normal child of God, live holy, and gain eternal life. However, God had more in store for me. The last thing I expected to be was a deaconess. After sharing an experience with a pastor, she said to me, "Ask God what He will have you to do. He did not put you through all this without a purpose." I was sharing another experience with a contractor of the Jamaican government who built bridges all over the island. When I was through, he said to me, "Woman, God made you for a special purpose." He was not a Christian, and he defined who he really was, yet realizing that from speaking to me, there was a genuine God from the one he knew. As it is written in the scriptures, the devil knows there is one God and tremble. During our encounter, he had difficulty in building the bridge, and the construction would not stand. I advised him on how and what to do. After multiple failings, he finally adhered to my advice. The bridge was a success. Although I was not an engineer, I knew about the area and the secret of the landscape. I was a blessing to him in his line of work. Unfortunately, he passed away one month after the completion of the bridge.

Before my ordination to deaconess, I reviewed my life and accessed the trials that brought me success and great achievements. I spoke to God as I would a friend, and I asked Him why He allowed me to go through all the trial and tribulations. Why wasn't I allowed to achieve my goals without all these obstacles? Why didn't I know You then like I know You now? He replied to me, saying, "The universities could not teach you, the Bible studies and seminars could not train or guide you, you had to go through it personally. I have other sheep that are trapped in similar situations, and you can empathize with them to show them the way out." When my pastor announced my ordination, I was shocked along with the congregation. I asked him why. He said because the Holy Ghost told him to do so. I did not want this appointment like so many other positions that I had evaded however this time, and I was dumbstruck, unable to move. I knew that God had done this himself. I was reminded of Jonah and how he tries to hide from God; however, we all know that when God gets ready, you have to move. No devil in hell, or any form of hindrance, can stop you. He makes the rain fall on the just and on the unjust. He gave us all equal opportunities, he gave us all the same senses, and it is for us to utilize them. I was trained and ordained and excelled in my studies. It is for us to utilize and not look back on our setbacks; the sky is the limit, so spread your wings and be inspired and inspire others. Just keep your head when others are losing theirs. Trust yourself when all others doubt you. Encourage yourself as there will be times when there is no one else to encourage you but you. Be self-sufficient, confident, courageous, zealous, and hold on to your goals until you accomplish them. Remember, there will always be those who come to discourage and handicap your dreams. See them as a hurdle that you must defeat, and approach each day with courage. Make your life meaningful and leave disappointments behind. Reach forward for the best life has to offer. Work for the betterment of yourself, your community, and your country. Make and excel your marks in the footprints in the sand of time. Ask yourself, is this really where I want to be? If not, go where you ought to be. Triumph over disaster, walk with kings, and yet not lose your touch.

There is a time in life when you come to your crossroads; you have to decide to move on to victory, make the right decision, be inspired, and look at the positive achievement from others around you. They did it, and you can too. Above all, don't quit. When there is no money and the bills are high, you will just have to stick it out. The darkest hours are before dawn. Either you think for yourself or else others will think for you and take the power from you. The power of Christ within you is greater than the troubles and pressures that surround you.

Deaconess Winsome W. Brown-Blackford
E-mail to: zenedaamir@yahoo.com

50

Yvonne Hill

O LORD my God, in thee I do put my trust: save me from all them that persecute me, and deliver me.

—Psalms 7:1

In April 1996, I met the man I would marry in August 2001. The kids and I moved with him from Michigan to Georgia. I really enjoy being married and taking care of my husband and family. In December 2001, we had a fire in our apartment and lost everything but the clothes we had on our back. After that, we lived with two different friends, and it did not work. We stayed a short time with them both until I could not take it anymore. Summer of 2002, I decided to get our own apartment. I let my husband know that I could not do it anymore. The kids and I were moving, and I hoped he would move with us; he agreed. We had a mutual friend who was a manager at an apartment complex, and she was able to have us an apartment ready in just two days. This lady and I became the best of friends, and what a blessing. We lived there for a little over a year, and during that time, we began to start having problems. My husband started to hang out with friends and putting them before our family. We became pregnant, but due to stress, we lost our baby in December 2003. The miscarriage took a lot out of me. I was hurt, depressed, and felt bad because this would have been his first child. We talked, and he knew how hurt and sad I was, and he just wanted to see me smile. We decided to do something that we had been putting off for months. He told me that on my birthday, we would be in our new home. I was very excited, and working toward that took a lot off my mind, and that was a good thing. On March 27, 2004, we closed on our new home. We were both so happy we got to pick out everything from the carpet on the floors to the tile on the kitchen and bathroom floors, doorknobs on the cabinets throughout the house. This was truly a blessing sent from God. Things were going great for a while, then the hanging out with friends started back. I noticed a lot of them were single. He would stay out very late, sometimes up to four, five, or six in the morning. I would be up, worried that something might have happened to him. He was drinking a lot, and sometimes he would tell me he did not know how he made it home. I was so stressed thinking that I was going to get a call saying he was hurt. While all that was going on, I noticed a change in him, like he could not stand the sight of me. More arguing, late nights hanging out, and not answering my phone calls when I would call him started to happen. I would try to talk to him. I told him I'm married, but I feel lonely and that he was disrespecting me and acting like he didn't have a wife at home. He would start coming in early for a short time then back to his same routine. I prayed so much for him and our marriage. I asked God to change him so that he would so respect me, not only as his wife but also as a human being. My heart was so hurt, and I felt like it was my entire fault that my husband did not want to be around his family. At that time, I wanted God to change my husband. When I was worried about the wrong person, I prayed that God would change me and work on me and help me to keep my focus on Him and my kids and to remind me that I can only change myself, not anyone else. Also, what God has for me is for me. I had got to the point that I prayed to the Lord that if my husband's purpose was done in my life, then so be it; let His will be done. I just wanted to have peace. In December 2005, my husband was walking around the house rolling his eyes at me and just had an "I can't stand the sight of you" attitude. All this time, I did not know, but God was preparing me for what was about to take place. You see, I realized that all those nights I was by myself lying all alone and feeling lonely. God knew what my husband was about to say to me. I started working a full-time job, getting paid more than any other job since I moved to Georgia; I was being equipped. My husband told me he was not happy and wanted a divorce. When I heard those words, I did not react the way he thought I would. I did not react the way I thought I would. I just felt a relief, a heavy load lifted right off me. I told him thank you. He looked at me strange, but I said it again. "Thank you, now I know how you really feel, and I can move on." I had a hair appointment and would move out the room when I returned. That was when the disrespect really started. I was called out my name so much; he would holler at me and be all in my face, but God had prepared me right before the name-calling started. God told me not to say anything to him or look at him. I said, "God, you know me. I will cuss him out, so hold my tongue." God not only held my tongue, but He also took the fear away, and I was able to stand up in silence to this very big man. All I would say in my mind was, *You are not talking to me because I am a child of God, not the names you are saying.* I did not react the way my husband thought I should to the name-calling, It made him mad because it did not move me. Things got worse one night when he came home, and I think he just wanted to argue. He was looking for the safe with the gun in it, and I told him I moved it out of the house. He continued to argue and told me that I better go get it and bring it back. The kids and I left to go over to a friend's house that God had placed there for me to be able to go and get away when I needed too. My husband called my phone three to four times that evening, but that was strange to me because he had not called my cellphone or even answered my calls in about six months. I had a funny feeling in my stomach (which I later realized was the Holy Spirit.) I told my friend that something didn't feel right. She told me, "If you don't feel right, just put the kids to bed, and you go to bed." The next morning, my husband should have been on his way to work, but I guess he wanted to get us in the house. The kids did not want to go in. He came back to the house to check if we were in there. I did not know at the time what he was thinking, but the kids and I had to go back over to my friend's house and wait until he made it to work. I called to make sure he was there. When the kids and I got home to change clothes for school and work, my son and I were in the car. My daughter was on the front porch, and she pulled back the welcome mat only to find two knives. Later God revealed to me that my husband would have killed us all if I would have come home that night or even if he caught us in the house that morning. God had been telling me all along that I needed to move, but I was not ready to hear that let alone do it. I was still holding on to us working it out and making it work. But after that, I learned to hear God's voice and to listen and do what he says. I told God that I will do what He says, but I wanted a three-bedroom, two-bathroom house, and I could afford to pay $700 a month. Before I moved, my husband wanted to serve me my divorce papers at my job. God blocked it. Even though I lived and worked in the same city, I worked in a different county, and I could only get served in the county I lived in. I was also blessed with a lawyer that gave me a flat rate plus a discount. She even told me what to do legally before I even hired her as my lawyer. I found an apartment, but I did not qualify for it. I did not make enough money, but I walked out that office saying "that is what you think." My God says it is time for me to move, and He will supply my needs. I got a call to come pick up my keys; my rent was $710 a month. I could not tell the kids because I did not want my husband to hear them talking about it. I set up a move date with Two Men and a Truck to move me while my husband was at work. I also could not change my routine, so I got up like I was going to work and got the kids ready for school and dropped them off. I did have breakfast at Waffle House: hash browns scattered and smothered and a cup of coffee. I was able to go back to the house twice to get all my things out. I changed my cellphone number so he could not get in touch with me. A week later, my husband was fired from his job of over eight years, and he blamed me for that. Everything that my husband tried to do, God had me one step ahead. I knew what he was trying to do before he did it. The kids and I were able to go to Florida and South Carolina for vacation. While in my first apartment, my lights were about to be turned off. I called Georgia Power to work something out with them. I did not have all the money needed, but the lady on the phone was so nice she told me to see what I could come up with and give her a call back on her direct line. I did what I could and gave her a call back. I told her that I could not come up with the total amount to pay. You see, my bill was higher because of the transfer of lights from the house to my apartment. I did let her know that I was going through a divorce. The lady said that when she talked to me on the phone the first time, she could feel my spirit, and God had told her to pay whatever I could not. Not only did this lady whom I did not know pay my remaining balance, we also talked about my daughter going to cheerleading camp and I was unable to get the things needed on her list for the trip. We lived in the same area, so she asked me to meet her at Wal-Mart. I thought it was just a chance to meet her and her children in person to thank her, but to my surprise, we meet, and she placed $200 in my hand and said, "Let your daughter get whatever she needs for her camp." As my daughter shopped for her things, I could not hold back the tears of joy. God gets all the glory, honor, and praise; I know it was nothing but the Lord. The lady and I became the best of friends, and even though we don't talk all the time, we are still in touch with each other. See what can happen if you walk out on faith and be obedient to God. I was so thankful for my apartment, and I let God know that, but the area went bad. I needed to move my children out of that area. In March of 2007, I found another apartment that they said I did not make enough money to rent, but I had already been there. I knew that my God would supply my need again for shelter. The kids and I moved into our townhouse with three bedrooms and two and a half bathrooms. Rent was $699 a month. God favored me. My job contract was not renewed, so I had to start looking for a new job. I was told by the supervisor from corporate office to start looking for a new job, and if I had any interviews, I could go and that they would still pay me for my eight hours per day. God blessed me and the kids again. He supplied all our needs and then some. After being obedient to God and depending on Him for everything, I was able to give my daughter a sweet-sixteen birthday party on the army base, and her cheerleading coach paid for it. I just had to pay for food. My daughter was able to be on the cheerleading squad at her high school, and her coaches paid for everything. My son was able to play football at his school, something that he had wanted to do since we moved in our home in 2004. As I write this, tears of joy are coming down my face because I know that if it was not for God on my side, I would not be here, and I am so thankful for God's grace and mercy. Through this whole thing, my church family in Georgia helped me with food, paying bills, and just supporting me with whatever I needed. In September 2007 my divorce became final, and God truly blessed me. The same man who called me every name but a child of God and said I was unattractive paid for me to get my copy of our divorce papers. My divorce was final that exact day, nothing but God working it all out. Soon after that, God spoke to me and told me that I would be moving back to Michigan. "Don't take it as taking a step backward," He said. "I have to take you back before I can move you forward." Things have not been easy, but I do know that God had His hands all over me. In November 2007, I moved back to Michigan, and God really did some amazing things. I lived with my sister Angela. I found a job in April 2008 and an apartment in May 2008. Now I see exactly what God was talking about. I belong to Union Second Baptist Church, River Rouge, Michigan, and I am an active member. God placed people in my life to help me get where He wants me to be, and I was put in people's lives to be a blessing to them also. I received a certificate of completion in Biblical Counseling I-IV (2009-2011) from Christian Research Development, Rosedale Park Baptist Church, Detroit, Michigan, where I was completely healed and delivered. I was laid off in June 2012. God used this time to use me to completely walk out on faith and also not to worry what I look like in the process; God was working on my outside to match my inside. I just had to be obedient to Him, and He will handle the rest. I was part of Michigan Leading Ladies with two of my childhood classmates, Treva Sanders Gordon and Janine Folks Edward. I was taken out of my comfort zone, but that is when God can do His best work through us. I am a willing vessel for God. He has used me to bring forth the ministries Ladies of Faith, a support group for domestic violence women, and FreezePop Children Ministry, where we encourage children to be the best they can be and that they can do anything they put their minds into. This ministry is still coming together. God, have Your way. I am currently attending Geraldine Marvell Miller Wright Institute for Women in Ministry in Detroit, Michigan, and will be graduating in 2014. God is so awesome, and I have mega faith that He will do just what He said He would do.

Yvonne Hill

www.ladiesoffaith.net
Yvonne@ladiesoffaith.net

        For we walk by faith, not by sight.—2 Corinthians 5:7

Thoughts of a Leading Lady

Rosetta Perry

As a leader, I have had many challenges in the last fifty years, but I have always used persistence and perseverance, and I never take no for an answer. This attitude, in turn, inspires young people to step up to the plate. I never leave my office first and expect the employees to work five hours later. I was always first in and last out, hardworking, and pushing for more so the staff follows suit. I nurture young people, but I am fair and just and have found that my woman's intuition is one of my strongest traits.

I have an unconditional belief in my own abilities. I am known to take on tough assignments and excel in them while maintaining successful relationships.

I actively support many charities and always look for ways to give back to the Nashville community. I always listen and communicate and look for ways to work with people.

My education encompasses more than just a college degree. I have sought out those more experienced in their field and learned from them so I pushed ahead, learned what works, and avoided potential pitfalls. I found mentors who helped me make connections that would not normally be made. I have been able not only to be an expert in my industry but also to see the bigger picture and understand my role in the community. As a Leading Lady with vision, I saw the path ahead and inspired others to help them turn a dream into a reality. Shine on, Leading Ladies.

Contact Informaton:
Rosetta Perry
Publisher of the Tennessee Tribune
Nashville, Tennessee
www.tntribune.com

Thoughts of a Leading Lady

Cheryl "Action" Jackson

(Houston, Texas)

Every woman possess the capability of being a Leading Lady; however, they are rare and hard to find. When you encounter a Leading Lady, you will know her by the words she speaks. They are graceful, and they penetrate your soul. She is one who cares for her family and lives by the motto it takes a village, so she nurtures others as well. A Leading Lady is not what Hollywood considers when they cast for a role in a movie. As a matter of fact, she is almost the complete opposite. She is not a villain, vixen, or a home wrecker. She is graceful, powerful; and although she is in front of the crowd, she works even harder behind the scenes. Her words are never scripted; they flow up to the heavens, and those in her presence pay close attention to her. She commands respect; she is noble, proper; and she is a caregiver to the world.

Cheryl Jackson is an author, speaker, wife, and mother of two beautiful sons. She is the president of Minnie's Food Pantry and The Giving Movement organization.

Contact Information:
www.minniesfoodpantry.org

Thoughts of a Leading Lady

Janis F. Kearney

A Leading Lady is one who, simply because of her presence and the way she carries herself, demands our undivided attention. A woman of whom we expect great things because she consistently delivers greatness. A Leading Lady presents herself to the world with her best face forward. She loves herself, but she also loves others and treats others with kindness and understanding.

Janis F. Kearney, publisher of Writing Our World Press, author, and presidential diarist, grew up in the Deep South; she is the daughter of Arkansas sharecroppers and the twelfth of nineteen children. In her first memoir, *Cotton Field of Dreams*, the she wrote with unvarnished truth of her early years of poverty and struggle and the invaluable lessons learned from two amazing parents. In her second memoir, *Something to Write Home About: Memories from a Presidential Diarist,* Kearney relives a most unlikely in her life—her days as President William Jefferson Clinton's personal diarist, the first-ever to hold the position. In her most recent book, *Daisy: Between a Rock and a Hard Place,* Kearney chronicles the amazing journey of one of America's most unforgettable Civil Rights heroines—Daisy Gatson Bates, the face and voice behind the 1957 Central High Integration Crisis.

Contact Information:
Please direct inquiries to janis@writingourworldpress.com.

Thoughts of a Leading Lady

First Lady Mary Curlin

(Hopkinsville, Kentucky)

A leading lady is one who understands her worth, recognizing her ultimate source is Jesus Christ, who gives us the grace to conquer each day.

Lady Curlin is the first Lady of All Nations House of Prayer and has worked in ministry with her husband since its founding in 1985. She accepted her call to the ministry shortly thereafter, instructing believers in the way of salvation and the road to perfection. She promotes self-development and spiritual development, encouraging the people of God to better their lives and be all that God wants them to be. She also has a heart for pastors' wives regarding their personal walk with the Lord and the importance of their role in ministry. Lady Curlin is currently devoted to full-time ministry in intercessory prayer, traveling on the evangelistic field with Apostle Curlin, and serves as the ministry coordinator overseeing all facets of ministry operations at All Nations House of Prayer.

Contact Information:
www.curlinministries.org

Thoughts of a Leading Lady

Pastor Ginger Luffman

(Clarksville, Tennessee)

My idea of a Leading Lady is a woman with inner strength. One who faces life head-on and depends on God for guidance. She leads by example and is not demanding or haughty. She is willing to do any task, and none are beneath her. She radiates beauty from within. She does not push or shout for position or recognition but is elevated by God. Most Leading Ladies don't even realize that they are. A Leading Lady is on the front lines of the battle and not calling the plays from behind or on the sidelines.

Pastor Ginger has been ordained by Faith Covenant Ministries and Mark Barclay Ministries. She is also the leader of the Faith Outreach Ladies Ministry, Project LOVE. She is the CFO at Faith Outreach Church. Dr. William Luffman, her husband, serves as senior pastor. Due to her personal testimony, she has a heart to help women that have been broken down, battered, and abused. She is a strong woman of God, who leads by example, thus being a role model to many.

Contact Information:
www.outreachministriesinc.com

Memorable Photos of Leading Ladies

Leading Ladies photographed with State Senator Thelma Harper at Harper's Restaurant, in Nashville, Tennessee

Michigan Leading Ladies Conference in Detroit, Michigan

Celebrating with Michigan Leading Lady and Honoree Alesia Carter (center)

Dr. Dorinda Clark-Cole and Pastor Yolanda Morgan at Leading Ladies Luncheon in Detroit, Michigan

Leading Ladies group photo taken at Union Second Baptist Church in River Rouge, Michigan, with Pastor Wess Morgan

Leading Ladies Luncheon held at Jazz and Jokes in Nashville, Tennessee, in April 2012

River Rouge High School with the Dream Team

Pastor Wess Morgan in attendance at our conference in River Rouge, Michigan

Our visit at River Rouge High School

Leading Ladies Luncheon

Leading Ladies Janine Folks and Treva Gordon

Leading Ladies: Our First Conference

Michigan Leading Ladies Conference
October 4-6, 2012—*We Remember* . . .

This was our very first conference for Leading Ladies, and what a great success with Dr. Dorinda Clark-Cole, Pastor Yolanda Morgan, Pastor Wess Morgan, Bishop Anthony Alfred, Servella Terry, Eva Barnes, Janine Folks, Women of Transition, Yvonne Hill, and Treva Gordon.

Honorees included:
Minetta Hare
Robin Kinloch
Gina Stewart
Helene Waters
Georgia McPhaul
Robin Bossio
Alesia Carter

Thanks to Union Second Baptist Church and Pastor Kenneth L. and First Lady Lanay Brown, River Rouge High School and Superintendent Derrick Coleman, the *Telegram*, the Dream Team, and everyone who came out to support.

Ministers of music: Anton Cook, Nicole McKeage, Dionne Jermeia, Renee Craig, AnnaMaria, Gospel Group Newly Ordained, and Minister Bonshea Lawson and guest.

Workshop speakers: Valerie Foulks, Jan Newby, Dr. Lisa Fuller-Tweh, Elder Velma Jo Williams, and Sis. La Trina Alfred with encouraging words.

Special thanks to Mr. Kelvin Braxton of Braxton's Photography and to all volunteers and sponsors. We greatly appreciate you all for making this event a great success.

For more information about Leading Ladies, visit www.TrevaGordon.com

My Personal Goal List Here

"I am a Leading Lady."

_____

_____

_____

_____

_____

_____

_____

_____

_____

_____

_____

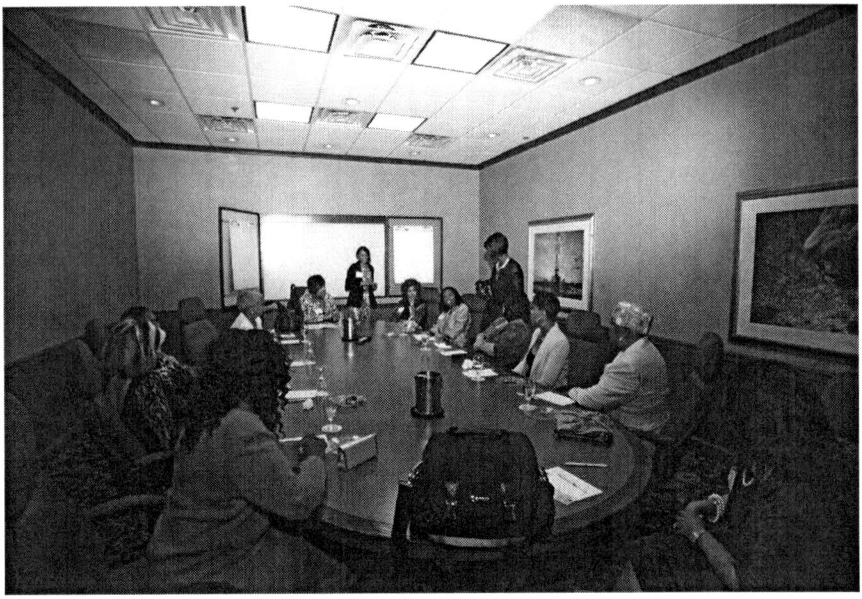

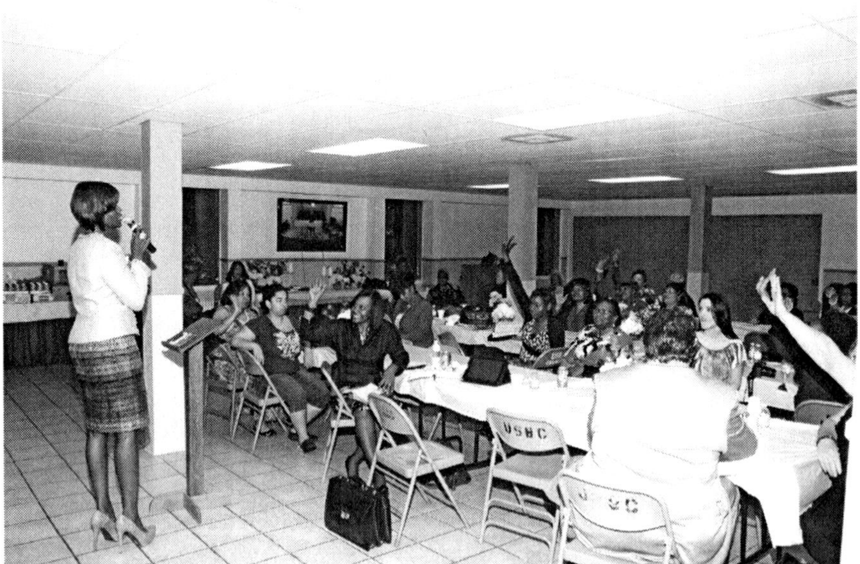
USBC

Leading Ladies inspires all women everywhere to *win* through its successful conferences, workshops, seminars, books, gatherings, and more.

For more information about Leading Ladies

or to support,

visit www.trevagordon.com

or send e-mail to: ccshopper@bellsouth.net.

To order additional copies of this book, visit

www.TrevaGordon.com